THE UNCOMMO

Vyvyan Deacon and spirit guide Dr Cheong

THE UNCOMMON MEDIUM

Vivienne Browning

SKOOB BOOKS PUBLISHING
LONDON

First published in 1993 by
SKOOB BOOKS PUBLISHING LTD
Skoob esoterica series
11a-17 Sicilian Avenue
Southampton Row
London WC1A 2JH

Series editor; Christopher Johnson
Design © Mark Lovell

First edition

ISBN 1 871438 42 X

Printed in Malaysia by POLYGRAPHIC

Acknowledgements

My thanks are due to the following for help supplying material and answering questions: John Arnold, Librarian Victoria State Library, Timothy d'Arch Smith, Atlantis Bookshop, the Australian bookshop Flinders, the Australian High Commission Library, James Bentley, Geraldine Beskin, Paul Beard, Mr Robert Bradford, Bill Breese, Ronnie Bunting, the British Library, the College of Psychic Studies, E. Stanley Brookes, my cousins, Esther Browning and Robert Browning, Debbie Cramer, John Day, Mary Dean, Julian Drewett of the Church's Fellowship for Psychical and Spiritual Studies, Jean Overton-Fuller, International P.E.N., R.A. Gilbert, Kenneth Grant, Bill Hornadge, Elsie Horstead of the Warburg Institute, Lucien Jenkins, Chris Johnson, Mark Lovell, Lucis Trust Library, Bishop Eric and the Liberal Catholic Church at Drayton House, Hubert Lestocq, Jack Lindsay, Nellie Lampeter, Brenda Marshall, Mitchell Library, Dr. D. Monkman, Psychical Research Society, Psychic Press, Mar Seraphim, Martin Starr, State Library of New South Wales, National Library of Australia, Phyllis Monument, (nee Pateman), Arthur Nethercott, Graeme T. Powell, Joint Copying Project Officer of the Australian High Commission, Mark D. Powell, Kathleen Raine, Keith Richmond, Francesca Schmitt-Charteris, the Scout Association, the Theosophical Society Library, David Redstone, John Symonds, Gregory Tillett, Orrin P. Walton, the Revd Gordon Wilson, Caroline Wise, Gerald Yorke.

Chapter One

I see crowds of people, walking round in a ring.
Thank you. If you see dear Mrs. Equitone,
Tell her I bring the horoscope myself:
One must be so careful these days.
T.S. Eliot, *The Waste Land*

ALL HIS LIFE controversy, scandal and adulation followed him. He worked as a medium; he dealt in patent medicines; he was friends with both the Theosophist Bishop Leadbeater and the occultist Aleister Crowley. He lived in a world where the early socialists and the trades unions, Spiritualist chapels, vegetarianism and other, more eccentric, diets, communes, naturism, Freemasonry, Rosicrucianism, Rational Dress and a thousand and one other earnestly pleaded causes all drew on the same audiences and signed up many of the same members. He was Vivian Deacon.

The son of William Cornelius and Elizabeth Deacon was born on 9 August 1895 at 9 pm. 'I fancy Polly Bune said it was one minute past', wrote his mother, when forty years later she was asked the exact time for Crowley to do a horoscope chart.

The confinement took place at Totterdown Farm, near Newbury in Berkshire, the home of farmer Frederick Stephen Bune, a distant relative. Calling a baby Vivian was thought by some friends at the time to be daring, for Oscar Wilde's son was called Vyvyan and any suspicion that the child might have been named after the Wilde boy would have been frowned upon. But Elizabeth Deacon explained that the name Vivian was chosen because it meant 'Living One': her first son had died in infancy.

Elizabeth had in fact been introduced to the Wilde family by her cousin Robert Browning in the 1880s, following her father's death. Through them she had also met the young Yeats and, through Golden Dawn connections, Arthur Machen and Algernon Blackwood. She shared

1

Constance Wilde's interest in the occult and had attended séances with Violet Tweedale, author of *The Cosmic Christ*, granddaughter of eminent Spiritualist Robert Chambers and, like Yeats, a member of the Golden Dawn. Gladstone, who claimed that 'Psychical Research is by far the most important work that is being done in the World' and who had attended séances in Mrs Tweedale's home, was another mutual friend. The Browning family were themselves part of a circle that was interested in Spiritualism, in Abramelin and Eliphas Levi, in Mesmerism, Swedenborgianism, Rosicrucianism and Freemasonry. The Browning Society, the Metaphysical Society, the Theosophical Society and the Society for Psychical Research often turned out to have members in common. William Kingsland, a leading Theosophist, was the biographer both of Browning and of Madame Blavatsky. W.T. Stead, the campaigning journalist and Spiritualist had a brother, Herbert Stead who became warden of the Robert Browning Settlement in Walworth after its inauguration 1895. Vivian's mother also met the young James Ingall Wedgwood at this time. Brought up by his maiden aunt, a regular correspondent of Robert Browning, Wedgwood was a rising star in the Theosophical Society. Years later he was to be one of Vivian's teachers.

In 1895 Elizabeth lived in Christchurch Terrace as back-to-back neighbours of the Wildes, who lived in Tite Street. (Oscar Wilde had been known to refer to Christchurch Terrace as 'the shadier side of Tite Street or worse'.) During the spring of 1895 Oscar Wilde was away from home in the period of his trial and Vivian's mother sympathised strongly with his wife. She felt this must have resulted in the life-long attachment her son had for Oscar Wilde and his family.

Vivian was born with an unblemished almost blue-white skin, explained by the family as being 'one layer too few'. Having lost one child, it was perhaps inevitable that Elizabeth should see her second child as delicate. As a result, he had a strange, isolated upbringing which marked him for life. He would grow up separated from other children, a solemn child mixing most readily with adults.

His mother registered him at Newbury as Vivian Hereward Rowden Deacon and his home address as 8 Christchurch Terrace, Chelsea. On the birth certificate the father's profession was given as 'Domestic Nurse'. He was always known as 'Dr Deacon' to patients and he gladly acquiesced in being given this status. Printed cards were issued, announcing that 'Kelly & Deacon' were medical practitioners specialising in electrical therapy at 42 George Street, Portman Square,

London W1. Charges, in that lost currency of shillings and pence, were from 7/6 to 12/6 per treatment. The length of a session varied between fifteen and forty-five minutes. The treatments listed are those which were modish at the time: hypnosis, mental suggestion, spinal adjustment, hand and electric combined massage, electric vibration massage, high frequency violet ray, faradic current, zone therapy and curative exercises. (It was during this period, that elsewhere in Britain Aleister Crowley's Plymouth Brethren father fell ill and received electro-homoeopathic treatment.) Vivian professed to have inherited an interest in medical matters from his father and he too would follow a career in unconventional forms of healing, although less consistently than his father, for he would always have too many interests in life to be able to pursue any one thing steadily.

Cornelius Deacon was a generous man, tall, big-built, genial and impressive. Rumour circulated that his noble bearing was attributable to his being the natural son of the Marquis of Bute. It was another example of a kind of social standing being conferred on him and again, it was not brushed aside.

'Corrie' had married Elizabeth Browning on 2 September 1893 in the Parish Church of Holy Trinity, Southampton. Neither of the two was young. The groom was thirty-one, the bride a little older. In an attempt to close the gap in ages, her age was recorded as thirty-three, although she had turned thirty-four the previous July. The father of the groom was William Deacon, Gentleman, and the bride's father was Reuben Browning (deceased), Accountant. By 1895 the couple was resident in Chelsea.

In an autobiographical interview years later, Vivian would say that his father died when he was very young. (Certainly, there are no records of them being together as a family after a single photograph of the three, where Vivian is looking miserable, perhaps jealous at his father's unaccustomed presence.) As a small child I always believed that this was the case. It therefore came as a considerable surprise to me later to meet my grandfather. The truth of the matter was that Corrie early established a pattern of working away from home and this developed until his absence was complete.

With her husband working in London, Elizabeth was recording in old exercise books the minutest detail of her surviving son's progress. 'He was never any trouble to look after. As soon as he was dressed he would entertain himself,' she wrote: there is no mention, though, of his playing with the children of the Bune family, or indeed with any other small children. He was playing on his own, with his mother watching, continually fascinated by her son's slightest action. 'He was very fond of piling things up on his little square wooden chair, as if he were building something – and as soon as he began his morning play, if I passed him or came up to him he would call out, "Away, away Marmee!" and wave his hands about as if he did not want any interruption or intrusion.'

He was a clean child who could not bear to have his hands soiled. After playing in the garden, 'he came running... stretching out his dear little hands, crying pitifully, "Look Marmee, dirty, dirty". If he had been playing with the mould he was most eager to have his hands washed.'

On one occasion Vivian disappeared, leaving his mother in a panic. She found him with Mr Wilton, an old man, playing soldiers. Vivian had on a three-cornered hat and Mr Wilton had a paper hat from a cracker. After that, these two companions were called 'old soldier' and 'young soldier'. The young soldier held the wooden bar from his high chair like a gun and the old soldier brandished an upside-down broom in battle with the foe. The inspiration for the battles was news of the skirmishes in South Africa including the Jameson Raid, as told by the numerous cousins who had settled in Africa in the middle of the century.

His mother would take Vivian on visits to her cousins in London. They were ardent royalists and in 1897 they celebrated Queen Victoria's Diamond Jubilee. (Royalty and the Church of England were a preoccupation of Elizabeth's.) There were also visits to the seaside in summer, Broadstairs being a popular choice.

With his father away so much of the time, Vivian was left with a keen need for the interest and attention of older men. (Perhaps even his relations with Leadbeater many years later were affected by this need.) The old soldier may have been a strange beginning, but a stay at Shelley Farm, in the village of Colegate, Sussex, when Vivian was eight years old, was remembered for the interest the local vicar took in him. He became infatuated with the boy and frequently called to take him on long country walks to look for fairies, or wood spirits. He was the Revd William Horsfall, coincidentally the name of the patron of Browning's poem 'Mr. Sludge the Medium'. Vivian was fascinated by the idea of nature spirits and by the ability of the Vicar to see psychically, and his own facility for psychic vision was nurtured at this time. Horsfall was of gentle character, with a beautiful tenor voice. Vivian was impressed by his psychic vision and his eloquence when describing the Eleusinian Rites.

At this time, perhaps in imitation of this father substitute, Vivian used to hold religious services in the play-room, conducting them as seriously as those conducted in the Church of England. He wore a surplice (his night-shirt) and the servants joined in the service at times. This combination of religion and theatre, or playacting, was to continue throughout his life. (Oddly enough there is a story that as a small boy Robert Browning, to whom Vivian's mother was related, came home from an early visit to church, donned a mock surplice, stood in an armchair and gave such a hell-fire sermon that his baby sister was frightened into tears, at which he ordered sternly 'Pew-opener, remove that child'.)

After the death of Victoria, Elizabeth settled for most of the years to 1908 in Broadstairs. Vivian did not attend school. The lack of discipline and the fact that he never had to discover a place for himself in a conventional setting left him able to develop his mediumistic abilities, but unable to settle to steady, regular work. He was to drift passively from one set of circumstances to another all his life. In Broadstairs his education was confined to the local Sunday-school and religious instruction alternating with drama and free expression taught him by the Revd Mills, rector of St Mary's Church and another father figure for Vivian. The rector proved to be perhaps the greatest initial influence on the lonely child. It was common knowledge that the area was associated with the introduction of Roman Christianity into southern England. It was at nearby Ebbs Flete that St Augustine and his missionaries landed on 7 August 596. Less than eighteen months after his arrival, 10,000 people were baptised in the mouth of the Medway. In this area Vivian became familiar with the early Christian Mysteries and Gnosticism. Through the Revd Mills Vivian met the Archbishop of Canterbury, who was visiting.

The lessons with Revd Shapley Mills were hardly formal. He was amazed at the gift of memory little Vivian had. He could recite word-perfect whole chapters from the Bible and soliloquies from Shakespeare after hearing them only once or twice. But if Vivian was unusual, so was the rector. He ran a very successful amateur dramatic society which performed at the local Royal Palace Theatre. The services he ran were so idiosyncratic that they attracted a good deal of comment, becoming a local *cause célèbre* and eventually being raised in the House of Commons.

Every morning at 10 o'clock adults and children alike would assemble in the venerable chapel of St Mary's for a full hour of devotional exercises. Well in advance, so that passers-by could be alerted that something was about to happen, seats were arranged on the sand in semicircles, and after the hour's devotion they would all set out for the sands. The services provided an opportunity for everyone from the youngest to the oldest to participate in lively entertainment. As the chapel was the meeting place for the start of the procession, additional people were attracted along the way. It was here that Vivian learned the hymns he was never to forget. They would regularly appear in his hymn sheets.

When the skies were grey and darkness loomed, the vicar led the gathering back to the sheltering comfort of St Mary's chapel. There would be a parade of coloured lights, Chinese lanterns, illuminated bicycles, which went in procession through the various streets. The meetings varied, with fancy-dress and a thelemic atmosphere of 'Do what thou wilt'.

Because of the popularity of Broadstairs as a holiday resort, the local theatres were able to attract the famous names of show business, Lewis Waller's company, Beerbohm Tree and the Terrys, and Vivian saw every possible performance. Goethe's *Faust* with music by Coleridge-Taylor made a lasting impression. He was even coached in Shakespeare soliloquy and fencing by Sir Henry Irving not long before the great actor died. As an adult Vivian's repertoire of Shakespearean speeches - including Othello's court-room plea, Henry V before Agincourt, the successful pleading of the little prince to Hubert not to put out both his eyes – owed much to Henry Irving. In particular the 54 lines from Henry V Act I Scene Two, where the Dauphin has sent a consignment of tennis-balls as a snub and Henry asks of Exeter, 'What treasure uncle?' and receives the reply 'Tennis-balls, my liege'. The pregnant pause before the sarcastic and scathing reply of the monarch was of such alarming length one feared a stillbirth – but how effective and hypnotic! I swear I could hear a voice in the silence repeat '*tennis*-balls?' (with something of the quality of Dame Edith Evans' 'A *hand*-bag?') followed by another pause before the words, spat out between clenched teeth, 'We are glad the Dauphin is so pleasant with us'. It was a spellbinding performance.

Vivian's first poem was composed when he was eight years old. Just before Christmas he had been shopping with his mother in the late afternoon when the sky is night in England at that time of the year, and the street lights give a special magic to the occasion. He was attracted by the sad face of a woman at a window he was passing. She was looking out with apparently unseeing eyes as the people bustled by. Her sadness haunted the little boy who, in his hours of devotional studies had learned to observe the needs of others.

I know one who sits alone by a window looking out,
And I fancy I could tell you what her thoughts are all about:–
How she wandered here and there, just a little year ago
With a glad mysterious air, and a visage all aglow.

I know one whose cheeks get wet, as the people hurry by
With their bundles and their wreaths, and I fancy I know why!
Just a little year ago, she came home with bundles too,
Which were hidden high and low from two sparkling eyes of blue,
But the room is quiet, and still, – where a baby played about!
I know one who sits – alone, by the window, – looking out!

With encouragement from all quarters to express himself spontaneously, the natural sequel was that he rapidly developed as an inspired speaker between the ages of eight and ten, and in this guise made his contribution to the open-air services on the sands.

One Sunday he took his place as usual among the open-air congregation where a lay preacher regularly held the service and preached. On this occasion the preacher did not arrive at the appointed time. After several minutes it became obvious that no speaker was coming. Without hesitation Vivian walked to the platform and started to preach. When he finished speaking and was feeling very bewildered, a woman came up to him, shaking her fist at him, stating he had been possessed by the devil. Others came to congratulate him and thank him. One particularly kind woman showed she understood what had happened, by comforting him with an explanation that what he had shown was a rare gift; he was one of the very few people who could be used by others, as she said, 'on a higher plane'. This accusation of demonic possession was a charge also levelled at Vivian's contemporary Krishnamurti. The latter, like Vivian, grew up close to his mother (who then died when he was ten years old), did poorly at school, was privately educated, after the Theosophists had discovered him, and became one of Leadbeater's pupils. When the time came that Krishnamurti began to teach something that Leadbeater's close colleague Wedgwood felt was at odds with Theosophy, the latter whispered to Mrs Besant that this was the voice of a black magician speaking through him.

When Vivian became famous as a Spiritualist medium and was asked to describe his development, he gave as examples of the three phases of trance his experiences as a child on the sands at Broadstairs, which earned him publicity in the *Daily Mirror* as the 'Boy Preacher'. The progression to going into a trance was firstly the urge to speak spontaneously as himself, inspired; secondly the awareness of a voice within which uttered words he felt compelled to express aloud but which were not necessarily words he understood; thirdly the vacating of his body to enable it to be taken over. When this occurred, he was oblivious to what was happening or what was said and regained consciousness as if waking in the morning without the memory of dreams. This experience as a child is the first occurrence of the theme of the 'hollow one', an openness to being taken over by something outside of himself, which is the other side of the same passivity which left Vivian unable to be a success in worldly affairs, a theme that was to remain one of the constants of his life.

Little of the typical boyhood was present in Vivian's life to date, with his bias to religious education and friendships with adults, usually clergymen. Not that he was always solemn – he enjoyed frivolous things, such as visits to the local minstrel shows, theatre and music hall.

There are signs in his mother's note-books which appear to be deliberate clues to significant events which she wanted someone later to know about. But somehow her courage seems to have deserted her, for whole pages were torn out. One piece of paper very carefully torn at a precise point reads frustratingly 'A serious record happening at Broadstairs in' - there is not even a date one might work from. She obsessively recorded regular and ordinary occurrences, as if concerned to prove that her beloved boy was essentially the same as the other boys in the Sunday school that he attended regularly. Yet she was able to note tellingly that 'none of the boys liked him because he was so attentive and never had to be corrected'.

Meanwhile, as the Rector grew in popularity for his social activities, so among his critics did he grow in notoriety for his unusual services. In March of that year things came to a head. D. Brymer-Jones, member of parliament for Swansea, rose in the House of Commons to ask the

Attorney-General if his attention had been drawn to a public service held on Sunday 3 March 1907 at Holy Trinity Church, Broadstairs, in the diocese of Canterbury, in the course of which 'illegalities' were committed. Among those listed were 'The wearing of one or more mass vestments, the use of portable lights,' (these were not specified as the tapers, candles, flares, torches or Chinese lanterns such as were organised for the parades), 'the ceremonial mixing of the chalice, the introduction of a ceremonial closely resembling the lavabo, the elevation of a consecrated wafer... the introduction of secret prayers and the secret reading of the Last Gospel... at which there was no communicant except the celebrant... and reference was made to illegal ornaments'.

It was at this time that an event took place which was to have the profoundest effect on Vivian's life. By 1907 he must already have been told that his father was dead, for that year his mother married again. Vivian and his stepfather were, perhaps not surprisingly, incompatible. The boy did not enjoy losing the monopoly on his mother's care; her second husband John Chamberlain intensely disliked what he viewed as his stepson's religious mania. Vivian began to run away from home, perhaps attempting to escape his stepfather, perhaps to win back his mother's undivided attention, or perhaps in imitation of his own father's absences.

In June 1907 Mrs Henrietta Grace Baden-Powell stayed at the Grand Hotel, Broadstairs, for two weeks the year preceding the founding of the Boy Scouts' Movement by her son, the hero of Mafeking. Vivian's constant absconding from home at that time brought the personal interest of the Baden-Powells and led to Vivian's being allowed to join the camp at Humshaugh the following year.

One picture survives of Vivian in uniform among a group of Scouts clustered around their leader, attentive to what B-P is saying. This picture at Humshaugh Camp is the last evidence of his being in Britain. Vivian's name does not appear on any of the official lists in *The Scout* at 12 September 1908, but it was known that there were at least two other lads included unofficially by Lord Baden-Powell. Vivian did not forget his kindness at what was a traumatic period of his life. He had, for however briefly, found another father substitute.

Chapter Two

What is Love - the divine Love of which the – the great
singer teaches us in Proverbs? It is the rainbow that comes
after the dark cloud. It is the morning star and it is also the
evening star... ah, what indeed is music but the voice of Love!
                                        Sinclair Lewis, *Elmer Gantry*

O N A SUMMER'S DAY in the weeks leading up to a hot
Australian Christmas, the children of St Peter's School,
Melbourne, were rehearsing in the Old Trades Hall. It was
1912 and the world seemed safe. The idea of a war in
Europe was unthinkable. Vivian Deacon, now a tall, good-looking boy
of seventeen, and his middle-aged friend Roy Redgrave had plans to
give elocution lessons and they were looking for premises. The older
man, an established actor and producer, was Vivian's new father figure
and the two were sharing digs. When Redgrave had suggested to
Vivian that they teach elocution, Vivian, with his lifelong enthusiasm
for the theatre and performance of every sort, immediately agreed.
They entered the hall and found the school rehearsal in progress.

A twelve-year-old girl was singing. Vivian stared at her in fascina-
tion: a picture that hung in his lodgings showed just such a girl walking
along a path through the blue sky with angels guiding her steps. The
girl on the platform sang sweetly. She was small, with shoulder-length
hair and she seemed to have stepped out of the gilt frame of his picture.
Vivian wanted to meet her and he asked for her address. He was an
elocution teacher, he explained; the girl's voice was promising.

The staff were sufficiently impressed by the pale, serious young man
to give him the name and address of the little girl. She was the daughter
of the Revd Philip Lew Tong and she lived in Cardington Street, in a
suburb of Melbourne called Carlton. Her name was Eunice. What they
did not tell him was that her family were bringing their daughter up
in a strict, religious atmosphere where social encounters were not

encouraged. Her father was the son of a Chinese lady of noble birth who had fallen in love with a businessman, an exporter of foods. They had sent their son to be educated in a mission school and trained for the ministry in Canton.

The family presented a respectable face to the world. They had few friends. They worked diligently. The Revd Philip Lew Tong was regularly not at home, for he worked as the minister in Bendigo, which meant his being away for days at a time: another absent father, that recurring feature of Vivian's life. Mrs Baker, the grandmother, had a scrubbed appearance. Her face was weathered by time and worry. Eunice, though, had been brought up to look more than merely clean. She was taught to be neatly presented. Hard work might have calloused her grandmother's hands, but Eunice's had been cared for. Eunice practised the piano, sewed and studied the Bible. The only interests outside the home were Church, the Salvation Army and the Temperance Hall where little Eunice could always be relied upon to sing one of the typical sob songs of the period such as 'Don't go down in the mine, Daddy', and songs of the suffering of families through the demon drink. It is a sad irony that her own marriage would itself at times suffer the effects of her husband's use of alcohol and other drugs.

To this God-fearing home came Vivian Deacon. Would the young girl care to take elocution lessons, he wanted to know. The Revd Philip Lew Tong was not impressed by the information that his daughter's voice was promising and Vivian was sent on his way. When he returned, he was armed with religious tracts. This time he added to his arguments the idea that Biblical passages would form the basis of the elocution and the lessons would be a form of Bible study. At this point his early lessons with the Revd Mills came to his rescue, for Vivian had studied the Bible as a boy and had an excellent memory. He turned out to know more of the Bible off by heart than even the Revd Philip Lew Tong and could answer any query with an apt quotation from the scriptures. This time they were impressed.

His first visit to Cardigan Street was on 26 January 1913. He was soon able to have an intimate friendship with a girl who until that time had been so sheltered from the world. His first letter is dated 21 February 1913 and pointedly headed 'c/o Temperance Hall'.

My very dear Eunice
It seems to me years since last night. Today I have started to write a short play for you to act in. Be of good cheer and comfort to your dear mother.... Always remember that I am thinking of you and praying for you. I want you to pray for me too. I will come and see you as soon as possible. Learn your piece for Sunday. Good-bye my little sunshine until to-morrow
Mispah your Vivian

Less than a week later another letter was received from Vivian. He is concerned that Eunice should pray for her mother. There is no mention of her being 'of good cheer and comfort' to her father, perhaps because of the latter's being unenthusiastic about having Vivian as his daughter's elocution teacher, perhaps simply because fathers continued to be a difficult subject for Vivian. This time, in place of the reference to temperance, there is mention of the Theosophical Society's 'International Order of the Star in the East', which had been founded early in 1911 with Krishnamurti at its head and Annie Besant and Charles Webster Leadbeater as its guardians. Mrs Besant, who had been a clergyman's wife until she admitted to losing her Christian faith, had then worked as a social reformer. Asked by W.T. Stead to review Madame Blavatsky's *The Secret Doctrine*, she found reading the book converted her to Theosophy. Since that time she had travelled the world, lecturing on 'The Coming World Teacher'. The formation of the International Order of the Star in the East had been announced by Mrs Besant upon her bringing the newly discovered Krishnamurti to London. Vivian's registration card for the Order was dated 9 October 1912 and signed by Krishnamurti and by J.R.M. Conkey, the national representative.

My dear little Eunice –
You told me you wanted the enclosed card so I am sending it to you, also some papers about the Star in the East, keep these until I see you next. Pray for your dear Mother.... Kindly remember me to Tim, your Mother and Mrs Baker.
With love until we meet yours for ever and ever
Vivian
X Mispah X
P.S. Write to me, do.

Enclosed was a folded card listing lectures arranged by the Theosophical Society, Besant Lodge, Collins Street, Melbourne. Mr Deacon was advertised as giving a lecture entitled 'Re-incarnation in Robert Browning's Poetry' on 21 May, a week after a Mrs Daniell was lecturing on 'Mystical Fires'. The objects of the organisation were listed:

First: To form a nucleus of the Universal Brotherhood of Humanity without distinction of race, creed, sex or colour.

Second: To encourage the study of comparative religion, philosophy and science.

Third: To investigate the unexplained laws of nature, and the powers latent in man.

On the plain back was written in ink, 'This is to request the honor (sic) and pleasure of your presence on 21st May at my lecture Yours Vivian'. Then he had written 'To Eunice Lew Tong' and underneath he had drawn a star, surrounded by a ring and finished off by carefully writing in block capitals, STAR OF LIFE.

Eunice attended the lecture. Thereafter she regularly attended the meetings, as the constant companion of the young orator whom some elderly members of the Society thought could well be the very world teacher to prepare for whose coming the International Order of the Star in the East had been formed. Vivian had travelled to Australia in his early teens. He always claimed to have run away from home to join a group of actors going to India and to have visited the Theosophist centre at Adyar. Certainly on his arrival in Australia he was quickly in touch with the Theosophists there. Baden-Powell knew many Theosophists and had appointed Annie Besant Chief Scout Commissioner for India, following amalgamation with the Besant scouts. Vivian's family was itself closely associated with the Society, but it is possible that B-P was the means by which Vivian was put in touch with Theosophy in Australia.

On 5 August 1913 Elizabeth Chamberlain made a note that she had given to her son, possibly as a birthday present, three letters written by the poet Robert Browning, none of them personal to her, namely two business letters to her father Reuben and a letter to her sister Christina on the death of a younger brother. There were also some photographs from the family album. These were part of a collection sent to his mother after the death of the poet's son Robert Barrett Browning in Asolo, 1912. Vivian, a natural showman, knew a reliable source of publicity when he saw one and was not slow in putting the letters to work.

Commanding the front page of *The Herald*, Saturday 16 August were the headlines BROWNING LETTERS, then in progressively smaller print headings: 'Relative of poet, Resident in Melbourne, Interesting photographs.'

The reporter found Browning items interesting and newsworthy. But surprisingly enough the article about three letters of Robert Browning turned into a profile of Vivian Deacon and his unusual beliefs and opinions, in which both Theosophy and temperance played a part:

Vivian Deacon is a mystic, and believes in reincarnation and the Law of Karma. He is a tall young man, olive complexioned, with raven hair and dark shadowy eyes.

'The Star of the East', the five-pointed emblem of the society formed by Mrs Annie Besant, but which is not restricted to Theosophists, and which confesses to the belief in the coming of a Christian all-world teacher, is worn by Deacon. But he distinctly states that he differs from the Theosophists on many subjects. His principal disagreement is in connection with the Hindu boy, who, at the expense of Mrs Besant, is being educated to be the sarcophagus of the soul of Christ reincarnated on earth.

This is his creed – 'I believe in reincarnation and the Law of Karma and its Hindu teachings. Karma is the absolute law of justice. What a man sows he will reap, if not in this incarnation, then in the next. I believe in God as personal and impersonal; as Logos, the All and the Infinite.

God is Love, and if you are sceptical you will say, How can God be love when that new-born baby dies after all its mother's sufferings? I say the death of that baby was in obedience to the Law of Karma. It may be that the souls of baby and mother re-incarnated were paying for something in a past incarnation. God made the law and it is in effect.

By and by the perfect race will be born – the Karma will be complete, the lesson will be learned. The greater souls among us have learned more of their lessons. Do you remember Rabbi Ben Ezra?'

This kinsman of Robert Browning also tilts at the agnostics and the scientists: 'Intelligent folk disbelieve Church theology,' he says. 'Why? Because it is insufficient. I tell you these scientists, these free-thinkers, these agnostics, these nothings-at-all are all soul-hungry and tired – for want of a God.

My intention is to form a Browning Society somewhat on the lines of the Theosophists, but we will practise and study from the teaching in the poems. We shall endeavour to obtain a knowledge of God, not merely intellectual, but in every fibre of our being, so that we know he is. The astral body will need training to develop the astral sense and enable students to roam the astral plane. A scientist or physician must have special training in the mental and manual work required.

So must the astral sense be trained. I shall take classes. I have a special system. Under the old methods either the optic nerve was strained or people went mad. The systems were principally fasting, crystal gazing and Hindu concentration. Mine will be of a meditative nature.

I believe in suggestive hypnotism. As Buddha says, "That which a man thinks, that is he."

In spite of doctors I believe in old Mesmer and his theories of animal magnetism. I am a vegetarian and have studied psychology therapeutics and practise total abstinence from alcohol and tobacco.'

Although talking with the fluency and confidence of middle-age this young man, seemingly in the early twenties, is but eighteen years of age this month. Although he numbers leading Theosophists among his friends, sceptics among his pupils, and enthusiasts among his followers!

The enthusiasm of the article almost suggests that the journalist himself was about to drop everything and become a follower of the charismatic young man. Illustrating the article was a photograph of Vivian, his hair parted in the centre, the style Leadbeater favoured for his pupils.

On Thursday 28 August 1913 Eunice sent Vivian a letter embellished with an ink-drawn shining silver five-pointed star under the address and the time 10.40 carefully recorded:

Dearest Vivian

I received your beautiful letter this morning, and was very pleased to hear from you, your letter is not too serious, religious or too long, but it is rather short. I like your 'lecture' (as I may call it) very much.

I received a book and letter for you by post this afternoon, they were from Mrs Daniells, how I know is because of the post marks and her writing.

15

Do not worry about me for I am quite well and hope that you are the same.

I have not lost the ring and I still wear it, the wattle blossom is alive and kicking.

I have to do Latin for homework tonight and I have not finished it, it is very hard and I have no one to help me, and I will soon have to go to bed.

With best wishes from all and love from me, I am yours for ever
Eunice
'Mispah'
'Dieu te benisse'
'God bless you'

From the very beginning of their relationship, the pattern was established of Vivian disappearing for weeks at a time. (The example of his father was clearly important.) Sometimes he would write to tell her that he was making and selling patent medicines. Another time he would be lecturing or making odd stage appearances. He always had several different ways of earning a living and several protectors. J.C. Williamson was a theatrical manager who could offer the odd engagement. E.W. Coles, the owner of the Coles' Book Arcade, was a spiritualist to whom Vivian could always turn for help; he helped develop Vivian's talent as a trance medium. Coles used to allow Vivian to borrow books without charge and would also pay him small commissions when Vivian brought in friends to buy books. William James Chidley was a single-minded sex reformer, always campaigning and always being arrested for refusing to stop publishing his controversial views. Vivian and he often used to meet in the Book Arcade and discuss philosophy and naturism between Chidley's many incarcerations in prison or mental asylum. Sister Veni Cooper-Mathieson was the voice of New Thought: when Vivian was in Sydney he stayed with her. With links to Mesmerism and its mediumistic ideas of healing through the animal spirits of the healer affecting those of the patient, New Thought had begun in New Hampshire with Phineas Parkhurst Quimby. Emphasising healing through prayer, New Thought was a belief in the universal and supreme power of good and taught that humanity was a spirit dweller in the human body. Among Quimby's pupils was Mrs Mary Baker Eddy, who founded the Christian Science Church; she, Ella Wheeler-Wilcox, Evelyn Underhill and Sister Veni were vice-presidents of the International New Thought Alliance.

16

Coles Book Arcade, also known as 'The Poor Man's University'

Born in America in 1873 or 1874, married at sixteen, a mother at seventeen, Sister Veni had fled an unhappy marriage and in 1903 came to Western Australia as an evangelist, starting the Women's White Cross and Moral Reform Crusade. In 1910, the year that Vivian arrived in Australia, she 'resigned under inspiration' from her work in Perth. In 1912 she obtained a certificate of ordination in the Church

Universal and the following year established this church in Perth. 1914 saw the publication of her novel *A Marriage of Souls*.

Vivian had by this time also made contact with the Esoteric Section of the Theosophical Society and thus with Charles Webster Leadbeater. A former Church of England clergyman and a disciple of Madame Blavatsky, Leadbeater had split the Theosophical Society in 1906, when it was discovered that he had been encouraging two pupils in Chicago to practise masturbation. In a world that was terrified of homosexuality and believed that masturbation led to blindness, madness or possibly both, this caused an uproar. Leadbeater was allowed to resign his membership of the society quietly to avoid too much public fuss. Two years later, when Annie Besant became the new president, she succeeded in having him reinstated.

In addition to the Theosophists, the New Thoughtists and the naturists, Vivian had also already discovered the teachings of Aleister Crowley and had begun to practise Crowleyan magick. It was a rich brew of influences, but not an unusually eclectic one for the times.

His mother had by now come to Australia to find him and sometimes he would go to stay at her home at Ferney Creek, Bayswater. His stepfather was now never mentioned.

The image of himself as delicate, which had affected him since birth, continued. He suffered frequent chills, nose-bleeds and faints. In spite of this delicacy, Vivian took work for a brief period as a docker in Port Melbourne. The other men were amused by his long hair and his delicate long slim white fingers, the nails kept scrupulously clean. Yet when a fight did break out, Vivian came off rather well and after it there was no more mockery. Behind the delicate manner, there was a perfectly robust masculine identity. Before long some theatre work turned up and he left the docks.

Usually he had only small walk-on parts. These would often be in Lewis Waller's company, with Madge Titheradge, Charles Quartermaine and Frank Wolfe. But again his memory came to his rescue, for his knowledge of Shakespeare made him a perfect understudy. His largest actual performance was as the Archbishop of Canterbury in *Henry V* in 1913 when the appointed member of the cast was, in one of the theatre's oldest traditions, indisposed.

He was often asked to give a recitation at charity bazaars or as interval entertainment at lectures or other public events. His repertoire of Shakespearean monologues had not varied much since his days with

Revd Shapley Mills, but new from his studies in Coles' Book Arcade were passages from Oscar Wilde, especially the 'Ballad of Reading Gaol', 'Charmides' and the 'Harlot's House', and from Wilde's fairy stories and plays. For music hall and in pantomime he performed his sketch 'My Brother Willie' based on Oscar's brother who was often said to have behaved like a village idiot in a public house. He also recited Browning.

He sang a duet composed by himself, but based on Charles Mathew's sketches, where he dressed partly as a man and partly as a woman so that he could present a different character to the audience by turning from one side to the other. He varied the verses to fit the occasions and topical themes. This comic figure of two contrasting genders recalls the two sidedness of Vivian's own nature, with his outward delicacy, in which he had been brought up to believe, and his ability to hold down jobs – and give a good account of himself in a fight – on the docks.

Having the ability to go into a trance at an early age, Vivian was a capable participant in hypnotism acts. He had mastered sleight of hand, learned about Houdini's muscle-control and manipulation, and about conjurers' magic, and was able to adapt himself as an entertainer to a variety of audiences.

With Coles' Book Arcade as a resource, all the books that he needed could be obtained, whether he wanted to study for the Theosophical Society, or for the New Thoughtists and Sister Veni's Church Universal, or for Leadbeater's classes. Even the works of Aleister Crowley were available through Vivian's friend Frank Bennett in Sydney. Vivian read with enthusiasm Blake, Tennyson, pre-Raphaelite poetry, Shaw, and writers of the Western esoteric tradition such as Cornelius Agrippa. He studied alchemy and Crowleyan magick, parlour tricks and conjurers' magic with equal glee. He loved the novels of Marie Corelli. Her *The Sorrows of Satan* was successfully adapted by Vivian's friend Roy Redgrave as a 4-act play; her Ziska left Vivian and Eunice convinced they had known each other in a previous incarnation. One book of short stories which Vivian carried with him on long journeys was *The Soul of Judas*, by Douglas Price, whom Vivian knew through the International New Thought Alliance. He used to say the title alone was the perfect thing for making conversations start with fellow travellers.

In his letters to Eunice, now turned thirteen, Vivian returned to his 'shut-in existence' and to 'the time drawing near for my Ministry of

Healing to commence'. At this time he records a number of physical symptoms – fever, sickness, near-death, dramatic loss of weight – all things undergone by other initiates in the Esoteric Section of the Theosophical Society. His close friends now were all either in the Theosophical Society or part of the wider circle of mystics. At Kilsyth there was a school 'Allawha'. There were boy nurses and examinations given by people with qualifications in mysticism. His mother visited him there, for she was very familiar with the workings of the Golden Dawn and had believed in a special destiny for her son from birth. At the Ibis Lodge Vivian had been preparing for his 'Christos Initiation'. (The Ibis was a bird venerated by the ancient Egyptians as a bird sacred to Thoth, known to alchemists as Hermes Trismegisthus. It might also have appealed to Leadbeater for its habit of cleaning its anus with its beak, for Leadbeater insisted on daily enemas for himself and his students. Under his influence Vivian acquired a red rubber tube and a blue-rimmed enamel enema.) Vivian wrote from there, telling of illness, shedding blood and fasting, as he underwent symptoms similar to those suffered by Krishnamurti and the other Theosophists who underwent initiations. He took a vow of two years' celibacy.

The day following his initiation, he wrote to Eunice, using for the first time their secret names for each other. Vivian felt that his spirit had progressed throughout many incarnations and now that his spirit was on the final incarnation he sometimes used the name 'Christos' in correspondence with Eunice. It was from this time that he first began to spell his name 'Vyvyan' and for the rest of this book, this is how he will be referred to. This was the spelling used by Wilde's son and he may in part have been influenced by that. He was certainly always very interested in Wilde: his mother used to be acutely embarrassed by his public readings of Wilde, at that time still an unmentionable author. When talking about the change later in life, he used to joke punningly that it was to do with a change from more 'I's' to more 'Y's', from greater selfishness to greater wisdom. In addition there was the symbolism of the 'Y' as the division of the Left Hand and Right Hand Paths. (Pythagorus, whose name is associated with this symbol, was revered by the Theosophists.) The photographs taken after the initiation show him in white robes, his hair brushed back, giving a blessing. In contrast to these, there are others dating from the same time, showing him as a blood red fiend in a Crowleyesque pose. It is this division between the Godly and the Satanic that the 'Y' symbolised for him. When Eunice answered letters for him, she always continued to spell his name as it appeared on his birth certificate, partly perhaps because she did not approve of changing one's baptismal name, partly perhaps because she was never happy about his decision to explore both Right and Left Hand Paths.

While Vyvyan took the name 'Christos', Eunice sometimes used the name 'Ziska'. They had both read Marie Corelli's novel of that name, in which the eponymous heroine appears at a Cairo fancy dress ball dressed as the mistress of Araxes, one of the early Kings of Egypt. 'She is sinuous, beautiful, enthralling, but has the eye of a vampire bat and the soul of a fiend. Men worship her, women hate her, all fear her and the young French painter who so resembles Araxes, falls passionately in love with her but not, he feels, for the first time.' Vyvyan remembered being a priest in Egypt, called Memnon, in a previous incarnation and remembered the hypnotism of the young boys in the temple so that they could report what was happening miles away. He was later to call himself 'Frater Memnon' in connection with his Christian Mystics of the Rose Cross. The statue of Memnon in the Egyptian desert had an Aeolian harp on the top of its head, and when the wind blew strongly, it sighed or hummed. This seems to symbolise beautifully the 'attuned receptivity' of the medium.

In the beginning of their friendship Vyvyan had given Eunice a ring which she was to keep all her life. It was only an inexpensive, adjustable metal ring, with a Chinese symbol in gold on turquoise as a kind of signet. On the cover of a blue penny exercise book ('The Champion') they recorded their devotion. Written on the top half, faded and torn from the bottom half are the words:

Trust me darling always and I will always trust you, my own love Eunice X X X X
To Eunice Lew Tong –
I hereby promise that I will be your husband because I love you more than anything else on Earth.
Vyvyan H.R. Deacon
Vyvyan Vyvyan

Vertically in the left-hand margin Eunice added:

N.B Vyvyan kept the other half of the exercise book cover on which I avowed my love and promise, 1914.

Vyvyan's half, however, has not survived.

In 1914, while volunteers queued in Australia to join the armed forces, Vyvyan gave Eunice the Theosophical handbook *At the Feet of the Master* by 'Alcyone', the name used by Krishnamurti as a pen-name when publishing something written in trance. In her preface, Annie Besant declared that the small book was 'the first written by a younger Brother, young in body verily, but not in Soul. The teachings contained in it were given to him by his Master in preparing for his Initiation, and were written down by him from memory – slowly and laboriously, for his English last year was far less fluent than it is now.' Vyvyan wrote on the flyleaf: 'To Ziska with Love from Christos. My beloved Leader and President.'

Vyvyan was busy the year war began. His weekly timetable, showing a characteristic mixture of health care and spiritual advancement, reads:

Monday 8 pm, Nights with Great People.
Mr Deacon or some other lecturer will deal with the life and works of various celebrities, living and dead.

Tuesday 8 pm, Lecture on Health.
Mr Deacon deals with the Prevention, Cause and Cure of various ailments.

Wednesday 8 pm, Meeting for Spiritual Advancement.
A written application with a fortnight's notice must be given by anyone desirous of partaking in this meeting.

Thursday 8 pm, Every alternate Thursday Mr Deacon gives a lecture to Ladies Only, and on the intervening Thursday to Men Only.

Friday. Business hours until 10 pm.

Saturday 3 pm, Conversazione. This ticket admits.

Notice: At all meetings except Wednesday, a collection to defray expenses etc will be made.
To ascertain the Name of Subjects etc, see Meetings and Lectures column in *Age*.

At this time Vyvyan was publishing leaflets such as 'A Talk about Health' and 'Man, Know Yourself.' For those with problems there were endless Consultations Free, though any herbs prescribed were charged for.

Among Vyvyan's disciples one of the most devoted was Bomberg. Bomberg had dark curly hair, a large well-shaped Jewish nose and dark expressive eyes with long black lashes. He used to suffer from terrifying hallucinations, possibly due to drugs. Vyvyan was a calming influence on him. Once, when he was chased by invisible pursuers, he found himself driven to run faster and faster until at last he collapsed, cringing in fear. While others struggled in vain to convince him there were no pursuers, Vyvyan on the contrary accepted that the pursuers were there and gave him the strength to turn, face them calmly, inhale deeply and dismiss them with chosen magic words.

On Thursday 31 December 1914 in the *Labour Call* (printed with a bright red cover), appeared an advertisement for 'the only White Herbalist in Australia who has a really thorough knowledge of Oriental, as well as of American and English Herbs... Mr Deacon has an Expert Optician always in attendance.' Occupying two columns of the same issue was an article by 'Vyvyan H.R. Deacon' on the subject of tolerance, specifically towards the Germans.

In March 1915, Eunice's father died. For her spiritual solace Vyvyan recommended the Order of the Star of the East, which he himself had joined in 1912. On 25 May 1915, Vyvyan had arranged for Eunice to be enrolled by his friend T.H. Martyn who, as national representative of Australia, signed her card personally. He was visiting from his home in Sydney, where he was the main support of the Theosophical Society. The stamped signature of Krishnamurti appeared as the Head and the State Secretary, N.R. Ray, signed it at the side.

After the death of her husband, Eunice's mother became more anxious about her daughter's friendship with Vyvyan. It is noticeable that on Tuesday 21 September 1915, Eunice did not put her own address at the top of the letter, but c/o 114 Lygon Street, her grandmother's shop. It is likely that the correspondence became clandestine for a time and she was receiving Vyvyan's letters at her grandmother's address, because against her mother's wishes. On 22 October for Eunice's fifteenth birthday present, Vyvyan sent her another Theosophist book, this one entitled *In His Name* by C. Jinarajadasa, a protégé of Leadbeater who worked with him and Annie Besant and travelled around with them lecturing and writing. This particular book Vyvyan found expressed so much that he wanted to say that he started to underline it in odd places and ended up by underlining most of it. Eunice wrote two letters of reply, suggesting that there was still a ban on correspondence. 'Dear Vyvyan,' ran the official letter, 'Mother has permitted me to write to you thanking you very much for the book you sent me for my birthday.' By the time this reached him Vyvyan had in fact already received a letter from Eunice, one which she must have written as soon as she picked up her present from the shop. The tone of this one is of course very different: 'I received your charming letter yesterday and your dear, sweet little book this evening. Thank you very much for both and also for the kind, helpful thoughts you sent me to-day.' In another letter she told Vyvyan something about her mother that she found curious: 'It is a very strange thing that mother feels your presence; often when we are going out she says she can feel you walking near us.' What this glimmer of insight tells us about Eunice's mother's feelings about Vyvyan, though, it is impossible to guess.

In 1915 Sister Veni urged Vyvyan to move to Sydney. There, she insisted, he could quickly establish himself as a teacher, healer and lecturer through her patronage and his links with New Thought groups. Vyvyan knew that his connections with Leadbeater would be of help in such a move, for Leadbeater, after a long lecture tour, had settled in Australia. Living in Sydney since 1914, Leadbeater stayed with Mr and Mrs Martyn and used the large Independent Order of Odd Fellows temple in Elizabeth Street. In the twenties, as the head of a community, he settled in a mansion on the shore of Sydney Harbour. Leadbeater was still writing articles for Theosophical magazines, but had also begun to operate as a leading member of what was to become the Liberal Catholic Church. The Old Catholic Church had broken away from the Roman Catholic Church as a result of the refusal of some to accept the doctrine of papal infallibility, defined in the Vatican council decrees of 1870. As a result, the Old Catholics were able to claim apostolic succession and it was this that attracted Leadbeater, for he believed that the Mass released occult forces. Once raised to the episcopate, however, he and Wedgwood increasingly began to operate an independent church, staffed partly from within the Theosophical Society; this was the Liberal Catholic Church. Vyvyan, meanwhile, was continuing weekly training classes in the Esoteric Section of the Theosophical Society. The difficulty was that unless they married, Vyvyan's moving to Sydney would mean that he and Eunice would inevitably be separated.

Since the death of Eunice's father, there was no money coming in. Her widowed mother was left stubbornly defending the family against both poverty and gossip. Vyvyan himself still had no regular income, no capital and no prospects, but Eunice's mother must have decided that he would nevertheless be able to support a wife and that marriage would at least legitimise the unstoppable secret correspondence. Perhaps she thought he would settle down. In any case, she knew that she could no longer support her daughter. On 5 January 1916 fifteen-year-old Eunice Mary Lew Tong, who had less than a month previously appeared with long flowing hair in her school photograph, and twenty-year-old Vyvyan Hereward Rowden Deacon came with their mothers and a few friends to the Congregational church, East Melbourne. His mother had declared herself appalled at the thought that Eunice might get married in school uniform. This led to difficulties, for the poor girl had no other smart clothes. Eventually Vyvan's mother came up with some drab cast-offs: a coat, a hat with a torn veil, and an old string bag. The results were so truly awful that one can only wonder at her motives. After all, this was her adored sole surviving child that Eunice was taking from her. In addition to being dressed up in a ragbag of old clothes, Eunice's beautiful long hair was all cropped off, for the same reasons: long hair was suitable for schoolgirls, not for brides and married women. The result was not that she looked older, just poorer. Vyvyan himself, meanwhile, was looking ill and emaciated, for he was still weak from the ordeals surrounding his initiation.

They were married.

Chapter Three

Now they are old, now they are young. They change all
in a moment as their thought changes. It is sometimes a
terrible thing to be out of the body, God help us all.
W.B. Yeats, *The Words Upon the Window-Pane*

ON 15 JANUARY 1916 Vyvyan put his wife on a train for
Sydney. They were moving to Sydney, but he was not quite
ready to go himself. She was to travel on ahead of him and
he would join her there shortly, he assured her. Still
wearing the old clothes his mother had found and insisted she wear,
Eunice boarded the train miserably. She was confused at his sending
her away so soon. They had been married for ten days.

Among Sister Veni's New Thought followers in Sydney, were
Norvald Brown, a hairdresser, and his wife Inez. They had been very
impressed by Vyvyan when they had met him, so they agreed that
Eunice should go to stay in their rooms behind the hair-dressing salon.
The Browns were vegetarians and Eunice lived with them on a diet of
peaches and nuts. They gave Eunice fresh clothes and she was able to
discard the ones she had worn at her wedding. She read Lamb's *Tales
from Shakespeare*. She went to the Independent Order of Oddfellows
temple to hear Rani Susani lecture on Truth and to the Majestic Picture
Palace to see Mary Pickford in *Cinderella*. Eunice wrote daily to her
'darling husband Vyvyan', waited for news of him and watched the
boats in the harbour. After just over a week he arrived.

The Browns could not make room for two people, so Vyvyan turned
to Sister Veni. Through her he was introduced to the Pateman family,
who lived in a large house in Coogee, a suburb of Sydney. They were
offered two unfurnished rooms, but as the young couple owned only
the clothes they had arrived in, it was decided that the Patemans' two
young daughters would go into the empty rooms with a pair of camp

beds, leaving their bedrooms, with two small single beds, to Vyvyan and Eunice. Vyvyan had business cards with the Mount Street address printed, to promote his herbal and metaphysical work.

Vyvyan had again met up with his friend Roy Redgrave and through him was able to pick up some acting work. *Under Fire* by Roi Cooper Magru was opening at the Criterion Theatre under the management of J.C. Williamson Theatres. Nothing to do with the Henri Barbusse novel of the same name, this was a wartime piece about the invasion of Belgium and Vyvyan had a walk-on part as a Belgian peasant. Roy Redgrave also walked on while he was busy preparing for the next production, *On Trial*, in which he had a lead part. Because of Vyvyan's work as a herbalist during the day and theatre in the evenings until very late hours, Eunice was left alone a great deal.

Sister Veni was an enthusiastic organiser and founder of institutions, centres and orders: in addition to the Esoteric College, her interests in 1916 included the Truth Centre, the Church Universal, the Home of Truth, the Bethany Healing Rooms, the Universal Truth Publication Company, the Bethlehem Children's Home (For Children of Universal Love) and the Order of the Prince of Peace, this last being the province of one Brother Ariel, or Joseph Cooper, the husband (or common-law husband) of Sister Veni Cooper-Mathieson and the source of the first part of her surname.

The Saturday afternoon after Eunice had arrived in Sydney there was a reception for Dr Julia Seton on the lawn of the Esoteric College and Home of Truth, which was housed at 39 Brown Street, Paddington, Sydney. Julia Seton, the vice-president of the International New Thought Alliance in the USA, was a popular speaker and a dynamic character and more than two hundred guests came to hear her. She was given to urging her audiences to respond to life with endless love. 'If a discordant condition comes into your life – just love it away! Flood a cold heart with warm love and melt it.' Such advice was always received very well. The reception was followed by a service in the evening, which ended with the Doxology, a New Thought practice and one Vyvyan was to keep to all his life.

The following day, Sunday, Vyvyan was free from engagements and read Dr Seton's book *Freedom Talks No.1* while sitting on the balcony with Eunice. She, he noted, was menstruating at the time. This was no idle observation, but one which reflected his involvement in magic, for in sexual magic the bodily fluids are of great importance.

Women are thought to be at their most lucidly vatic at this time, possessed of a force which men can absorb through sexual contact, particularly cunnilingus. The cakes of light for the Mass of the Holy Ghost should always be prepared by a woman during this phase of the menstrual cycle.

After tea Vyvyan had an engagement at Leigh Hall to speak on 'The Christ that is to be', a familiar Theosophical theme. Over 30 people attended and the lecture was so well received that he was engaged for the following Sunday. He was paid five shillings for the lecture by the local organiser, one Mrs Weeks. James Harradine Pateman had gone with Vyvyan to listen to him talk and Vyvyan afterwards remembered that they had an intense conversation on the way home on the subject of Crowley, black magic and New Thought.

The following morning, while Eunice took Julia Seton to the Home of Truth, Vyvyan went into the city centre with Mr Pateman. The latter went off to a day's work at his office at Wunderlich's and Vyvyan made his way to the railway station, for he needed to arrange with a carrier to send his black tin trunk out to Coogee for one shilling and six pence. Once that was done, he returned home for tea and afterwards went to the theatre for that night's performance of *Under Fire*. When the play closed in April, Vyvyan did not audition for any more parts, but concentrated instead on building up his career as a lecturer and herbalist.

With printed cards to publicise himself, he began to be more widely involved among Sydney esoteric groups. At first much of the healing work was inevitably voluntary, an essential part of building up good-will and developing a network of patients and contacts. Unfortunately he was therefore reliant on the odd few shillings paid for the patent medicines some clients bought from him and for the occasional lecture: this was not enough to keep himself and Eunice in food, let alone pay rent. In addition therefore he worked with Mrs Pateman at Sister Veni's Bethany Rooms when needed. The Bethany Rooms were a centre for healing and women and girls expecting illegitimate babies would often arrive and stay through their confinement. Now that he was no longer auditioning for walk-on parts, he was available for evening meetings with Sister Veni or Leadbeater, with James Wedgwood of the Liberal Catholic Church or the Crowleyite Frank Bennett, or with the incomparable Chidley, whenever the latter was released from captivity.

Mr and Mrs Pateman had made a pact never to turn away anyone in need, so life must have become increasingly difficult for them when

Vyvyan had no regular work. Things grew more serious when Australian enthusiasm for the war grew into an anti-German hysteria, of the same kind that infected so many of the allied countries. Mr Pateman's German employers Wunderlich were forced to close. Mrs Pateman's advancing pregnancy, with a baby due in September, added to their responsibilities, and they decided to move to a more modest house eight miles from the city in Bankstown in June 1916.

This was the reason I was given for my parents having to move on. One of the Pateman's daughters, Phyllis, though, recalled Vyvyan and Eunice being asked to leave even before June, however, and remembered that it all stemmed from Mrs Pateman's being offended by something Vyvyan had said to her when she was resting one afternoon. Whatever the reason, Vyvyan and Eunice now had to sleep in the changing rooms of Wyllie public swimming baths, in Coogee. During the day they used to sit in the cheap coffee-houses and cafés that were the natural resting place of the homeless and the unemployed. There was an atmosphere of mutual support in these places and those who happened to find themselves briefly in funds would pay for those in worse circumstances. Mockbell's was a favourite with Vyvyan and his dilettante acquaintances. Mr Mockbell had established a string of coffee-shops in cellars, lit by murky electric globes, where you could spend all day over a tin mug of coffee costing fourpence. Between five and six o' clock people with no stable address would be 'At Home' to friends at Mockbell's and messages and letters could always be left there for regulars.

Vyvyan obviously could not readily work from the changing rooms. However, as Frank Bennett, James Wedgwood and the Revd Cocks (who was to become a member of Vyvyan's Rosicrucian group) needed laudanum and cocaine from time to time and Frank Bennett also wanted heroin, these three, none of them poor, agreed to set Vyvyan up in a small shop at 3 Junction Street. With a pharmacy at their disposal, none of them now had to worry unduly about where their next supplies were coming from. Frank Bennett was by now the appointed representative of Aleister Crowley, responsible for promoting the Ordo Templi Orientis, of which Crowley had become the chief, in Australia. The Temple's members required drugs for sacramental use in specific rituals. Bennett subsequently died of heroin addiction in 1932. Crowley's *Fountain of Hyacinth* gives an account of his own struggle with an addiction that began with a prescription for asthma. The poet Michael Hamburger recalls, in his autobiography

String of Beginnings, meeting Crowley in a deserted boarding house in Hastings, a meeting during which Crowley drank large quantities of whisky or brandy and kept disappearing behind a screen to inject himself with heroin.

Eunice always insisted that if Vyvyan took drugs at secret O.T.O. rituals at that time it was never apparent to her. She did, however, recall that in 1914 a clergyman gave him, without his knowledge of the inevitable effects, an aphrodisiac which produced an erection lasting longer than forty-eight hours, causing Vyvyan almost fatal distress. What the clergyman's intentions were in doing this, I never discovered. The leaflets and patent medicine bottle labels that survive from this period are innocuous enough, being for guaranteed influenza cures and a popular gripe water called 'Babies' Blessing', a herbal remedy for sciatica and a hair tonic among other things.

Julia Seton had returned to the States in May, leaving Sister Veni's eloquence in full spate. She preached without notes and the words flowed easily. She wrote fluently for her magazine *The Revealer*. Her motto, *Veni, Vidi, Vici*, from which she took her name, was one she lived up to, drawing crowds wherever she went, with her impassioned oratory and her controversial behaviour. There were rumours of roof-top orgies, oddly enough, given her strict insistence on total abstinence from sexual intercourse by all the pregnant women who were patients at the Bethany Healing Rooms. Of pregnancy she wrote: 'Men that truly love their wives do not make these unnatural and unholy demands upon them at this most sacred period of a woman's life and that of her unborn child.' She insisted that sexual intercourse during pregnancy was the cause of deformity in children, that the embryo had been distorted by the lust of the parents. This was almost pure Chidley.

In June 1916 yet another Chidley case was before the public. He would from time to time be conditionally released. The condition was always that he should not return to selling his book *The Answer* in public places or preaching his ideas. Although it was pointed out that Chidley, being obsessively loyal to his ideas, was increasingly gaining public support as a martyr, he was, after a brief spell of freedom, again sent to Kenmore Asylum and Vyvyan spoke in protest in Domain, a small park surrounded by art galleries and the usual place for public meetings, and Sister Veni continued to pronounce what was in effect Chidleyan philosophy from the platform without being censored.

On 8 August 1916, the day before Vyvyan's twenty-first birthday, Chidley was released quietly from Kenmore Asylum into the bosom of his Sydney followers. In spite of Chidley's public support with letters to the press, open-air meetings held by his supporters and disciples in Domain and politicians pointing out that the martyrdom of Chidley was making the law unpopular, Chidley was re-arrested on 23 September 1916, on a breach of licence. Again he was incarcerated. This time his spirit was broken. The inflexibility of the Law had proven intolerable, for what life was there for Chidley if he could not disseminate his message freely?

Two days after his arrest, while he was in Reception House he wrote his final message to the world:

> You have looked on for five years and seen me done to death by fools, quacks and rogues (including unjust 'judges') Well, listen: every word of my book *The Answer* is true.

He went on to plead with the people not to let those who had crushed him, crush his book.

> The human race must return to (1) natural coition, (2) to nudity and (3) to a natural diet: fruit and nuts only; and each of these depend upon the other two. Only thus can you obtain mutual Joy, Love, Content. Bring children up naked and on fruit only – clothes do more harm than is supposed. The skin serves a natural function – through pores keeping you warm in winter and cool in summer.

He urged publication and reading of his book and his *Confession* of which Havelock Ellis held a missing chapter.

> Mine has been an unhappy life, but it contains a moral, namely, that all my misery comes from that 'erection' in boys and men. Farewell! W.J. Chidley.

Being locked up with the insane, forced to eat prison diet and to wear prison clothes was a life Chidley could not endure. He attempted to end the ordeal by what he must have considered preferable; a few days after writing his last message he tried to kill himself by setting fire to his clothing after drenching it with kerosene. His guards were too quick for him to be successful. They ensured he suffered only minor burns, but the will to live had gone irreparably. He died at Callan Park Mental Hospital on 21 December 1916, aged 56. He was not forgotten by his friends. A follower called James Stewart ('John') Shirlaw opened a commune and meeting place in a magnificent old house called Ivycliffe in Berrys Bay, North Sydney, with tropical gardens going down to the water's edge, where people could go bathing. Life there was lived as near to Chidley's ideals as possible, with talks on Nietzsche, Steiner, sex and health reform. The commune survived for six years after Chidley's death in 1916, during which time Vyvyan and Eunice were founder members and periodic residents.

Meanwhile a New Thought conference was held in Brisbane in October 1916, under the guidance of Grace Aguilar, and Sister Veni established 7 October as Australia's New Thought Day, for Australia, she used to teach, was the 'land of the dawning'. Sister Veni by now ran a boarding house 'Non-pareil', in Merriwa Street, Katoomba, and here followers of New Thought could stay and join in the New Thought activities. 'Non-pareil' was also the place to which some of Vyvyan's followers would come, like author James Bunn, working as a ship's steward.

There were always mysteries in the New Thought movement. Things would happen, people would suddenly come or suddenly be expelled and one was left guessing at what lay behind these events. A friend of the Pateman family, Edward Crester-Wilson was librarian of the Truth Library. Tall, dark and good looking in a cadaverous sort of way, he lectured for the New Thought Centre on concentration. 'We always knew that he had been involved in something unpleasant, though it was never quite clear exactly what' Phyllis Pateman recalled. (Not that anything would have worried Sister Veni, for she could seem pretty shady herself.) On the 16 November 1916 he wrote in Mrs Pateman's autograph album, a few weeks after the birth of baby Julia. (The page was decades later sent to me by Phyllis.) After comparing the qualities of truth, wisdom and power he concludes that love surpasses these qualities: 'it guides us always into the fullness of greater realities, leaving us neither desolate nor in despair, but alive to the greatness of each successive change that makes for progress. Let us never forget that the crown of life is love. E. Crester Wilson 16/11/16.' Then there was an announcement in *The Revealer* that he no longer occupied the post of librarian. The announcement having been published, Sister Veni went away for three months' holiday at the end of 1916. In fact, both Crester-Wilson and Mr Pateman broke off all contact with Sister Veni because of the illness of the younger Pateman daughter Evie, which they both attributed to some kind of black magic. They were perhaps beginning to guess that Sister Veni had joined forces with Frank Bennett as Crowley's representative of the O.T.O. in Australia in 1915, receiving her certificate from the South African branch in November. In addition to the suspicions of black magic, there were rumours that she and Frank Bennett and others had been seen naked on the roof of her house.

Sister Veni was now running a publishing company. She offered correspondence courses on sex education (twelve lessons called 'The Sacred Science of Sex' would arrive at the home of the anxious student in a series of plain envelopes), for which she charged high fees. At the same time, and perhaps the two were connected, she moved the Home of Truth Esoteric College to Mount Victoria in the Blue Mountains in order to convert the old Esoteric College building into a maternity hospital able to take up to twenty-four patients, with a roof garden and a view across Manley Point. The cost of running such a maternity home must have been high, even with the then modish starvation diet which passed for a healthy regime. Patients had to survive a fortnight taking nothing but orange juice, followed by a second fortnight in which they were limited to two apples a day. On Vyvyan's advice, raspberry leaf tea was also made available in the orange juice fortnight, as this was thought to strengthen the muscles of the uterus. Such fasting and frugal dieting was not a fetish peculiar to Sister Veni. Chidley was another enthusiast for spartan food. In the twenties and thirties the early health farms and nature cure houses, such as Champneys, near Tring in Hertfordshire, run by Stanley Lief, and Dr Issel's Swiss Clinic, believed in total cleansing of the body by fasting and irrigation. As we have seen, Chidley's influence clearly remained with Sister Veni after his death, both in her attitude to diet and her blaming infantile paralysis and similar afflictions on the 'depleted vitality on the part of the father' or 'an excessive indulgence of carnal passions on the part of both parents, which is a shock to the nervous system.'

As part of the changes organised by Sister Veni, the library was sold off. The July-September issue of the *Quarterly Revealer* for 1917, declared:

> IMPORTANT ANNOUNCEMENT, the Progressive Thought Lending and Circulation Library together with the Complete Book Stock of the Truth Centre has been purchased by COLES' BOOK ARCADE, 346 George Street, Sydney, where the Library is now carried on.

Until 1916, Vyvyan had been involved with Sister Veni's New Thought and Church Universal work and she had prepared him for his spiritual initiation pending the settling of Leadbeater and Wedgwood in Sydney. His marriage left his relations with Sister Veni far cooler. He still worked with her in healing and supported her work with visiting New Thought exponents such as Dr Julia Seton and Grace Aguilar. But his chief spiritual involvement was by now with Wedgwood and Leadbeater.

On 13 February 1916 James Ingall Wedgwood, Theosophical

convert and refugee from Anglicanism, was ordained in London as a bishop in the Old Catholic Church. The first choice of bishop to officiate at Wedgwood's consecration had been Arnold Harris Mathew (himself consecrated bishop in Utrecht 28 April 1908), but he had declined to ordain a man who held authority in the Theosophical Society, so Wedgwood turned instead to Bishop Willoughby, assisted by Bishops Gauntlett and King. As soon as Wedgwood had been ordained he headed for Sydney, passing on the Apostolic Succession to his friend Leadbeater on 22 July 1916. Such wanderings of the episcopacy were not unknown at this time. The Outer Head (or chief on earth) of the O.T.O. Theodor Reuss was created a bishop of the Gnostic Catholic Church by the French Dr Encausse, or 'Papus', and he in turn seems to have passed the honour on to Aleister Crowley.

Wedgwood was at this time in his early thirties, a good-looking man with a magnetic personality and a dark appearance inherited from his mother, a Spanish woman who married into the Wedgwood pottery family, in which there were several members with an interest in Spiritualism. Wedgwood had been admitted to the O.T.O. in 1912 by Theodor Reuss at the request of John Yarker, an obsessively dedicated English masonic enthusiast, appointed Masonic Grand Constable of England and associated with the secret Masonic orders among which the O.T.O and the Golden Dawn had their roots. It had been from Yarker that Reuss, who later recruited Aleister Crowley, obtained the charter for the Berlin Grand Lodge of the Masonic rite of Mizraim and Memphis. (Earlier in his life Reuss had worked for the secret service in Germany, spying on Karl Marx, whose daughter Eleanor considered him dirty and vulgar.) Wedgwood and Marie Russak, the private secretary of Henry Olcott, one of the two founders of the Theosophical Society, had in 1912 established the Temple of the Rosy Cross, an adventist, strongly ritualistic group with an interest in cabbala, freemasonry, and astrology; he dissolved the group in 1914. With Vyvyan's training in the early Christian Mysteries and in the Ancient Order of Oriental Templars, he was well placed quickly to be on good terms with Wedgwood and Leadbeater.

Three days after Leadbeater's ordination, he wrote to his friend Annie Besant, president of the Theosophical Society to speak of his joy at having Wedgwood arrive in Sydney:

> He himself had so guided events as to produce this curious result, that a branch of the Catholic Church, having the Apostolic

Succession in a form which cannot be questioned, should be entirely in the hands of the Theosophists, who are willing and eager to do exactly as he wishes... This was a method of bringing over the Holy Orders of the old plan into the new one... gradually drawing round it those who love the Catholic ritual, but want a theosophical interpretation of it and of the doctrine of the Church.

They began to reconstruct the Liberal Catholic Ritual and Liturgy. On 5 September 1916 Leadbeater wrote of their efforts:

All the greatest poets of the age ought to be at work on it, not a couple of obscure though earnest gentlemen... It must conform exactly to the old thought-form and yet contain no word that is untrue, no thought derogatory to the Love of God and the dignity of man who is part of him.

On the nights between 11 and 12 December 1916 the revised ritual of the Mass was submitted to the 'Lord Maitreya' and the instructions received were 'to preserve the old thought-form and the working of the old magic – the effect of the various acts at different stages...' The Liberal Catholic Church thus began to have a life distinct from that of the Old Catholic Church in which it had grown like a cuckoo. Although Christian in its origins, Jinarajadasa, a Buddhist by birth and closely involved with Theosophy, was among a number of non-Christian sympathisers who used to attend and speak at services. Annie Besant herself also used to address services, being led to a seat of honour beside the altar. George Arundale, another Theosophist who was excited by Liberal Catholic ritual, was later ordained and became a bishop in that Church. Arundale had been brought up by his aunt Francesca Arundale. A severe woman in steel-rimmed spectacles with whom Krishnamurti lodged for a time when in England as a boy, she was the first Englishwoman to enter Co-Masonry, the movement growing from a French Masonic Lodge that had been suspended for admitting women in 1882. Arundale himself had once been promised by Leadbeater the role of Buddha on the planet Mercury in his next life, though to Arundale's distress this opinion had been revised in 1913 when Leadbeater prophesied that one of his discoveries, a Brahmin boy from South India called Rajagopalacharya (who had, he declared, been St Bernard of Clairvaux in a previous life) would occupy this position.

The Church had its first constitution adopted at a joint meeting of the Episcopal and Clerical Synod held on 20 April 1916. It was published under the imprimatur of Bishop James Ingall Wedgwood, Bishop of the Old Catholic Church with the title *Constitution and Rules of the Old Catholic Church in Great Britain*, subsequently issued with a cover bearing the name Liberal Catholic Church.

To understand the real merit of Wedgwood as a living presence it is well to know his effect on those who knew him. The Revd T.W. Shepherd first saw him at the Queen's Hall in Upper Regent Street, London, in the summer of 1924, when he and other distinguished members of the Theosophical Society were seated in a semicircle behind Mrs Annie Besant while she addressed a meeting. It was a practice to 'give support on the Inner Planes' and it seemed to work. 'As the lecture drew to a close, the atmosphere was electric. For my part I was aware of a splendid influence coming from Bishop Wedgwood.' Revd Shepherd was a school-boy at the time. He next saw him in October 1927 when he was the principal guest at a service at St Mary's Church. 'It was a Mass of the Holy Spirit with Bishop Wedgwood as the celebrant. It was the first time I had seen a full High Mass according to the Liberal Catholic Rite, which was a great experience in itself, but the memory of hearing the Mass sung by Bishop Wedgwood, of catching the inflection of speech and of witnessing the perfection of his movements, still enthrals me. I realised then that I had witnessed a hierophant of the Christian Mysteries at work.' Writing in the *Liberal Catholic* the Rt Revd Gerrit Munnik ends his 'Personal Glimpses of Bishop Wedgwood':

> The German psychoanalyst Dr Groddeck, when trying to analyse the case of Bishop Wedgwood, said that he was a real live 'saint'. He should be considered as such in the Liberal Catholic Church.

Vyvyan always treated him with reverence during his training in the traditional early Christian Mysteries with the same emphasis on ritual and the science of the sacrament given by Vyvyan's first religious teacher the Revd Shapley Mills. There was a very special relationship between Wedgwood and Vyvyan, apparently beyond time and space. Although I cannot recollect anything said, I sensed an atmosphere that was not of this world when I was in a room with the two of them twenty years later when Wedgwood was dying of syphilis.

Leadbeater returned from New Zealand, where he had been on

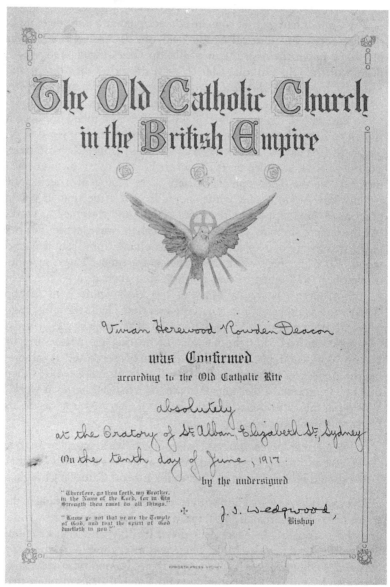

The Old Catholic Church
in the British Empire

Vivian Herewood Rowden Deacon

was Confirmed

according to the Old Catholic Rite

absolutely

at the Oratory of St. Alban, Elizabeth St., Sydney

On the tenth day of June, 1917.

by the undersigned

"Therefore, go thou forth, my Brother,
in the Name of the Lord, for in thy
Strength thou canst do all things."

"Know ye not that ye are the Temple
of God, and that the spirit of God
dwelleth in you?"

J. J. Wedgwood,
Bishop

EPWORTH PRESS SYDNEY

tour, on 11 February 1916 and in the spring of 1916 Vyvyan renewed his relationship with him although they were now colleagues more than teacher and pupil. When Wedgwood consecrated Leadbeater to the episcopate, Vyvyan, who was himself occasionally given to wearing a surplice at the Liberal Catholic services, took part as an observer. The two priests assisting Wedgwood were D.M. Tweedie of Adelaide and J.B. McConkey of Melbourne, both of them friends of Vyvyan. The latter was national representative of the Star in the East and as such signed Vyvyan's registration card. McConkey had lectured for the Theosophical Society in the arcade of Flinders Street, Melbourne in 1914 and had known Vyvyan at least five years.

The ceremony took place at Crendon, the home of Gustav Kollerstrom, an eminent Theosophist and the father of Oscar Köllerstrom, then aged thirteen and one of the four boy witnesses. He was Leadbeater's first pupil when he settled in Sydney in 1915 and he remained his principal one. Vyvyan was well acquainted with the family and was baptised and confirmed by Gustav Köllerstrom before being reconfirmed by Wedgwood, at the oratory of St Alban, Elizabeth Street, Sydney on the 10th June 1917. Eunice too became a member of the Old Catholic Church, being baptised by the Revd Köllerstrom and confirmed by Bishop Wedgwood. The large official cards headed 'The Old Catholic Church in the British Empire' were filled in by Wedgwood himself.

Leadbeater seemed to found or co-found as many orders as Aleister Crowley gave himself titles. With great success he instilled life into the Order of the Star in the East, the Lotus Circle, the Servants of the Star, the Golden Chain and the Order of the Round Table. The latter was a youth organisation where 'knights' were to practise chivalry and bravery, with Christ as their King Arthur. The Round Table was formed in four groups according to age: pages, companions, squires, who wore blue collars and knights, who wore red. (Leadbeater liked to be known as the Senior Knight.) It was a ceremonial organisation and the children loved it. The order is still in existence in Auckland, where there are enough children to make it worth while in the Theosophical Society.

Vyvyan attended the Esoteric Section of the Theosophical Society at least once a week in addition to the Sunday services when he himself was not lecturing. On many occasions he remained behind after lectures or services for private meetings. In the early days when he was a pupil he would go into a trance on occasions, or discuss with Leadbeater previous incarnations, Leadbeater as a former student of Pythagoras, Vyvyan as a priest in Egypt and as a boy in the temple

From a later shop in Junction Street

being hypnotised to tell what was happening miles away. Vyvyan had always possessed the faculty of astral travel.

He felt sorry for the ageing Leadbeater and was always close to him. Perhaps as a result, the idea of Vyvyan marrying had been anathema to Leadbeater. As things turned out, the old man became fond of Eunice too, in his own way. After all, at fifteen she was still younger than some of the girls who later on, in 1922, joined the children's group at Leadbeater's Theosophist Sydney commune, the Manor.

At this time home was the rooms behind Vyvyan's dispensary and consulting rooms at 3 Junction Street. Eunice would get up every morning early to start the household chores, which included daily scrubbing of the floors in an endless struggle to keep the dismal place clean. If Vyvyan had to lecture, or visit a client, or eat, or rest, then she would take over the running of the shop. His interests always came first. As Vyvyan spent so much time at the Oddfellows temple in Elizabeth Street, she applied for a job at Mark Foy's, the department store opposite. She worked in the handkerchief department, where her work included embroidery and crocheting round the edge of handkerchiefs. One of her first customers was a surprised Mrs Pateman. With Eunice working at Foy's, they were able to pay rent for one room at 3 Junction Street.

On 10 January 1917 Vyvyan joined the Sydney Lodge of the Theosophical Society. On 8 July 1917, Eunice too joined the society (she had been a member of the Order of the Star in the East since 25 May 1915) and was issued with an enormous membership card signed by Vyvyan's friend Mr Martyn. That same month Leadbeater, who had been living with the Martyns since 1914, was asked to move. Mrs Martyn had become more and more nervous of his obviously close involvement with his young male pupils, including their own son. An outbreak of scarlet fever in the family gave them an excuse for quietly asking Leadbeater to leave. Mr Martyn wrote privately to Annie Besant that he was concerned by what he had seen of Leadbeater's activities, but Mrs Besant had already weathered Leadbeater scandals and was not to be rocked by another one. In the event, the old man and Oscar Köllerstrom, still his favourite pupil, moved together into a flat attached to the society's headquarters in Sydney Lodge. Adyar's report of the 1917 Sydney Convention was able to report: 'The storm-centre of the whole Theosophical campaign in Sydney is, of course, Mr Leadbeater.'

If Sister Veni's interest in the sexual magic of the O.T.O. had been nervously clandestine, the same cannot have been said of Frank Bennett, who advertised, in the press, a Sunday meeting at 7.30 pm in the Oddfellows temple, a lecture on 'The Mystic Quest', (always a popular subject among the New Thought and occult groups). Frank Bennett's advertisement resulted in a jocular article in *Truth* on 1 April 1917, lampooning the whole affair with headlines in four lines of printing descending in size: 'A MAGIC BAND, The Viceroy of Baphomet, AND THE WHOLE OF THE LAW, Mystic Merry-Andrews in Our Midst'. The article was by 'Spookologist', who declared he had attended the meeting to see how the 'Magic of the Ages' was getting on. 'Evidently it is progressing a little – perhaps because Sister Veni Cooper-Mathieson's New Thought Temple has shut up for some reason, thus scattering the New Thought stock abroad like sheep without a shepherd. Or should it be goats?' Continuing in this cheery 'no nonsense' vein, the article went on to mock the 'brilliant yet cryptic advertisement in the *Herald* re different methods of development – 'New Thought', 'Theosophic', 'Rosicrucian.'

Spookologist declared himself 'rather disappointed, as the Viceroy of Baphomet is a dull sort of person, ponderous in his utterances and talked all around his subject. Seated behind the table he looked but middle-aged and very tame.' Bennett gave a brief history of how he came to represent Crowley, spoke of the Rabelaisian creed of 'Do what thou wilt shall be the whole of the Law,' and told of the order's opening the door to 'marvellous and WONDERFUL THINGS.' Bennett dismissed first New Thought, saying it was not progressive and second Theosophy, because, he said, 'its results were all negative. One had only to look at Theosophists to realise they were nonentities.' After Bennett spoke of the use of the will, people began to ask questions and interrupt one another in debating fashion. 'Sir Frank F. Bennett' (the title was bestowed by O.T.O.) spoke of the 'penchant for taking poison enough to kill 44 men,' and Spookologist stated 'that the A.A.O.T.O. has a big chance of finding itself in the giggle-gaggle house if it is not extremely careful.' The reporter learned from the literature the rule of the order that 'The private purse of every brother should always be at the disposal of any brother who may be in need.' Of the O.T.O. teachings Spookologist wrote, 'what it all means Baphomet's viceroy only knows.' He concluded the article, 'Sufficient for Spookologist to say that the Sunday evening's entertainment was the dreariest and deadliest he ever struck and that if Baphomet's viceroy does not introduce some gaiety, or conjuring or parlour tricks into his show, it will frizzle into nothingness. Not that this would be a calamity for the city of crazy religions.' 'Baphomet', the name adopted by Crowley, is probably originally a variation of 'Bapho Metis' and was used to describe the goat god allegedly worshipped by the Knights Templar. The name is also read by some as an inverse acronym for 'Templi omnium hominem pacis abhas', and by others as containing the meaning 'Father Mithras', so concealing a Templar sun cult.

Frank Bennett was corresponding frequently with Crowley now, giving him progress reports on the latest developments in Sydney, primarily of course the response to the public lecture in April. On the 1 May 1917 he wrote on his O.T.O. headed stationery, though citing the address Oddfellows temple, reporting that at least one person had paid and there were three candidates for the Minerval Degree, which was 0°, the degree preceding the First Degree, but no-one known intimately to Vyvyan was mentioned. The Lodge was to be called the 'Rosicrucian Lodge', although Crowley himself did not much like the choice of name. Perhaps it reminded him of the Rosicrucian roots of the Hermetic Order of the Golden Dawn from which he had been driven by his opponents in that organisation, among them W.B. Yeats. Notes and comments Crowley made at that time showed that he was aware of Frank Bennett's hovering between the O.T.O. and the Theosophical Society. He reminded Bennett that the Theosophical Society would expel him if they learned of his O.T.O. association.

Frank Bennett was already offering for sale many volumes of Crowley's works, including the *Equinox*, in the bohemian cafés where Vyvyan and Eunice had spent time while homeless.

Vyvyan (who was knowledgable about the O.T.O. and whose contacts with it were independent of Bennett and preceded Crowley's becoming Outer Head) had established 'J' Lodge of the Rosicrucians in Australia and to this his small group of followers used to come. Vyvyan had assumed the Browning Rosicrucian inheritance after the death of Robert Barrett Browning. From 1917 Vyvyan held weekly evening meetings of 'Christian Mystics of the Rosy Cross', usually at the home of Mrs Grace Victor in Sydney. Mrs Victor, vice-president for the New Thought movement in New South Wales, was a devoted follower of Vyvyan, who would stay the night at her house when he was unwell. He also frequently slept at the shop premises while Eunice slept at the flat. It may seem surprising that Mrs Victor should supply the meeting-place for Vyvyan's C.M.R.C. meetings, but Rosicrucian, New Thought, Golden Dawn, Theosophist, Gnostic and Liberal Catholic groups often had overlapping memberships and fellow travellers. Æ (George Russell) was never a member of the Golden Dawn, but because of his friendship with Yeats and his consequent interest in its activities, few remember this technicality.

The close links between the C.M.R.C. and Crowley are suggested by Vyvyan's designs for the headed stationery and application forms for the Christian Mystics of the Rosy Cross: they are undoubtedly similar to those of the O.T.O., which Frank Bennett was certainly using in his correspondence at this time. The lists of names of those attending the meetings, which Eunice always carefully recorded in her diary, never in fact included Frank Bennett, although there were frequent personal meetings between the Bennetts and the Deacons. Moreover, Eunice was now sleeping and, with a full-time job during the day, living separately from Vyvyan. She did not take part in these meetings and the list of people she met in connection with them is not likely to be comprehensive.

Regular members whom she did record, apart from Mrs Victor herself, included Nellie Bell, a member of a well-to-do occultist family who had a large house (with health spa facilities) at Roseville, where Frank Bennett intended having a temple; the Revd Cocks, who had visited Vyvyan in February 1914 at Allawha, Kilsyth during his initiation period; Bomberg, who also visited Vyvyan at Kilsyth and took photos of Vyvyan at the end of his ordeal; Mr Buijs, an affluent, widely-travelled occultist and an admirer of Crowley who married Nellie Bell; and Mr Vincent Pantin, a tall, well-spoken gentleman, usually dressed in a pin-striped suit worn with a bowler hat and, when the weather demanded it, spats. Like Frank Bennett he met the Deacons socially. He had an estranged wife and children living in Sydney with whom the Deacons were equally friendly. Most of these people were Theosophists and also supported the Liberal Catholic Church, which Vyvyan attended on Sundays.

Papers surviving from the time of the 1914-1918 war indicate that the rituals that were used were based on Crowley's O.T.O. and that Frank Bennett was the channel of this influence. Nevertheless, it is important to note that according to Gerald Yorke the 1915 certificate citing Sister Veni gave her equal status with Frank Bennett to receive the details of ritual for the various degrees. By 1919 Vyvyan's business card, which declared him to be an author and lecturer, bore the Greek letters chi omega theta. By gematria, this adds up to 1409, making it a cypher for 'agape esti ho nomos', or 'Love is the law'. Gerald Yorke believed Chi Omega Theta was likely to have been Vyvyan's name or motto in the O.T.O.

Those who came seeking membership would sign a form stating that they understood that the O.T.O. was a secret order:

> ...pledged to the high purpose of securing the Liberty of the Individual, and his advancement in Light, Wisdom, Understanding, Knowledge, and Power through Beauty, Courage and Wit, on the Foundation of Universal Brotherhood.

This form of wording would have appealed to members of both the Theosophical Society and the Church Universal. There is also acknowledgement of kinship with Freemasonry. Once an applicant had filled the Preliminary Pledge Form, the ritual for the Minerval Degree was carried out. The stage would be set with a conical tent, within which was seated Saladin, dressed in oriental costume. In front of this presiding figure was an altar in the form of a well covered with a coping-stone, on which were laid the *Book of the Law (CCXX)*, a sword, and a platter of bread and salt. On Saladin's right hand would be a seat. The tent was lighted by a single candle, or in its place there could be a palm tree. There followed questions and answers and the swearing of the oath of secrecy, accompanied by the symbolic sharing of bread and salt and the acknowledgement that in breaking the oath he may be 'mutilated and no more a man'.

The candidate was told that he had arrived 'at a time when freedom was about to deliver the decisive combat against the forces of superstition, tyranny, and oppression.' His sustenance would be the *Book of the Law*, and whose nature is indicated by the expression that Crowley borrowed from Rabelais and made his own: 'Do what thou wilt shall be the whole of the Law. Love is the law, love under will.' These phrases were used to open and close correspondence between members of the fraternity and are still instantly recognisable by students of Crowley. Candidates submitted voluntarily to the discipline and organisation afforded by the Order, fulfilling a philosophical paradox. 'The regulations of our Order are strict, even as the sinews of your arm are firm. Were your sinews loosened, you could no longer move your arm. Chafe not, therefore, at the apparent restrictions which your obligations place upon you. They are designed solely to enable you to do your will... Thou hast no right but to do thy will. Do that and no other shall say "nay". We unreservedly place power in your hands.'

A banquet followed the initial ceremony. The ceremony was symbolic of the soul's journey. Those who progressed to the third degree, named 'Devotion', drank a mixture of blood and laudanum in some branches of the O.T.O. (The taking or supplying of certain drugs aroused less comment then. Opiates were used by many individuals, both famous and unknown in the eighteenth and nineteenth centuries. In fiction, Sir Arthur Conan Doyle's Sherlock Holmes was shown as regularly turning to opium.)

Vyvyan and Wedgwood certainly conducted O.T.O. rituals, but they kept the entire matter closely concealed. It may have been that the C.M.R.C. run by Vyvyan at Mrs Victor's house was not a front for the O.T.O., or a secret lodge of the order, but literature published later by the C.M.R.C. certainly suggests that it was something of the kind. Traditionally the Rosicrucians never used sex in their workings, but the O.T.O. did. It would be understandable for the New Thought followers to be Rosicrucians, but not Oriental Templars. The O.T.O. regarded Theosophists as 'Probationers' and Freemasons as 'Students' in the early stages of the Order's structure of degrees. The probable explanation is that different amounts were revealed to different individuals.

It should not be assumed from the overlapping membership and the frequent borrowing of terminology that can be observed happening with the different esoteric groups, that mutual respect and tolerance was entirely the rule. On 28 June 1913 Aleister Crowley had bitterly criticised Leadbeater, Krishnamurti and Annie Besant, citing in particular allegations concerning Leadbeater's relationship with Krishnamurti. A copy of this diatribe, in purple ink, survives from that period. Aleister Crowley returned to the attack in a letter to the American Montgomery Evans II in 1926:

> About Krishnamurti. There is no objection on my part to pederasty as such. This is a totally different matter. It is a question of the following practice, which I class as black magical because it is unnecessary, unrecommended from the magical standpoint, and likely to arouse highly undesirable forces as being in opposition to the Law of Thelema.
>
> The practice consists in hypnotising a boy and masturbating him while in that condition. He then becomes lucid. You will find it broadly hinted at in the reprint of the Introduction by Wilmhurst to 'A Suggestive Inquiry into the Hermetic Mystery' by Mrs Southwood.

Vyvyan and Krishnamurti were born within a few months of each other and each received training from Leadbeater. It would be logical to surmise that their treatment by Leadbeater was similar. Vyvyan certainly admitted that Leadbeater had regressed him to previous incarnations. (A belief in reincarnation – and indeed metempsychosis, but not personal immortality – was central to Theosophical thought. Krishnamurti as 'Alcyone' wrote an account of previous lives dating back to Atlantean times.) There was no sexual activity officially linked with the teachings of the Esoteric Section. But Leadbeater's having been required to resign from the Theosophical Society certainly confirms his having carried his own sexuality into his esoteric practice. We know from his past that Vyvyan was particularly susceptible to the influence of older men, father figures that filled the void left by his own father's disappearance from his early childhood. My own recollection of Leadbeater is of his being rather creepy, in contrast with the attractive Wedgwood.

At the close of 1917, Vyvyan and Eunice celebrated New Year's Eve at the home of Mrs Grace Victor. Eunice retained very vivid memories of Mrs Victor's close questioning of the relationship between the young husband and wife. Like Sister Veni, she believed strongly in celibacy, particularly for religious teachers. Eunice, perhaps out of loyalty to her husband's religious position, perhaps simply out of social embarrassment (she was still only seventeen, after all), always denied that she and Vyvyan had a sexual relationship. Nevertheless, Mrs Victor, perhaps not fully convinced by these protestations, went with them on their wedding anniversary and scrupulously monitored all the activities.

On Monday evenings Eunice went to Mrs Victor's for singing lessons, learning from her the songs, 'My Task' and the 'Cobbler's Song' from *Chu Chin Chow* which were to number in her repertoire with the Indian Love Lyrics then in fashion ('Pale Hands I love' and 'The Temple bells are ringing'). Mrs Victor also provided hospitality at her home at Mc Mahon's Point for Vyvyan's consultations and on Wednesdays, unless Vyvyan had to lecture elsewhere, for his special meetings of the Christian Mystics of the Rosy Cross. On Thursday evenings Vyvyan had his special Esoteric Section of the Theosophical Society meeting after which he returned home very late, or went on to Revd Cocks's place or had some other reason to stay elsewhere.

It was in the early part of 1918 that Vyvyan Deacon qualified as an orator from the Esoteric Section of the Theosophical Society and the Orators' Training Class supervised by Mr Grieg, who in 1929 was defined as secretary of the Independent Sydney Lodge and devoted much of his time to following Leadbeater and reporting on any misconduct. He became the secretary of the Loyalty League, which was founded in August 1921 to urge a return to the principles of Theosophy.

Vyvyan had several books on hypnotism, self-hypnotism, suggestion, auto-suggestion, Coué, Mesmer and Charles Baudouin, but most important of all appears to be a foolscap exercise book of eight lectures, dated February and March 1918 and the subjects of the lectures were ones which were used by Vyvyan on many occasions thereafter:

1. Suggestion, dealing with the lucidity of vision of microcosms under the microscope and ending with a sonnet by Ella Wheeler Wilcox, a Vice-President of the I.N.T.A.

2. The idea and its material equivalent, dealing with the law of suggestion.

3. The four laws, quoting from Herbert Spencer and dealing with tribal customs, suggestibility, relativity, expectancy and automatism.

4. Automatism. About the creative power of thought – its place in achieving the Philosopher's Stone and the Elixir of Life.

5. The physical mechanism. The need for change and comparison

in order to define. 'We are all factors in one great whole; there will never be perfect or permanent equilibrium while any one factor is out of poise.'...'Mind is the root substance behind all form...' There is reference to the effect of experience on the physical – reminiscent of Chidley.

6. Man – know thyself. The three planes of consciousness – the seer, the act of seeing and the thing seen. The use of a 'key note' by which Joshua brought down the walls of Jericho. The divine paradox that all things apparently external are internal – seen in the wisdom of Krishna when he told his disciples – I am the seed of all existing things. In me behold the universe, animate and inanimate.

7. Telepathy. Someone seeing written symbols can translate them into the original thoughts. Telepathy is similar.

8. Application. The harnessing and directing of thought.

Their room in Junction Street did not have many facilities for comfort or entertainment so that leisure hours were spent at one of the many picture houses, such as McIntyre's, the Majestic, the Orpheum or the Australian Theatre. Sometimes there were friends or patients waiting for their return to the shop. At the start of the new year Eunice was tired and frequently unwell. Vyvyan's meetings were reported as successful. Saturday 5 January 1918 was their second wedding anniversary. It was her half day so Vyvyan met her from work and they went to Vancluse Bay, where they visited Wentworth House and Tomb before going down to the beach. On their return home they met Mr Buijs who had just returned from a sea voyage. He had visited Shanghai among other places and gave Vyvyan and Eunice a print of Crowley's Aiwass, a monochrome on which Eunice had written on the back 'Mr Buijs, Shanghai'. The keyword for the month of January was 'peace' and their anniversary went unmarred. Eunice gnomically recorded 'Anatomy Lesson' in her diary. Later she was to tell me that they were celibate throughout the first two years of their marriage; with the second wedding anniversary things began to change and this change brought consequences.

On Sunday afternoons Vyvyan usually went to the meeting of the Order of the Star in the East. In the evenings on Sunday he delivered his lectures at Kenilworth Hall (which was run by their friend Mrs Godwin, who lived next door to it) although for a few weeks he attended Irving Cooper's Sunday evening addresses in preference as they formed a short series he did not wish to miss.

One morning after Vyvyan had fainted and stayed at Mrs Victor's house, Eunice called on her way to work to see how he was. He had been ill in the night, but had fallen sound asleep and woke just as Eunice was leaving for work. She returned home at night, but Vyvyan did not come home after his Esoteric Section meeting of the Theosophical Society. Her only comment after diary entries recording these events was a trusting 'God bless Vyvyan and make him strong!'

On Sunday 20 January 1918 Vyvyan attended the Liberal Catholic Church in the morning. In the evening he gave his first big city meeting at the beautiful Theosophical lodge room in the G.V.C.O.K. Building in Pitt Street. He and Eunice called afterwards at Mrs Victor's house from which Eunice retired feeling ill at 11 pm. When she returned home from work on the next day Monday at 6 pm. Vyvyan had not returned home from where he had stayed the night at his mother's home. Eunice went to Mrs Victor's house for her Monday night singing lesson. She had dinner at a vegetarian café on the way home and did a 'little ironing with great effort.' Vyvyan's absences always left her depressed and ill. When she went to bed, she wrote the keyword 'peace' three times and ending 'God help me!'

Vyvyan was participating in all the Theosophical, Star in the East, and Liberal Catholic services as well as taking his own meetings of the C.M.R.C. and, with Eunice's help, running the shop. On Wednesdays, throughout February and the beginning of March, Vyvyan held a series of lectures on psychology at the Streathfield Theosophical Lodge. He also gave lectures there on Sundays. His subjects included the Christian Mysteries, mind-consciousness and super-consciousness.

Also on Sundays Vyvyan's old friend Mr Pateman, who had broken with Sister Veni, was nevertheless now hiring a hall at the at the Oddfellows temple for a series of eight lectures in February and March 1918. His daughter Phyllis used to play the piano for the hymns and hand out hymn-sheets or pamphlets. The platform was shared with Edward Crester-Wilson, as was the office at 337 Pitt Street, where private interviews and absent healing could be arranged by appointment. They provided suitable literature, but also recommended Coles' Book Arcade. As with all these groups 'funds urgently needed' is stated on their leaflet. The attendance at the Sunday night lectures did not justify the hiring of the Hall so other arrangements had to be made at the end of March 1918.

On Thursday 14 March 1918 Eunice recorded in her diary an event which was to effect their lives considerably. 'Did not rise until 6.30 am. Business. Had tea in town then went to pictures in City. I returned home, but V not back. I made wonderful discovery re certain matter tonight. "Ye shall become as a little child before ye can enter the kingdom of heaven." The coded style of the entry gives some indication of Eunice's feelings. She found herself barely able to talk to her husband about being pregnant; in later years she was still unable even to mention 'stockings' without a euphemism, I remember her once asking my sister to move her 'shopping'. She was of course entirely forbidden to tell anyone else, out of fear of how people would react. After all, Mrs Victor was still being reassured that the young couple continued to have no sexual relationship. Vyvyan's constantly being away began to upset her more and more so that when, the following Wednesday, Vyvyan was at home with her, she was more, not less, depressed. Sister Veni's and Chidley's strictures on the consequences of lust for the health of mother and baby were clearly terrifying Eunice, for Vyvyan stayed with her that night and she recorded: 'We retired early, but I never in my life spent a more miserable night. Karma alas! I must go away for a while or my health will completely give way.'

Eunice continued working at Foy's, where she was stocktaking. Vyvyan's mother and John Shirlaw, the founder of the Ivycliffe commune called, but Eunice went to bed leaving them discussing Rudolph Steiner. This high initiate of the O.T.O., also a 97° Memphis and Mizraim Mason, had been a secretary of the German section of The Theosophical Society from 1902 to 1912. He had then broken away, with most of the German Lodges, to form the Anthroposophical Society.

Eunice was acutely lonely. Vyvyan continued to stay frequently at his mother's home and after meetings he would often be a guest at Mrs Victor's. When going to deliver lectures for the Theosophical Society, he would spend the weekend away with friends. She would be left to come home after a day's work to a dark, deserted shop.

Sometimes she would find Vyvyan at home, though Mrs Victor would often be there, as if chaperoning the couple. Eunice always preferred to busy herself in another room, leaving them to talk. Vyvyan made an effort to be more of a companion for Eunice. He still attended his speakers' training evenings and kept his appointments, but gave more time to her. He would stay in to read her Oscar Wilde's poems. They already ate out regularly, since they had no cooking facilities nor the means to pay fuel bills; now he began taking her on to the pictures and the theatre.

Sometimes they would go to lectures together. On Tuesday 26 March she went with Vyvyan and his mother to Mrs Needham's lecture on 'Michael, Angels and Architecture'. But the strained atmosphere of those days is indicated by Eunice's recording that the day was unusual, since that night's supper 'did not end in a nightmare'. On the Thursday she accompanied Vyvyan and his mother to a Theosophical Society reception, where Mr Spice put on a juggling show. (No doubt Spookologist would have approved.) The next day the first meeting of the Annual Convention of the Theosophical Society was opened by Leadbeater and the three of them went to hear him. After lunch Vyvyan stayed for the second half of the meeting and an Esoteric Section special meeting, but Eunice went on to the Royal Show.

Though Vyvyan may have quarrelled with Mrs Pateman, both Vyvyan and Eunice had visited the Patemans earlier in the year to see their new baby, named Julia after Julia Seton of the New Thought Alliance. When they heard Eunice's news, they invited her to stay the weekend with them: it was a rare treat to be brought breakfast in bed and made much of. When she returned home, Vyvyan was not there to meet her.

All through April Eunice recited the verse:

> God is Love. His love surrounds me
> In his Love I safely dwell
> 'Tis above, beneath, within me
> God is Love and all is well.

She would use Peace, Wealth, Strength, Health, Happiness and Success by turns in place of the word Love. Vyvyan again tried to take Eunice out more, but it was usually in the company of friends like Nellie Bell, Mr Buijs, Mr Pantin, Mr Spice and of course Mrs Victor.

Thursday 11 April was Eunice's last day at Foy's. The girls from her department gave her half a dozen handkerchiefs and Eunice felt quite sorry to leave. Vyvyan had a meeting of the Esoteric Section to attend that night so Eunice went to the pictures alone.

Mrs Victor, meanwhile, had become suspicious. She had several weeks earlier perceived a Màdonna-like quality on Eunice's face. Had Vyvyan continued to practise total abstinence? Eunice, embarrassed and loyal, protested he had. When Eunice gave up work, the hint that she was pregnant became too strong and Mrs Victor suggested that Vyvyan had remained pure, so he was obviously not the father. On discovering that Vyvyan sometimes put Bomberg up for the night, Mrs Victor decided that since Vyvyan was celibate, then here was the obvious father.

Eunice's confinement was due at the beginning of September. Vyvyan as usual took responsibility for all health care. As in Sister Veni's maternity home, he prescribed fresh orange juice daily, raspberry leaf tea to strengthen the muscles of the uterus and swimming as the ideal exercise. But on the question of a midwife, Eunice, supported by women friends, struck and Nurse Tudor was booked for the delivery.

Vyvyan was still not making enough money to support a family. An influenza epidemic kept him busy enough, but brought in very little money. He contributed a weekly subscription to the Theosophical Society, but was not paid for the work he did for the Order of the Star in the East. He was reliant on the money from the medicines and herbal remedies sold in the shop, on fees for lectures to the Theosophical Society or the independent groups that engaged him.

In May Vyvyan and Eunice asked their landlord Mr Klussendorf if they could have a flat: at the shop there was only a consulting room and a bedroom with two single beds. A couple of days afterwards, when Eunice came home from shopping at about 4.30 pm, she could smell smoke. A neighbouring room, that belonged to Mr Klussendorf, was on fire. Vyvyan sent for the fire brigade, who soon put out the fire, but not before it had spread to the shop and left the bedroom so damaged by water that it was impossible to sleep there. They were able to spend the night in the flats, but Vyvyan nevertheless held a meeting of the C.M.R.C. on the premises.

The next night, when they returned from visiting patients at Ryde, they found the flats locked and had to make up a kind of bed in the shop. The little girl next door had been entrusted to give them a key and she had forgotten.

Vyvyan began going out regularly with Vincent Pantin. They always went off late at night, and it frequently ended up with them being ill the next day, Vyvyan having collapsed in the street, and Pantin having to be put up for the night in the shop. Sometimes Eunice slept at the flats to avoid the two men, leaving them to sleep at the shop. These various outings were certainly to do with preparing Pantin for a lecture and on the 16 June they all went to hear him lecture at the Oddfellows temple on Vyvyan's pet subject Esoteric Christianity. The lecture went well, but Pantin never attempted another; he was not a natural public speaker. At the same time Vyvyan experimented with Frank Bennett and Wedgwood in consciousness-altering drugs. Vyvyan, as a pharmacist, did not find it difficult to provide the materials. They also sought lucidity through hypnotism and self-hypnotism.

Monday 10 June was the last night that Eunice and Vyvyan slept at the flats, for the shop premises had by now dried out. Vyvyan no longer enquired about alternative living quarters. Instead, he, Vincent Pantin and Frank Bennett were having frequent talks, whispering in corners and falling silent whenever Eunice came into the room. On Wednesday 19 June, Vyvyan told her the first plan. He and Pantin were going to see about some work out in the country, 8 miles from Wyalong. It was menial work, but it was paid work.

From his job at Wattle Brand Eucalyptus Oil Coy, Vyvyan wrote to Eunice:

> It is now 8 pm and have just finished tea (potatoes boiled in skins and cocoa) and feel quite tired out. They are very short-handed here so to-day I did not go out cutting, but remained behind to help distil the Eucalyptus. At 6 am I lit the boilers and from 7-7.30 washed and had breakfast and then worked until 6.30 pm with an hour's break for lunch. We did nine 200 Gallon tanks to-day, four in the morning plus five in the afternoon. The process is to lift the iron lid off tank, empty into cart with pitchfork, cart to heap, empty cart then refill tank with new leaves; turn on steam, leave for two hours, meanwhile go on to next tank, and so on all the time. My limbs are aching and I can hardly write.

On Friday 5 July, when she went into the city to collect herbs bought with money from the first cheque from Vyvyan, she found the streets were decorated in honour of a thousand wounded soldiers who were expected: it was a rare reminder of the Great War still being fought on the other side of the world.

While he was away for those couple of months, Eunice began to enjoy deputising for Vyvyan, making up medicine according to his instructions, dealing with patients and comforting those who normally turned to Vyvyan, such as Mrs Reinhart whose seven-year-old son had died. She wrote to one of Vyvyan's patients at Ryde, a Mr Anderson and visited him, sharing her tending duties with Mrs Victor. Eunice, more businesslike than her husband, kept accounts, recording all the money sent her and the deposits paid on medicine.

On Vyvyan's return, apart from a Members Only meeting with Mr Rodgers at the Theosophical Society, his main preoccupation was with a patient who had been given up for dead by doctors. Vyvyan had cured many hopeless cases and believed Mr Deane would be no exception. However, after rallying for a day or two, on Tuesday 20 August he had a relapse. Vyvyan tended him, then went to visit another patient at Ryde, before returning to spend the night with Mr and Mrs Deane. Mr Deane died at 4 am. Vyvyan washed him and prepared him for his coffin before returning to Eunice at 6 am. He spent the following nights, until the funeral the following Thursday, with Mrs Deane as she was afraid to be alone with the coffin. He had suffered the first death of a patient under his treatment. That night Vyvyan was unwell: he had fainted in the street.

Eunice continued to clean and tidy the shop at 3 Junction Street every morning and play the piano in the afternoons. A week after he was back, she learned of Vyvyan's second plan. He and Frank Bennett had acquired new shop premises across the road at 46 Junction Street. Though in the last stages of pregnancy, Eunice helped with the move. During the next three days Vyvyan was back lecturing for the Theosophical Society at Streathfield.

Eunice was safely delivered of a baby daughter at 10.45 am, 11 September 1918. Mrs Linton, the first caller, announced that Vyvyan would be coming soon, which he did and stayed until late at night. They called the baby Hypatia, after the Alexandrian Greek Neoplatonist philosopher, murdered by a Christian mob, who had been the eponymous heroine of a novel by Charles Kingsley. She was called by her second name Sybil from the earliest days and when I found out her birth certificate had Hypatia as a first name I nicknamed her 'hippo'. Perhaps Leadbeater suggested the name. He would have known that it was a favourite of Annie Besant and her friend (and partner in the *Fruits of Philosophy* contraception scandal) Charles Bradlaugh. Besant had declared that eloquence was one of her greatest attributes because she had been practising oratory for over twelve thousand years, being most eloquent during her incarnation as the philosopher Hypatia. (Considering her earlier death on the orders of Bishop Cyril, it was generous of her to go on to write, in the later incarnation of Besant, a book on *Esoteric Christianity*.)

Vyvyan could not stay with Eunice long; a couple of times he was unable to come at all. Often he had patients to attend to. On Sunday

15 September Wedgwood wanted Vyvyan's participation in the services at the Liberal Catholic Church and again Vyvyan's visit to Eunice was cut short.

Mrs Pateman came one afternoon to invite Eunice and the new baby to stay with them for a holiday. That evening Vyvyan read to her the *Rubáiyát of Omar Khayyám*. He became unwell at the prospect of her going away.

Eunice spent four weeks, playing with the three Pateman girls. She was only five years older than Phyllis and they played like sisters, dressing up, going to the pictures, eating ice-cream, playing the piano or listening to records ('Peer Gynt' was a favourite). She gave Phyllis the sheet music of 'The Maidens Prayer' and they played it endlessly to each other. Years later Eunice could still play it from memory; it was one of the pieces I played to Vyvyan during his last illness.

Mr Pateman held regular meetings at Campsie. Eunice stayed with the children so that Mrs Pateman could attend lectures. On 10 October Mr Pateman had a long private discussion with Eunice on the subject of Crowley, the O.T.O. and the Theosophical Society. He was concerned for her and Eunice did her best to reassure him.

On Eunice's eighteenth birthday, 22 October 1918, Vyvyan arrived at Bankstown in the afternoon, bringing gifts for his wife. They included an amber necklace, which Eunice treasured all her life. He told her how much he longed for her return. He stayed to tea then took Eunice and Sybil for a four-mile walk in the country before she saw him off on the train home.

When Eunice came back, they were invited to Mrs Lumley's for a weekend in which they could swim and laze in the sun. They lay in bed together and Vyvyan read her some Oscar Wilde. On Sunday 10 November, Vyvyan went to his lecture at Burwood in the evening while Mrs Lumley took Eunice home. The following morning, Monday 11 November, the ferry boats woke them with their sirens. 'It is declared that Austria has surrendered,' Eunice noted. 'The people are quite excited and are making as much noise as possible to celebrate it. Flags decorate private houses as well as shops and the hotels are closed to the merrymakers.' The great excitement continued into the following day when peace was officially announced. 'Anyone might know miles away something has happened the ferry boats are making so much noise'. Wednesday 13 November became an official holiday. A procession passed the shop, where Eunice was working while Vyvyan taught his class at Burwood.

The postwar influenza epidemic was already beginning: by the end of it, more people had died than had been killed in the Great War. Vyvyan began to advertise his patent medicines; boys were hired to distribute pamphlets:

There is a certain, sure and positively infallible cure for this complaint. It is DEACON'S INFLUENZA SPECIFIC. Mr Vyvyan Deacon, after much careful experimenting has discovered the best and only certain cure for this disease to be a unique combination of certain rare Oriental and Eastern herbs. For the following reasons Mr Deacon has made this invaluable medicine in tablet form:

1. To insure accuracy of dose.

2. Because tabloids are tasteless and easy to take anywhere thus insuring regularity of dose.

3. Because in this form the rare and volatile herbs used retain strength and purity for any length of time.

Price 2/- per Bottle By Post 2/3.

Deacon's Influenza Specific came with a money-back guarantee.

On Sunday 24 November Vyvyan went round to Frank Bennett to borrow a book of Crowley's poems, from which he quoted to his audiences. He read some of the poems to Eunice that afternoon in the Botanical Gardens before going to the Oddfellows building where he was engaged to lecture on 'Theosophy, spiritualism and Christian Science'.

Vyvyan and Eunice used to go to Domain together, but once there they separated. Eunice went to the art gallery while Vyvyan listened to the speakers.

Committed to optimism and convinced by New Thought of the power of positive thinking, Eunice would never talk about those things she was unhappy about – indeed, she seemed to be struggling not even to think about them. Not surprisingly, she left a good deal out of her diary. But from the beginning of December Eunice allowed herself to be 'tired'. She no longer went to hear Vyvyan lecture in the evening, being too tired. She dosed herself with raspberry leaves (loyal as ever to Vyvyan and Sister Veni's health rules). Entire days were being left blank in her diary, but the daily treatment by Vyvyan of a certain Miss Key is steadily noted. During the sessions with this particular patient, Eunice usually took Sybil out for a walk.

Vyvyan went to the Conservatoire, where Miss Key was taking part in a concert. When Eunice was too tired to go to hear Vyvyan lecture at the School of Arts on 'What Poets have done for Progress', Miss Key was there. Eunice spent the day with her friend Miss Etherington while Vyvyan had an engagement to lecture at Burwood. Vyvyan also declared he was feeling tired and ill. Then Miss Key came for a game of cards. Eunice went with Vyvyan and their friends to the Kings Hall to hear Mr Rodger's address: Miss Key went too.

Christmas Day they spent quietly at the shop and Vyvyan's mother came round with a Christmas pudding. On Boxing Day they went on a picnic to Narrabean and Eunice was very happy. The next day Miss Key was back for further treatment and went with Vyvyan to the Liberal Catholic Church. Eunice became unwell again. There was a New Year's Eve party: Miss Key was one of the guests. Eunice was not sleeping and on Monday 30 December she had what she called an occult experience: whatever it was (and she always refused to elaborate) it clearly had a pivotal role in what followed. Eunice had been struggling to say nothing to anyone and to write nothing in her diary, but notes on a crumpled sheet of airmail paper, starting 17 January 1919, indicate that away from her diary she was in fact secretly (almost in secret from herself) writing down the forbidden thoughts. Phrases like '...but oh the blow is so cruel' are still just legible. By now she was desperately asking friends for advice. 'Miss Key called. No better,' is one sad entry. Friends were able to do very little. After a private talk, one friend took Eunice to the pictures hoping it would cheer her up. Eunice persisted with struggling to 'forget. I love Vyvyan too much to let him go.' In later years the most she usually admitted was that Vyvyan had begun to eat meat, drink alcohol and smoke whereas she was a total abstainer from all three. Perhaps more to the point, she also indicated that she was always restrained where sex was concerned. Finally, on a day when he did not return home until 1.30 am, they became reconciled and there was no further mention of Miss Key.

Vyvyan applied for his baby daughter to be baptised in the Liberal Catholic Church. This was the year that the Liberal Catholic Liturgy was published and Irving Steiger Cooper was consecrated Bishop in St Alban's Cathedral, Sydney. Vyvyan had been attending Irving Cooper's lectures, knowing that they were leading up to this consecration. Vyvyan's worn, treasured copy of the *Liturgy of the Liberal Catholic Church* is inscribed 'Vyvyan H.R. Deacon, 46 Junction Street, North Sydney, N.S.W. Australia. First used by me on Sunday

July 13th 1919 at St Albans Church on the occasion of Revd Irving S. Cooper being raised to the Episcopate as Bishop for the United States of America.'

Vyvyan was particularly close to Wedgwood at this time, studying the Egyptian Rite of the Ancient Mysteries with him and Leadbeater, who later established a ceremonial movement known as the 'Egyptian Rite of Ancient Freemasonry' consisting of six degrees. A knowledge of Krishnamurti's (or 'Alcyone's') *At the Feet of the Master* was required by candidates. The Fourth Stage was the Temple of the Rose and the Cross. The Fifth Stage was the Outer Temple or Temple of the Dawn, followed by the Sixth Stage, the Inner Temple or Temple of the Star. These rituals were originally drafted by Wedgwood, though clearly he drew on existing traditions. There was, for example, the masonic rite of Memphis and Misraim, which John Yarker had drawn together and from which the Berlin lodge, of which Hartmann (who became a follower of Madame Blavatsky) and Reuss (who became outer head of the O.T.O.) were co-founders, took its name. Vyvyan's copy of *At the Feet of the Master* was stored after his death together with a large five-pointed star on a golden cord. In the centre of the star was a hand with a red garnet heart in the centre, suggesting a wound. On the back of the cross was deeply etched 'Presented by the Officers and Brethren of the GOLDEN GIRDLE to Bro Vyvyan Deacon WM Sydney 17.10.17. Wedgwood had written in his *New Insights into Christian Worship* that just as the Son of Man was girded round the breast with a golden girdle, that is to say with the company of the Saints, so the ornaments of the altar were God's faithful people who shone with the beauty of holiness; we may be reasonably confident that the star was from an order established by Wedgwood.

Rumours had begun to spread that Wedgwood and Leadbeater had been sexually involved with the young men and boys receiving religious instruction from them. Leadbeater had taught boys how to masturbate, he invariably slept with a boy in his bed, had a boy in his bath with him, insisted on communal bathing at his home and was given an enema each morning by one of his pupils in the presence of the others while they were all bathing together. The resulting scandal cast a shadow over the ceremony at St Alban's and the appearance of the liturgy. During the year both Leadbeater and Wedgwood began to show the strain under which they were living, with Wedgwood doing less and less. Both the Theosophical Society and the Liberal Catholic Church were affected by this brew of sexuality and black magic.

In July 1919 Eunice and Vyvyan went to live at Ivycliffe, the commune run on Chidley principles. Vyvyan took with him a copy of Aleister Crowley's poem 'Hymn to Pan', an invocation to an obsessing deity written five years earlier, which had been published at the end of March in the *Blue Equinox*. Vyvyan had received his copy via Frank Bennett. Moving in, Vyvyan and Eunice asked for single rooms. Sometimes the Schott family would visit them.

At Ivycliffe, most of the residents and visitors were in their teens and twenties. An exception was 'Diogenes', nicknamed because he sunbathed in a trough resembling a bath, and emerged dressed in a loincloth. This was one of the sunbathing troughs that were intended to allow residents discreetly to sunbathe naked; I later saw them in use at Champneys in the thirties. Although to themselves the residents appeared eminently respectable, the fact that Chidley's name was linked with the premises aroused curiosity. Sightseers came to peer through the bushes in the hope of being shocked or finding something scandalous they could report to the authorities: eccentricity was the most they could claim to have found.

Rooms were rented by members, who could choose whether to cook for themselves or join communal meals in the dining room and kitchen. There was a library, which Vyvyan's arrival had helped to fill, and a large drawing room with a piano where people used to gather.

Frank Bennett's friend, A.C. Curtis, who had sometimes minded the shop at 46 Junction Street, moved in after Vyvyan and Eunice. Meatheringham, who wrote poetry and spoke regularly in the open air at Domain, came and stayed for a time and there was also old John Brigden, a man in his eighties, who by 1920 moved to lodgings outside the commune though close by. There were also some Russians who stayed at Ivycliffe, immigrants on whose behalf Vyvyan had corresponded on 6 May 1919 with the secretary of the Australian Labor Party, P.C. Evans.

Vyvyan continued to give consultations and offer herbal treatments during the day, and to address meetings most evenings on New Thought, Theosophical and, increasingly, Spiritualist platforms. The Spiritual Scientist Society of Sydney (President Mr G.W. Nettleton, Secretary Mr Haldane, Treasurer Mr Maskell) recorded at a meeting on Saturday 12 June that the previous six months had proved 'an unbounded success' and it was noted that Vyvyan Deacon's lectures were well attended: the subjects had included 'Thought Power and Fate' and 'Religion of Common Sense'. The influence of Leadbeater and Wedgwood showed not only in small things, such as wearing evening dress, but also in the hypnotic style of oratory he had developed.

On Thursdays and Fridays Vyvyan visited Auburn to lecture, attend patients and deliver medicines. The pattern of being away from home continued with him often not returning on Thursday nights. Sometimes he had missed the last train, or the weather was too bad, or the fares were so high, or the journey was too long to make late at night and then return the next morning. He was always able to stay with friends, sometimes with the Schott family.

In August 1919 Vyvyan left the Junction Street shop and began renting an office at the Oddfellows centre. Frank Bennett, working daily through the week, was as much part of the scene as he was in 1918, because when Bennett was free at the weekends Vyvyan usually had two lecture engagements daily, so Vyvyan and he arranged to work shifts in the shop.

Some undisciplined verse that Vyvyan wrote in an exercise book during August 1919 suggests that he was passionately involved with at least two young women at this time. There was a 15 line acrostic on the words 'May for I love thee' and odd snippets to a certain Lily: May Schott and Lily Lingwood-Smith are the most likely candidates. May Schott was part of his circle of friends in Auburn and he used to stay with her family. Lily belonged to the Order of Light Christian Spiritualist Church Adelaide and Melbourne and she had appeared with Vyvyan on the Spiritualist platform together in Melbourne. Their mutual regard was no secret.

Normally Eunice made no comment when Vyvyan stayed away, went missing, came home ill from excess of some kind, or was evidently seeing another woman. Sometimes she would decide he had gone too far and would leave him and stay with friends for a time. Towards the end of 1919 Eunice took Sybil and left Vyvyan at Ivycliffe to stay with friends indefinitely. From Ivycliffe Vyvyan, drawing on the same rhetorical skills he had built up in his lecturing, tried to lure her back.

While listening to the music tonight my thoughts turned to you and to how and where we first met in this life. It seemed to me that Life is one vast Garden – God's Garden – and we each are sent into

Vivian aged about 1½ holding
the wooden bar from his high
chair.

With his mother, Broadstairs,
about 1905

Humshaugh camp
August 1908.
Vivian is indicated
by the flag Baden-
Powell to the right.
Courtesy of the
Scout Association.

Vivian after 'Christus' initiation,
Allawha, Kilsyth.

Sister Veni Cooper-Matheson

A theatrical group,
Sydney, Spring 1914.
Roy Redgrave second
from left, Vivian far
left, note centre part-
ing hall mark of pupils
of C.W.Leadbeater.

the garden to pluck one flower – that's the purpose of descent into matter. The troubles of life are the needful wind and rain to scatter the seed and nourish it. The dark spaces of the world are the protecting nooks that shelter many a fruitful piece of land, and you dear heart, what are you? Why! You are the little flower I have plucked in the garden of life so that I could press it to my burning lips. Come back to me soon for I want you so – I need you badly. You are the first girl I ever really loved and no-one can ever take your place in my heart...

There have been days and nights that were terrible since you left me, days full of gloom and nights full of terror. Days when I seemed in a dream and nights in which I could not sleep. Days when my mind would not think without pain and nights when I dared not cease to think lest the pain be too great. So come to me dear one that I may be near you, come to me soon lest I should go mad. For I need you near me – the feel of your presence – the sound of your voice – such sweet music to me.

She read the poem 'Brunette' which he had dedicated to her in the first flush of their relationship. In later years, whenever she felt lonely, she would copy it out, almost as if it were a talisman, substituting 'sweet for wee':

> My wee little bud from the bed of dark roses,
> So soft is thy cheek when it lies upon mine,
> So sweet is the blush that thy face now suffuses,
> It makes me awhirl, like a draught of red wine.
>
> My little wee bud from the bed of dark roses
> The light in your eyes I am sure is divine,
> The smile on your lips a flirtation proposes,
> And bliss follows fast as I press them on mine.

By Christmas, she was back at Ivycliffe.

That year Vyvyan received an elaborate Christmas card from Bishop Leadbeater and a signed photograph of Krishnamurti.

At the beginning of January Vyvyan received a letter from Thomas Campbell of Auburn conveying the unanimous agreement of the annual meeting of the members of the church there to retain him as lecturer for the next six months, holding Thursday night meetings in the Auburn School of Arts and confirming four Sunday lectures in

January and February. Travelling to Auburn was already part of Vyvyan's growing involvement with the Ordo Templi Orientis. After the entry in her diary for 17 March 1920, where she writes about Vyvyan's visits to Auburn, Eunice added simply 'M.M.M.', standing for Mysteria Mystica Maxima, a name closely associated with Crowley and the O.T.O. Eunice did not accompany Vyvyan. At Auburn he stayed with Jack White and his family, or with Mr and Mrs Schott – and their daughter May. White and Campbell were both long-term followers of Vyvyan.

Eunice was trying to fight back, by going away herself. Monday 5 January 1920 was their fourth wedding anniversary. Vyvyan arrived home early expecting to take Eunice out. She was not there. When she did arrive home, the surprise of her not having been there had sobered Vyvyan somewhat and he was very pleasant company all evening.

The following day, while Vyvyan was lecturing, old John Brigden called on Eunice, suffering from loneliness. The next Saturday he called again and this time his plight was pitiable enough for Eunice to tuck him up in bed for the night at Ivycliffe. When he got up the following morning to take himself home, he slipped on the stairs, cutting his head. He was taken to hospital unconscious, where Eunice visited him. He never regained consciousness, dying on Tuesday 13 January.

On the Tuesday evening 6 January, since Vyvyan had to take his occult class, Eunice went to Protestant Hall to report on a debate on the motion 'Spiritualism is Demonism', proposed by Revd Simpson and opposed by Mr Ford. Vyvyan decided to arrange such a debate in his occult class and on Tuesday 23 March the same Revd Simpson opposed the motion 'The Dead Can Communicate With Us' which was proposed by Professor Abbott.

On 14 January Mr Rushton, an American elocutionist, attended Vyvyan's lecture on the 'Religion of Common Sense.' After a good meeting Vyvyan went with Mr Rushton to his hotel, the Metropole. The next day he had not come home because it was too wet. Vyvyan had good reason not to go out in the rain. When he had holes in his only pair of black shoes, Eunice would cut out cardboard inner soles, inking in any parts which showed a light colour on the soles. When his suit became threadbare she would mend it. He never owned an overcoat and if he had to be reduced to one suit it would be an evening-suit which he wore under his velvet-collared Inverness cape in the evening, if necessary remaining at home until late afternoon. If his clothes got wet they would disintegrate leaving him nothing to wear in a world unready for Chidleyan principles.

Mr Rushton came home to dinner at Ivycliffe and, to Eunice's delight, recited Tennyson's 'Death of Oenone'. After his lecture on 29 January, Vyvyan again stayed at the Metropole with Mr Rushden, who then attended Vyvyan's occult class on his last evening in Sydney, before sailing home on Wednesday 11 February. While Vyvyan was out with his new friend, Eunice went to visit Mrs Pateman, who was making plans to go home to England with the girls. Eunice was still going as frequently as ever to the cinema, but was beginning to read more. She discovered Bulwer Lytton's *Rienzi*, Dicken's *Bleak House* and Frank Harris's biography of Oscar Wilde, choices reflecting her husband's influence. With her friend Miss Olsen she used to talk about New Thought and numerology.

Vyvyan was becoming gradually more closely involved with the Spiritualist churches: his central lecture in Auburn at this time was 'Spiritualism and the Bible'. In March there would be a Spiritualist rally at Protestant Hall and handbills were given out announcing that the speakers would be Mr Bradford, Mr Morell, Mr Oatis and Mr Deacon. When Sir Arthur Conan Doyle, an ardent Spiritualist, began preparing for a tour of Australia and New Zealand, it was suggested that someone should precede him on the lecture circuit. Vyvyan's reputation had reached New Zealand and prominent Spiritualist leader 'Joe' McLeod Craig came to Sydney to meet him. On Sunday 15 February, the day a letter on Spiritualism from Vyvyan was published in *Truth*, Eunice went to hear McLeod Craig lecture. Vyvyan was himself speaking both afternoon and evening at the Oddfellows temple and could not attend.

On Wednesday 24 March Vyvyan was not feeling well but he went to town and brought back for the night his friend James Bunn, who had just returned from a trip to America. Vyvyan developed influenza and began to run a fever. He rested for a time, but got up as he was keen to hear a lecture from the leading Theosophist Jinarajadasa, for he remained keenly interested in Theosophy. Vyvyan asked John Shirlaw to lend him the three pence fare: he refused. Still weak from the fever, Vyvyan was greatly upset at this but he took Eunice for a walk and a free boat ride. Despite having no money and being still unwell on the Monday, he went into town and stayed late with Pantin and Brennan. The following day Eunice was full of misgivings over where he had been the previous night.

Vyvyan resigned from the church at Auburn and for the first time took his own meeting at other premises instead. He still visited Auburn daily and he introduced Mr and Mrs McLeod Craig there. Both McLeod Craig and Vyvyan gave well-received addresses at Mason's Hall. With McLeod Craig's encouragement, Vyvyan was already preparing to visit New Zealand. He was keen for his office at the Oddfellows temple to continue while he was away and since Eunice had made up her mind not to go with him to New Zealand, they decided that she would take over both the office and the occult class. Vyvyan booked a passage on the *Manuka* and when sailing was delayed he took Eunice out to dinner at the Paragon Hotel. He gave her some brooches; her present to him was a walking stick.

On Saturday 29 May 1920 the *Manuka* left No. 5 wharf, taking Vyvyan to New Zealand and leaving his mother and Eunice waving on the dock.

Chapter Four

Or else it's - 'What's a "Medium"? He's a means,
Good, bad, indifferent, still the only means
Spirits can speak by.
> Robert Browning, *Mr Sludge, 'The Medium'*

VYVYAN ENJOYED the five day voyage. He conducted a service, gave a well-received lecture on 'Life after Death' and discovered there were several Spiritualists on board. He also wrote to Eunice with advice about how to run the occult class and keep up the dispensary while he was away. The 'psychometry' he proposes is the faculty of divining the history of objects, which are supposed to carry with them something of the aura of the people and places with which they have been in contact.

It would be a good idea for you to have a Psychometry Night at the Class and make them all hand an article to their right-hand neighbour and after 10 minutes' meditation tell in turn what impressions they get. Or you can get Mr Kennerdale to magnetise them and to suggest that they will leave their bodies but will be able to hear your voice as you describe where you are taking them astrally. Take them up through beautiful pale blue clouds and wonderful golden lights until at last you reach a wondrously white Temple into which you take them and introduce them to an old man with a white beard, a Teacher and you can leave them to Him for 10 minutes or a quarter of an hour. Then bring them back.

Don't get Hyos pills, from P.D. and Coy. but from Pattinsons: They are Colocynthis and Hys. I mostly buy a hundred there at a time.

The medications Vyvyan cites are a curiosity in themselves. Both the Hyoscyamine pills and Colycynthis could have been connected with childbirth and thus perhaps reflect a continuing link with Sister Veni, since both control the discharge of lochia. The twigs of the

What Says Modern Spiritualism?

Syllabus of Fascinating Lectures on Vital
and Thought Absorbing Problems of the Day

By the RENOWNED ORATOR

Mr. VIVIAN H. R. DEACON
In the SPIRITUALISTS CHURCH
WORCESTER STREET, W.

aromatic herb hyssop were used in Jewish rites, particularly to do with purification. Colcynthis, though, appears also to be able to cause priapism and to leave the patient easily open to the effects of alcohol. It is hard to be sure whether he was prescribing for a nursing home, a lustration or an orgy.

The boat arrived on Thursday 3 June 1920 at Christchurch, where the Worthington family was waiting to meet him. Mr Worthington worked as a gardener and the family were admirers of Sister Veni: their daughter Venetia was known as 'Veni' for short. The Worthingtons had a Temple of Truth in which orchestral concerts would sometimes take place. (I believe that this temple could have been a front for the Ancient Order of Templars.)

McLeod Craig had arranged for Vyvyan to be engaged as a lecturer on the Spiritualist platform, with a renewable three month contract that set Vyvyan's fee as half of any money brought in by his lectures. Vyvyan needed to ensure that his income would be enough for him to be able to support not just himself but also Eunice and the baby in Sydney. As soon as he received any money, he cabled some to her. It was urgent for him to begin publicising his presence as soon as possible. Within days the local paper announced:

> A visitor to Christchurch at present is Mr Vyvyan Deacon, a second cousin of the poet Browning. He is son of Dr Cornelius Deacon, of Croydon, near London. Mr Deacon, who possesses considerable literary ability and is the author of several works on poetry and art, is visiting this country on a lecturing tour on behalf of Spiritualism, as a forerunner to Sir Arthur Conan Doyle, who will visit New Zealand later.

In addition he arranged for the publication of pamphlets for his Christian Mystics of the Rose Cross and the O.T.O. His business cards, which interestingly enough began and ended with the Thelemic imperatives 'Do what thou wilt shall be the whole of the law... Love is the law - love under will', declared him a lecturer, teacher, healer and the 'sole custodian of the order of C.M.R.C. for Australia and New Zealand'.

Vyvyan also released the titles of his first lectures at the Spiritualist Church in Worcester Street West, titles which reflect influences beyond Spiritualism, the influence of Theosophy being still evident.

Sunday 6 June, What happens after death.

Wednesday 9 June, Your Aura and what it means to you - followed by Auric readings from audience.

Sunday 13 June, Spiritualism and Christianity.

Wednesday 16 June, Auras and Keynotes - followed by demonstrations from notes struck on piano by members of the audience.

Sunday 20 June, Spiritualism in the Bible.

Wednesday 30 June, The soul of things - a lecture on Psychometry and Psychometric demonstrations.

In addition to this there was a series of evening lectures on Thursdays, concerned with the Christian Mysteries. The opening lecture, rather startlingly, adapted as its title the motto which Crowley had displayed on his Equinox press volumes. We may be sure that few, if any, among his audiences and hosts will have known its source.

17 June, The Aim of Religion and the Method of Science.
24 June, Knowledge of God and how to experience Spiritual Consciousness.
1 July, The Living Christ. The Reality of his Presence.
8 July, Man the Image of God.
15 July, Christian Symbols - Interpretations.

Meanwhile, as 'Frater Memnon', he issued a pamphlet headed 'Rosicrucian Order of Freemasons'. This was in fact drawn from the INRI consitution issued eight years earlier in 1912. Theodor Reuss had been the chief author, though the document preceded the Crowley/Reuss reform of the O.T.O.: another indication of the significant links between Vyvyan and the O.T.O. One should also not neglect the fact that Hartmann, also a key mover in the O.T.O., had been very active in the Theosophical Society and was at one time very close to Madame Blavatsky (who had mixed feelings about him). The address given by Vyvyan was 'The Spiritualist Church'. One is left guessing how much his hosts knew about this side of Vyvyan's life.

During the past 25 years, constantly increasing numbers of earnest people and seekers after truth have been turning their attention to the study of the hidden laws of Nature.

The growth of interest in these matters has been simply marvellous. Numberless societies, associations, orders, groups etc, have been founded in all parts of the civilised world, all and each following some line of occult study.

While all these newly organised associations do good in preparing the minds of thoughtful people for their eventually becoming genuine disciples of the One Truth, there is but ONE ancient organisation of Mystics which shows to the Student a Royal Road to discover the One Truth. This organisation has permitted the formation of the body known as the 'ANCIENT ORDER OF ORIENTAL TEMPLARS'. It is a modern School of Magi. Like the ancient School of Magi it derived its knowledge from Egypt and Chaldea. This knowledge is never revealed to the profane, for it gives immense power for either good or evil to its possessors.

It is recorded in symbol, parable and allegory, requiring a Key for its interpretation.

The symbols of Freemasonry were originally derived from the more ancient mysteries, as all who have travelled the burning sands know. The ritual and ceremonies, signs and passwords have been preserved with great fidelity; but the real key has been long lost to the crowds who have been initiated, advanced and raised in Masonry.

Aleister Crowley.
The sign of Pan.

Vyvyan, Sydney 1919.

(Right) Bishops, 'JEM' Wedgwood (left) and C.W.Leadbeater, Sydney 1920.

(Below left) Vyvyan and Eunice wedding photograph January 1916.

(Below right)
The herbalist shop at
68 Queensbury Street
Carlton, 26.1.15.

The KEY to this knowledge can, however, be placed within the reach of all those who unselfishly desire, study and work for its possession.

The Symbols of Ancient Masonry, the Sacred Art of the Ancient Chemi (Egyptians) and Homer's Golden Chain are but different aspects of the One Great Mystery. They represent but different degrees of initiation. By the Right Use of the 'Key' alone the 'Master Word' can be found.

In order to afford genuine seekers after Hermetic Truth some information on the aims of the Ancient Order of Oriental Templars, we now print the preliminary instructions issued by the Fratres of this Order.

FIRST INSTRUCTION To all whom it may concern.

Let it be known that there exists, unknown to the great crowd, a very ancient order of sages, whose object is the amelioration and spiritual elevation of mankind, by means of conquering error and aiding men and women in their efforts at attaining the power of recognising the truth. The order has existed already in the most remote and prehistoric times and it has manifested its activity secretly and openly in the world under different names and in various forms; it has caused social and political revolutions and proved to be the rock of salvation in times of danger and misfortune. It has always upheld the banner of freedom against tyranny, in whatever shape this appeared, whether as clerical or political, or social despotism or oppression of any kind. To this secret order every wise and spiritually enlightened person belongs by right of his or her nature; because they all, even if they are personally unknown to each other, are one in their purpose and object and they all work under the guidance of the one light of truth.

Into this sacred society no one can be admitted by another, unless he has the power to enter it himself by virtue of his own interior illumination; neither can anyone, after he has once entered, be expelled, unless he should expel himself by becoming unfaithful to his principles and forget again the truths which he has learned by his own experience.

All this is known to any enlightened person; but it is known only to few that there exists also an external, visible organisation of such men and women who having themselves found the path to real self-knowledge, are willing to give to others, desirous of entering the path, the benefit of their experience and to act as spiritual guides to those who are willing to be guided. As a matter of course, these persons who are already sufficiently spiritually developed to enter into conscious communion with the great spiritual brotherhood will be taught directly by the spirit of wisdom; but those who still need external advice and support will find this in the external organisation of this society. In regard to the spiritual aspect of this secret order, one of the brothers says:

'Our community has existed ever since the first day of creation when the gods spoke the divine command: "Let there be light!" and it will continue to exist to the end of time. It is the Society of the Children of Light, who live in the light and have attained immortality therein. In our School we are instructed directly by Divine Wisdom, the Celestial Bride, whose will is free and who selects as her disciples those who are devoted to her. The mysteries which we are taught embrace everything that can possibly be known in regard to God, Nature and Man. Every sage that ever existed in the world has graduated at our school; for without wisdom no man can be wise. We all study only one book, the Book of Nature, in which the keys to all secrets are contained and we follow the only possible method in studying it, that of experience. Our place of meeting is the Temple of the Holy Spirit pervading the universe; easily to be found by the elect but for ever hidden from the vulgar. Our secrets cannot be sold for money but we give them free to everyone capable of receiving them.'

As to the external organisation of that society, it will be necessary to give a glance at its history, which has been one and the same in all times. Whenever that spiritual society manifested itself on the outward plane and appeared in the world, it consisted in the beginning of a few enlightened people, forming a nucleus around which others were attracted. But invariably, the more such a society grew in numbers the more became attracted to its elements, such as were not able to understand or follow its principles; people who joined it for the purpose of gratifying their own ambition or for making the society serve their own ends obtained the majority over those that were pure. Thereupon the healthy portion of it retired from the field and continued their benevolent work in secrecy, while the remaining portion became diseased and disrupted and sooner or later died disgraced and profaned. For the spirit had departed from them.

For this reason the external organisation of which we speak has resolved not to reveal its name or place to the vulgar. Furthermore for the same reason, the names of the teachers and members of this society shall remain unknown, except to such as are intimately associated with them in their common work. If it is said in this way the society will gain only a few members, it may be answered that our society has a spiritual head and that those who are worthy of being admitted will be guided to it by means of their intution, while those who have no intuition are not ripe for it and are not needed. It is better to have only a comparatively

70

small number of capable members than a great many useless ones.

From the above it will be clear that the first and most necessary acquirement of the new disciple is that he will keep silent in regard to all that concerns the society to which he is admitted. Not that there is anything in that society which needs to be afraid of being known to the virtuous and the good; but it is not necessary that things that are elevated and sacred should be exposed to the gaze of the vulgar and be bespattered by them with mud. This would only impede the society in its work.

Another necessary requirement is mutual confidence between the teacher and the disciple, because a disciple who has no faith in his master cannot be taught or guided by him. There may be things which appear strange and for which no reason can be given to beginners; but when the disciple has attained a certain state of development all will be clear to him or her. The confidence which is required will also be of little service if it is only of a short duration. The way of the development of the soul which leads to the awakening of the inner senses is slow, and without patience and fortitude nothing will be accomplished.

From all this it follows as a matter of course that the next requisite is obedience. The purpose of the disciple is to obtain the mastery over his own lower self and for this reason he must not submit himself to the will of his lower nature but follow the will of his higher, which he does not yet know but which he desires to find. In obeying the will of the master, instead of following the one which he believes to be his own but which is in reality only that of his lower nature, he obeys the will of his higher nature with which his master is associated for the purpose of aiding the disciple in obtaining the conquest over himself. The conquest of the higher self over the lower self means the victory of the divine consciousness in man over that which in him is earthly and animal. Its object is a realisation of true manhood and womanhood, and the attainment of conscious immortality in the realisation of the highest state of existence in perfection.

These few preliminary remarks may be sufficient for those who desire information concerning our order; to those who feel themselves capable to apply for admission, further instruction will be given.

For the true initiates who wanted definition 'Memnon' also issued a Treatise on Love:

True love ever doubts and yet doubts not. Whether it doubts or not depends entirely on the fact of its being either positive or negative, receptive or diffusive, and affects not the quality of the love.

Love has no qualities, only quantity – love is only different in degree, never in reality, in kind. Love is the great Transformer; it can transform anything – love and art are one. The truly great lover is a great artist – must of necessity be so. Art is expressing outward from within – so is love. Those who suppress expression know not love. A human being who never refuses love showeth great wisdom. A human being who never refuses to love shows greater wisdom. A human being who receiveth and giveth love is no longer human – provided ecstasy be reached.

I am the Way, the Truth and the Life – thus speaketh Love. To know truth the way is trodden; Life is the reward. Love is the only Truth, Love is the only Life.

Know that love knoweth no evil. Where evil is, love is not. Where true love is, evil cannot be. True love is a very healthy instinct. Those who follow it are very wise. Love is the Great Destroyer. Where shame is, love is not. People are only ashamed of ugly things. Love is ever very beautiful. Love destroys all sense of shame. 'I will', 'I live', 'I love'; thus ever speaketh the positive love. 'He wills'. 'He lives'. 'He loves' thus museth the negative love.

Love is the Great Creator, the Great Begetter, both point and circle, square and compass. Love is Jachin and Boaz. Love is also the secret pillar in the midst.

May it in you, be revealed to mortal eyes. Dost thou know, oh patient One, the Hidden Mystery, the secret. Oh! Prophet – dost thou know?

More has been said about love than about any other subject and yet there is nothing so little known nor so painfully understood. Van Dyke has already voiced the idea that there are many kinds of love. Love and Truth are in reality one and hence it follows that love can only be comprehended by means of paradox. All the opposites and extremes are utterly true of love. It aches with tears locked in the brain. It sings with a music like ten thousand nightingales all in sweet attune. It burns with a white hot passion and freezes the blood in one's veins by its intensity. All, all this and more can truthfully be said of Love.

Many who seek it find it not. Many who seek it not, think they have found it. Those who seek it, and those who seek it not, are in a world of delusion. Love comes – and it is irresistible. That is the one great fact of love.

Love is the only annihilator of Time. It is the great blender, the great destroyer. Love manifests not in this way or in that way, as limited Souls would have you think – but true love manifests in every possible way. It transforms evil, and makes it divine. There is something connected with love that is ever elusive; it floats in the Infinite Abyss.

Ah! Love divine how sweet thou art – thou art more beauteous and wondrous far than any flower.

Love is the means of attaining ecstasy – Ah! but it is the End as well. Love never leads anywhere – it is its own goal. Love is ever elusive, because the Hunter and the Hunted are one. Become that which you are – know yourself – so shall love be found. One should never think about love; one should never worry over love – love brooks not that. Express thyself. It is sin to hold thyself in. Express, express. Exceed the excess of excess and thou shalt know. Only he who has lived can love. Most people merely exist. Life and love are one. Love is the life.

We see here the doctrine of excess that was to cause such difficulties between Vyvyan and Eunice. Perhaps Vyvyan already knew Crowley's *Book of the Law*, with its rapturous cry of 'exceed! exceed!'.

When Vyvyan then prepared a descriptive programme for the following month's lectures, he was in fact drawing up a guide to his own personal interests and influences:

Sunday 4 July, The Message of Spiritualism to the World of Thought: Modern Philosophy – Christian Science – New Thought – Theosophy – the inclusiveness of Spiritualism.

Wednesday 7 July, The Geography of the Unseen Worlds: A vivid description of the Etheric, Psychic and Spirit Worlds, their size and relation to the earth, their importance to us.

Sunday 11 July, The Message of Spiritualism to the World of Science: Changes made and progress gained by Science – Facts already proved – New developments.

Wednesday 14 July, Self-Development and the Way to Power: We may be Nature's Slaves or the Happy Masters of Her Laws.

Sunday 18 July, The Message of Spiritualism to the World of Religion: The Hebrew Faith – Islam – Buddhism – Christianity – the Churches – Various Coloured Rays – the Pure, White Light of the Spirit.

Wednesday 21 July, The Modern Idea of God: Ancient ideas – Scientific Influence – The Modern Conception.

Sunday 25 July, The Message of Spiritualism to the World of Art: The Old Schools, the Realistic School – the Aesthetic School – Whistler and Turner – the Futurists – Effect of Art on the Community – the Power of Suggestion – Art in the Future.

Wednesday 28 July, The Secret of Happiness: Why we suffer – Change of Attitude – Sorrow Ceases – the Source of Joy – Life's purpose.

At first Eunice did not miss Vyvyan; life was easier without him. The money Vyvyan was able to send from New Zealand was not enough to live on but teaching the occult class and keeping up the dispensary seemed ready ways of earning more. She was still not her own person: her parents had brought her up to be obedient, not independent, and even with him away she was still Vyvyan's representative.

As is the way with evening classes, the very first class drew a crowd: thirty people turned up and Eunice had to direct eight to one taught by McLeod Craig, who was still in Sydney. The second week there were twenty members, the third week eighteen. After that attendance varied between thirteen and eighteen, some people leaving but others joining. Eunice started the class off with automatic writing, which was very popular. She brought in copies of *At the Feet of the Master* on one occasion. In all she conducted forty classes.

As well as the class, Eunice was also keeping up the herbalist work. She made a habit of taking the herbs she needed, together with a sieve and a saucepan, round to her friend Mrs Godwin, whose house was attached to the Kenilworth Hall. She began preparing the medicines there early each day and in the evening she would leave Sybil behind when she went to take one of Vyvyan's classes, calling back afterwards to finish the brewing. When this went on till late, they stayed the night. On 22 June Eunice had been able to pay seventeen shillings to Mr Nettleton at the I.O.O.F. building but by the middle of July the rent was proving more than she could afford and she was forced to hand in the keys. The weather was wet and cold that week. A wind blew all the time. It was a typical Sydney winter.

Eunice began making plans to leave Ivycliffe but while Frank Bennett, whom she had never liked, was away, she found herself much happier there than before. Finally, though, he was due back and she decided she would live with the Godwins, where Sybil would have a guardian and where there were two pianos. She made the final decision to leave on a damp Sunday afternoon in July. The following week she packed.

Eunice's last day at Ivycliffe was happy. There was a farewell party. Mr Shirlaw made a speech in her honour and Eunice was pleased to have Vyvyan's mother there to hear it. She wished Vyvyan would speak to her like that sometimes.

On Sunday 22 August she went with Mr and Mrs Godwin to hear a former priest speak but the meeting was already full so they went instead to hear Miss Miller and the materialisation medium Mr Bailey. On the Monday they were able to buy seats to hear a former priest, one J. Enright, who was accompanied by runaway nun Sister Lagouri. These people fleeing from holy orders were a powerful crowd puller, with their 'escape' story echoing *La Religeuse*, and people were still being turned away the second day.

She went to Roseville to stay with her friends the Bell family, whom she knew through occult circles. When she arrived home she found a letter from Vyvyan waiting for her with a ten shilling note enclosed as an extra present for Sybil. She cashed the latest cablegram wondering if she would ever see him again. It was now five months since Vyvyan left for New Zealand.

Her birthday was coming, so she went to stay with her family in Melbourne. The restricted world of her childhood had not changed but she found that after being married to Vyvyan for more than four years she was a different person. Conversations were strained and formal. On her twentieth birthday she received a cablegram from Vyvyan and heard there were letters awaiting her in Sydney.

In Melbourne she went to Oddfellows Hall to hear a talk on 'Why I am a Spiritualist' given by Revd Susannah Harris. Mrs Harris had been the pastor of a Spiritualist church in Columbus, Ohio. Accusations of fraud were levelled at her several times (in the US itself and then in Norway and the Netherlands when she visited those countries). She was to spend her later years in Britain. Though a poor education had left her semi-literate, she was an extraordinarily compelling presence and had given a test séance attended by Paul Beard, a co-founder of the London Spiritual Mission. Eunice and Vyvyan were later to get to know her well and came to look forward to her idiosyncratic letters. At the Theosophical Society Eunice met Mrs Daniell of the Ibis Lodge, who remembered visiting Vyvyan in the Kilsyth School February 1914. When she saw Eunice she was barely civil. Initiates, she explained coldly, were not expected to marry.

In New Zealand Vyvyan attended a lecture on modern drama at the Workers Educational Association and was himself hired to lecture on 'Psychology and Economics'. He wrote to Eunice that he was looking forward to this. With its vague receding echoes of Morris and Ruskin and its blend of Theosophy and Fabianism, Vyvyan's lecture proved very popular and Vyvyan was urged both to repeat the lecture and indeed to publish it as a pamphlet, which he later did when, in January 1921, he moved to his next centre of activities, Wellington. The tone of it gives some idea of what Vyvyan's lectures were like and its popular mixture of

Marx, Freud, Darwin, William Morris and New Thought (together with a strong New Testament flavour) is an indication of what people wanted to be told at that time.

The world today is faced with still greater and graver problems than those which confronted it prior to the recent war and the fact that those who represent the class termed 'capitalist' are striving in a hundred and one different ways to compromise with those who manifest Socialistic tendencies, indicates the gravity of the situation and the reality of working-class claims.

Whether the world finds itself plunged into absolute chaos or recovers itself and establishes a new order of things depends entirely on an accurate understanding of what lies behind the present industrial situation. In the past all attempts to change the economic basis have ended in failure. This is due to lack of thought and to the fact that attempts have ever been directed to the removing of effects rather than to the removal of the root cause.

Although it may seem to many an idealistic statement, yet I contend tonight that the cause lies in the world of thought and not in the objective world and I further contend that a thorough understanding of psychology would enable those who are confronted with the present economic situation to comprehend the root of the matter and thus to bring about the eradication of those things that are erroneous in our present system. Darwin, in his book on *The Expression of the Emotions*, shows in a very fascinating way the effects of thought on the physical body and modern science is coming more and more to realise that the thoughts that are individually or collectively held by people condition their environment and their physical appearance to a much greater degree than they formerly thought. Thought precedes action individually and collectively, and the action that follows thought, whether it be good or ill, is always the direct effect of the type of thought that was held. The French Revolution is an illustration of this fact. We find there that thought subconsciously held for generations by the masses of the people suddenly became dominant and the people were carried away by the thought instead of dominating it. The result was not altogether a success.

If the workers of the world are going to bring about a higher order of things, they must see to it that the change comes from a high mental attitude and not from that part of their consciousness where the baser thoughts reside.

It is well to remember that behind our present constitutional governments the economic basis is somewhat infirm and not altogether desirable but it is still more important to remember that behind the economic basis there lies the character of the people. If Socialism is ever to be established on earth it must be the Socialism that gives and not the Socialism that takes, and until men's characters are nobler, until they understand that the thoughts they think are potent in moulding the future of the world, until they understand the science of psychology and apply it to their economic life, any revolutionary change will prove the direst disaster instead of a change to a much better order of things. Economic change from below spells revolution and disaster; from above, means evolution and the raising of the whole level of humanity.

Man's consciousness can be divided into three. The conscious mind corresponds to the economic world, the object world, and is the mind one always uses in the present. Man's subconscious mind corresponds to the subject world and from the depths of the subconsciousness come the demands for those things that are termed 'the rights of the people'. In the subconscious mind is stored all memory of the past. Man's super-conscious mind corresponds to the ideal world and holds stored within it all the desires and possibilities of the future. Intuitions from the super-conscious mind might be said to emanate from the spirit of man – the highest part of him.

Viewing the constitution of man thus, from a psychological point of view, one is able to see how thought operates and is able to understand how easily the working-class movement can be misapprehended. These three parts of man's mind need to be utilised in his everyday life and to fail to feed one or the other means the stultification of the growth of the man and a killing out of an essential part of his nature. In olden times, when the workers were engaged in handicrafts, joy and pleasure were a part of their work. Now, with our modern machinery, that is no longer so. They are mere units in a crowd – mere 'hands'. A part of their consciousness no longer finds expression in the way it formerly did and it is this subconscious part of the worker's make-up that is protesting from within and sometimes without the workers knowing this. This causes them to feel resentment that a part of their nature is still bartered as a commodity, a part of their nature that they feel is a very real part of themselves, namely their labour. Great civilisations in the past have fallen through failure to understand that this is so.

The race today is at a higher level and whereas formerly civilisations were built on slavery and then in the feudal age on serfdom, in the modern world we have the proletariat movement. In the working-class movement today we find that the workers have become what is termed 'class conscious' and we must really understand from what part of their minds this class consciousness emanates. We must understand that the marxist philosophy has been accepted by the workers with all the fervour of religious enthusiasm. The reason for this is not far to seek. The part of their nature that has been starved by the present economic conditions was able to find an outlet in the study of the marxist philosophy and therefore the translation of Karl Marx's works affected the workers far more vitally and gave them an altogether different conception of things than it did to the so-called upper orders, and it is the result of constantly repeated thought along these lines becoming subconscious, automatic and suddenly dominant that has called into being the class-conscious movement today, and unless that part of man's nature that is dormant be given true nourishment, the dominant thought of the workers of the world is liable to carry them into chaos instead of leading them into their rightful sphere. The study of economics from a psychological basis is the only thing that can save the world from devastation and disgrace. We must learn that every thought we think raises or lowers the whole mental world. No man can live unto himself – no man can die unto himself. We are all our brother's keepers.

The workers of the world can never achieve anything so long as their spare time is spent in idleness, frivolity, or vulgarity. They must awake to the real situation and they must remember that upon them depends the fate of our modern civilisation. Each individual unit that tries to understand his own consciousness and turns his thoughts in an ideal direction is helping to raise the standard of humanity and is helping to bring about a higher state of affairs; for remember that thought always precedes action individually and collectively, and thought by constant repetition becomes subconscious, automatic and dominant, and in time dominates the life instead of the life dominating it. We are influenced all day long by suggestions for good or ill. Sight determines thought. The things we see we think about. That is why art and beauty are such a necessity among the workers today – because it is desirable that the workers should keep the concept that only the best is good enough for them, Socialism should mean not the tearing down or levelling down from above of all to one low standard but rather the raising up of all to the highest degree and unless the workers realise that because of the facts of psychology idealism is of practical utility, disaster will await humanity at no great distant date.

We can be carried along by the tide of evolution, we can work against it, or we can aid it. In olden days, before the science of chemistry was definitely established, we know how Roger Bacon was stretched on the floor of his laboratory senseless but he picked himself up and went on experimenting and now we have a science of chemistry and no one today is so foolish as to experiment without a knowledge of chemistry as supplied in our text books. So in the same way the laws of psychology and the truths of economics should be studied and understood by every worker in the world. Understanding the science of psychology and applying it to the economic life will rapidly bring about a change for the better, and will automatically present the true solution to the social question. If this is done, then out of the present state of things will arise a new age, when the ideals of Socialism will ultimately become realised and the brotherhood of man may be made manifest in a greater degree than ever before.

In the syllabus for October's lectures some reasons for studying Spiritualism were offered. It is remarkable for the insistence on optimism, a characteristic of the times, as we have seen with New Thought.

1. It solves the riddle of the Universe, harmonising the facts of Science with the fundamental truths of Religion.

2. It proves life worth living, by rendering it intelligible and demonstrating the justice and the love which guide its evolution.

3. It removes all fear of death and much of its sorrow; recognising birth and death, joy and sorrow, as alternating incidents in a cycle of endless progress.

4. It insists upon the optimistic view of life, proclaiming man the master of his own destiny; child of his past; parent of his future.

5. It demonstrates the power, the wisdom and the love of God; notwithstanding all the sorrow and misery of the world.

6. It brings hope to the hopeless, showing that no hope is ever wasted, no error irretrievable.

7. It proclaims the Fatherhood of God, hence the Sonship of Man and his ultimate attainment of perfection.

8. It declares the universality of the law of Causation maintaining that 'Whatever a man soweth, that shall he also reap in this and all other worlds'.

9. It regards the world as a school to which man incarnates until all its lessons are acquired.

10. It affirms the Brotherhood of Man and provides a basis of union for all who desire to work for its realisation.

11. It proves overwhelmingly the continuity of life beyond the grave.

Meanwhile, Sir Arthur Conan Doyle, for whom Vyvyan was paving the way in New Zealand, had arrived in Sydney. Macleod Craig gave Eunice tickets to the lectures. On 20 November she left Sybil with a friend while she went to the lecture on 'spirit photography'; she was interested but not greatly impressed by the man himself. Having made the ferry trip across the harbour she went on after to the Town Hall to hear the Revd David Simpson in reply to Conan Doyle. She went again to the Town Hall to hear Sir Arthur with Macleod Craig officiating. An audience of between four and five thousand crowded in to hear the author of the Sherlock Holmes stories speak. Eunice was not impressed by what he had to say, nor by his ability to hold an audience, comparing him unfavourably with Vyvyan.

The following Wednesday a group of Spiritualists went on a picnic together. A boat took them to Manley. Eunice was introduced by Macleod Craig to Conan Doyle but it was with his wife, Lady Jean Conan Doyle, that she got on well: Eunice spent most of the time telling her about Vyvyan. It would be easy to believe that Conan Doyle had Deacon in mind when he wrote 'Playing With Fire' in his collection of short stories *The Ring of Thoth*. There, Hervey Deacon, an artist who dabbled in the occult, was to have a séance in his studio. Deacon was:

> An ardent lover of everything which was outré... His work was all very clever and imaginative, fairies and animals and allegorical figures of sorts... Mythical monsters, imaginary creatures, heraldic emblems – a sort or weird, bizarre procession of them – with a Unicorn in front.

Deacon had been painting all day, trying to imagine what a real live unicorn would look like, and he painted him in and painted him out until he felt he had really captured him. Mrs Deacon had served tea to the guests, and the medium Mrs Delamere and the sitters took their places. The medium went into a trance.

> We had approached the most real and august of sacraments, that communion with the dead of which the fathers of the Church had spoken... Some huge thing hurtled us past in the darkness, rearing, stamping, smashing, springing, snorting...

When the door was opened for everyone to rush out, the creature, which arose from a green-yellow cloud, was seen to be a unicorn. Mrs Deacon was then found to be lying senseless, struck down by the sight she had seen rushing past her in the corridor. The story conveys the *power of thought,* one of Vyvyan Deacon's most popular lecture topics, for the unicorn, released by the medium, appears after the concentrated effort of Hervey Deacon to bring him to life.

You may if you please, imagine that we were the victims of an elaborate hoax... or a very real and terrible experience... you may know more than we do of such occult matters, and can inform us of some similar occurrences.

Although the story vividly describes a séance and could in many ways be a portrait of Vyvyan, Conan Doyle wrote the tale between 1899 and 1900, before ever hearing of Vyvyan Deacon.

On 1 December there were two letters from Vyvyan. The letters were quite open about how he was living in New Zealand. Eunice, shocked and upset by them and believing that everything was the result of what had happened in past lives, discreetly wrote nothing in her diary of what he had told her.

Vyvyan was feeling successful. He was earning enough money to support himself and send some to Eunice. He was a popular lecturer and had been awarded a six month contract. The clothes he was wearing at this time reflect his sense of confidence. Photographs show him in evening dress and opera cape with velvet collar, carrying a walking-stick and leather gloves. His lectures were as ever concerned with the search for meaning in life and the mingling of political and spiritual vocabulary is still characteristically there. But a new word has crept into the syllabus: 'race' was beginning to be one of the concerns of those searching. Emerging from the Social Darwinism of the late nineteenth century, a belief in racial identity was one of the talking points of the Twenties. By the Thirties, it would be part of government policy in some countries.

Sunday 24 April, The Spirit and Meaning of ANZAC. The part Australia and New Zealand have played in the life of the Race. Present day happenings. Future events. Impending Physical changes. The emerging of a new Race. The future that awaits us.

Wednesday 27 April, Scientific Evidence of a Future Life. Some of the scientific investigations that indicate the existence of an unseen world and future life.

Sunday 1 May, The Church Universal. A study of the past. Tendencies of the present. Indications of the coming of a world religion. Religion. Philosophy. Art. Science and Morality. The part of Spiritualism.

Wednesday 4 May, The Invisible World About Us. A lecture on the unseen regions beyond the grasp of the physical senses and the life we live after bodily death.

Sunday 8 May, The Coming King. Spiritual guidance. The mysteries. Vyasa. Thoth. Hermes. Zarathustra. Orpheus. Buddha. The Christ. The means of knowing Him.

Wednesday 11 May, Beyond the Border. Clairvoyance. Premonitions and other super-physical phenomena.

Sunday 15 May, The Problem of Today. Wealth and poverty face to face. The real cause of crime. Science. The use and abuse of machinery. Our duty. Merrie England (?). The Way out. Revolution v. Evolution. Self-sacrifice. The Reward.

Wednesday 18 May, Nature's Law of Justice. The laws of cause and effect as operating in the affairs of daily life, and the part played by thought and desire.

Meetings commence: Sundays 7 pm and weekdays 8 pm. For the weekday lectures an admission charge of 1/- will be made. An after-meeting is held on Sunday nights, when questions will be answered by the Lecturer. A special series of Sunday morning Lectures are delivered in the Church at 11 o'clock, on 'Methods of Psychic Development'. These Lectures are for members only. Join now.

Eunice was left not knowing how she felt about Vyvyan and could not decide whether to go to New Zealand, which would be joining him and accepting all that would bring, or stay in Sydney and get a job, which would be a step towards making her independent. She became very close to the Bell family, going with them to the Liberal Catholic Church on a Sunday morning, the Lotus Circle at the Theosophical Society in the afternoon and Theosophical lectures in the evening at the Kings Hall. On Sunday 24 April Eunice took Mrs Godwin's daughter Lucy to the Liberal Catholic Church as Bishop Wedgwood was officiating. She played the hymns in the afternoon for the Lotus Circle, then to the church again in the evening to hear Bishop Leadbeater's sermon. They held some services unique to the Liberal Catholic Church, using both priests and priestesses.

Twice in April she attended lectures by Dr Donald Anderson. He had a high reputation in the field of psychology and hypnotism and his lectures were always packed. He had used Vyvyan as a subject while he was studying him and Vyvyan had proved able to lecture clearly while under hypnosis. Argus, the 10-year-old supposed prophet with a phenomenal memory and second sight was on at the Shell Theatre. Eunice went to see him twice as well. As with many other performers, she was reminded of Vyvyan, who could perform similar feats with no problems.

Eunice paid her account with the Spiritualist Society. After handing the keys to Mrs Bailey, to whom responsibility for the occult class now passed, she concentrated on her college work. She studied sweetmaking and then later shorthand and typing. On 1 May she visited Mrs Frank Bennett and her family for the day. Eunice always dreaded having to cope with Frank who, under the influence of drugs, would usually make advances to her. She actually found Frank Bennett less difficult to be with than he always used to be and decided that he was at last improving.

Eunice had decided to write to Vyvyan and have the letter delivered personally by Mrs Howarth. In her own hesitant way, she was struggling to make her husband see how his behaviour was affecting her. In reply she received a cablegram which was enough to make her happy, though it still left her wondering what future there could be for them. He had written to say that his contract had been renewed after a committee meeting in March 1921 and as a result he would be staying on in New Zealand. Indeed, Arthur Miles, an occult student in his mid-twenties and the church's secretary, wanted Vyvyan to settle permanently in Wellington, where he was now based. The old pattern of staying away from home that he had inherited from his father was as strong as ever. Moreover, although Eunice had been left behind, his mother had gone out to stay with him in Christchurch and when he moved to Wellington, she went with him. It was as if he was reassuring her that he would never abandon her as she had been abandoned by his father. In later years he used to complain bitterly about her following him around, because he hated any feeling of being a mother's boy. It was, in fact, his mother who had been the main source of his interest in the occult, though he never admitted this in public; she was also his link with the Browning family's Rosicrucian tradition.

Perhaps to assure her that all was going well, Vyvyan sent Eunice a report on the activities of the Wellington Spiritualists' Church in which he was much praised. In fact, though, among the accounts of lectures, pentecostal meetings and occult classes, a note on the existence of an 'elocution and dramatic class' should have been enough to alert Eunice that Vyvyan had found another woman: after all, it was by means of elocution lessons that Vyvyan had first gained access to her.

During the last few months the Church has gone ahead by leaps and bounds. The membership, which was 49 members on the roll at the annual meetings held in January last, has now gone up to 119 on the roll at the present time. This is the number of financial members and does not include non-financial members or the one or two resignations that have occurred.

The Church has also recently commenced Sunday morning meetings at which our Leader and Teacher delivers some very fine talks on 'Methods of Psychic Unfoldment'. Our Teacher also conducts an enquirers' meeting after the usual Sunday evening service, where a pleasant half-hour is passed in asking questions and receiving our Teacher's replies.

The Elocution and Dramatic Class, which our Teacher holds on Monday evenings is growing in numbers. Already scenes from Shakespeare are in process of production and this night is eagerly looked forward to by the members of the Class as one of the most interesting and instructive week-night meetings.

Tuesday is devoted to the occult Student's Training Class, the logical outcome of the Eucharist, and those who attend are unanimous in saying that they do indeed there receive the Wine of the Holy Spirit and Bread of the Divine Presence.

After the lecture (on Wednesday) our Teacher comes forward and descending from the platform gives a number of treatments, for Health, Success and Spiritual advancement, to all who care to come forward. Only those who have been present on a Wednesday evening can adequately describe the feeling of power and spirituality that is there made manifest. Indeed it sometimes feels as if the Quickening Breath of the Holy Spirit had once more descended with a Pentecostal outpouring upon humanity. Quite a number of those who have received personal treatment thus, at our Teacher's hands, have testified to the almost miraculous benefit they have received therefrom.

During Easter in Auckland the Annual Conference of the National Association of Spiritualists was held. At this there were three representatives of the Wellington Spiritualist Church. Vyvyan and the young Secretary Mr A.H. Miles and a new elderly member a Mr Redell. The Conference was fully reported in the *Message of Life* but briefly, Mr W.C. Nation of Levin, New Zealand's grand old Spiritualist was elected President, Vyvyan Deacon was elected Vice-President and Mr Miles National Secretary.

Mr Deacon delivered three lectures to earnest and enthusiastic audiences. On Easter Sunday at 7 pm in the Arcadia Picture Theatre he spoke to over 800 people upon 'Spiritualism's Message to the Modern World'. On the following Wednesday, Mr Deacon lectured in the big

Town Hall on 'What Happens After Death' and at the close of the lecture answered several questions from members of the audience. Thursday evening was devoted by Mr Deacon to a lecture on 'Methods of Psychic Development', delivered in the Druids Hall to Spiritualists.

In conclusion, we would like to say that there is a distinct feeling of earnest zeal and spiritual force manifesting itself in our Church at the present time. And we cannot help feeling that glorious possibilities lie in store for us in the future. Banded together by no other ties than those of Divine Love, we press forward with eager faces turned towards the Light and our continuous prayer to Those who are our Leaders and Teachers in the Unseen World is, 'Oh, Masters of the Great White Lodge! From the unreal lead us to the Real, from Darkness lead us to the Light, from death lead us to a knowledge of Immortality.

When Eunice saw these accounts she was reading about a husband whom she had not seen for a year. She talked to Mrs Godwin about what she should do: her friend was in no doubt that a wife should be with her husband, that a temporary separation ran the risk of becoming a permanent one and that if Vyvyan insisted on being in New Zealand, Eunice must be there too. The next day she wrote in her diary 'Have been thinking over Mrs Godwin's suggestion last night, have decided to act upon it.'

When he first arrived in Wellington, Vyvyan found himself once again surrounded by new people. Olive Young, one of two daughters in the house where he had been lodging in Christchurch, began writing to him regularly, hinting at their previous incarnations together. She was about twenty years of age and, like Eunice, partly Chinese.

Mrs Margaret Stables, president of the Wellington Spiritualist church and heading the committee arranging Vyvyan's transfer, invited him to stay with her and her husband until he found accommodation elsewhere which suited him. Later she was to say that as soon as she opened the door to this tall, handsome young man, she realised that she had made a mistake in asking him to stay. Vyvyan's explanation for the difficulties he had with this woman was that she rather courted his attention and he did not respond. Whatever the truth of this, the fact that he was again going to be in conflict with the older woman who was his landlady and hostess, just as he had been in Sydney with Mrs Pateman, suggests an emerging pattern. Relations between Mrs Stables and Vyvyan were strained from the beginning. She was determined to maintain a high moral tone in the Spiritualist church and soon challenged him about rumours that he had been rather too friendly with some of the girls in the Christchurch congregation. Vyvyan tried to act as if he had nothing to hide. Aware that his hostess had been suspiciously watching the regular arrival of letters all addressed in the same feminine hand, he decided the best policy was confident openness. He made the mistake of showing her one in which Olive mentioned knowing him in a previous incarnation: Mrs Stables was not impressed.

Vyvyan set up his herbal and healing business at 1 Home Street. He had a secretary named Violet Johnson allotted to him. She had been a committee member of the church for several years although still only in her mid twenties and worked in the Lyceum teaching children calisthenics. Vyvyan asked Miss Johnson to pass a note to one of the pupils in the elocution and drama class, asking her to remain behind afterwards as he wished to speak to her. This was Isobel Sly, whom Vyvyan first had met in January that year at a Sunday school anniversary he had gone to with his mother, who had not yet returned to Sydney. He told 'Bella' that he was lonely. When he had been only nineteen, he said, he married a girl because she had no parents who could take care of her. She had stayed in Sydney with their baby daughter, rather than leave her friends.

Bella Sly was seventeen years old. She had been adopted from a children's home at the age of three and still did not know if she was an orphan or illegitimate. Her adoptive mother was living but her adoptive father had died. From his estate in the Public Trust Office she received an allowance. She worked as a shorthand typist.

Vyvyan told Bella her voice should be trained. He formed the drama class so that he could see her at the weekly meetings. Bella lived about a quarter of a hour's walk away from the church. Vyvyan used to take her home after class and after a service. They began going out with Vyvyan's secretary Violet Johnson and her friend Frank Rathbone. Then a scandal broke. Mrs Stables announced that she had heard that Vyvyan had been seen kissing Miss Johnson outside her house late at night. Vyvyan insisted this was a goodnight kiss, with no harm in it. Questioned by a severe Mrs Stables, he said that when Miss Johnson had a headache he cured it for her by mental suggestion. Mrs Stables immediately said that it was not proper for someone in Vyvyan's position to take girls home, nor to put them into a hypnotic trance when he was alone with them in the office. She arranged for Vyvyan to be followed by committee member, George Bodell, and a member of the church by the name of Clarke. When Vyvyan found out about this he threatened violence. Arthur Miles, the secretary of the Kent Terrace Wellington Spiritualists' Church and now the new National Secretary of the movement in New Zealand, claimed that he had been followed by the same two men, also at Mrs Stable's request.

As president of the Wellington Spiritualist church, Mrs Stables arranged for Vyvyan to be summoned before the committee, hoping its members would demand his resignation. Vyvyan admitted to seeing the girls home but denied this was improper behaviour. Violet Johnson was a 'nice and very good girl,' he insisted. Mrs Stables pointed out that Miss Johnson had accompanied Vyvyan to the conference at Easter; Vyvyan replied that they had stayed at different hotels. Without any direct evidence of impropriety, a vote resulted in any proposed action being held 'in abeyance'. Vyvyan asked the meeting to report his being followed.

After the Committee meeting both Mr and Mrs Stables resigned to devote their time to the exposure of humbugs. The elderly committee member Mr Redell, who had also been at the Easter conference, had taken his four children away from the Sunday school after hearing reports from Mrs Stables; he too resigned. Arthur Miles showed his full confidence in Vyvyan by renewing the contract for a further six months. Mr Fabling, the vice-president, took over the presidency.

Fabling was a salesman at Duthie's hardware store. One day he found a small stove had been charged to his account by Vyvyan. Vyvyan explained, when asked, that he had bought it for his room and had assumed the sum would be deducted from his fees. Vyvyan gave him five shillings towards the total owing and said he would pay a further five shillings a week. In fact, there were to be no further instalments. Vyvyan also borrowed £2 from Mr Fabling; this too was not repaid. Vyvyan always got on well with Mr Fabling, who later recalled guardedly 'We have to recognise that he had rather an attractive personality'. The next shock was when french letters were found in Mr Deacon's office. Mr Fabling again had to demand an explanation: Vyvyan said that they were for a friend. When he was asked about his relations with women he agreed that they chased him and to illustrate the point he showed Fabling letters he had been sent. In one, a young lady from Hataitai said he had swept her off her feet. Like Mrs Stables, Mr Fabling was not impressed.

When Vyvyan could not meet Bella immediately after the class, she would go off with Frank and Violet. He would meet them at a Chinese restaurant in Haining Street, about the only place open on a Sunday night. The fact that Vyvyan had been seen going into a Chinese restaurant seemed to be as much of a scandal as his owning contraceptives. To prove there was no harm in it, Vyvyan invited Mr Fabling to go with him one evening. Accompanied by the nervous hardware salesman, Vyvyan went to Haining Street, where the Chinese staff were friendly, for Vyvyan was a familiar customer. They were given bowls of Chinese food at which Fabling picked dubiously and without enthusiasm. When he admitted he had eaten enough, Vyvyan cheerfully reached over, took Fabling's bowl and finished it off for him. He was also worried about the news that on some evenings there were dancing girls in very scanty clothes: Vyvyan assured him that it was not Chinese etiquette for one to appear to look at them. Years later Fabling still remembered how strong the wine was.

On Monday 23 May 1921 Eunice received a letter saying Vyvyan was ill. This was the excuse she had been waiting for and on Thursday 26 May 1921 she sailed on the *S.S. Moraki*. The boat arrived on Monday at midday. She passed the ship's doctor's examination but was not allowed to land in Wellington at first because she was part Chinese. Mrs Howarth came to meet her on the boat but Eunice was detained on board all night.

The next day Mrs Howarth returned to see if she was free to go yet. Eunice had to go before customs and sign a declaration before the officials, still half convinced that something murky must be at issue where a Chinese person was concerned, finally allowed her into Wellington at midday. Mrs Howarth brought a car to take her and her luggage to Vyvyan's lodging.

She wrote to Vyvyan who was staying in Christchurch for a holiday with the Worthingtons. A week went by and she had no reply. On 4 June, because she had no word from Vyvyan, she wired the Worthingtons and heard Vyvyan had gone further south to Dunedin.

Walking around Wellington on her own, the place seemed to her to be dull after the bustle of Sydney. The people from the Spiritualist Church were courteous enough towards her and the lecturer taking Vyvyan's place while he was away came calling but the atmosphere was dreary. When after a fortnight she at last heard from Vyvyan, it was an angry letter: he was not pleased she had come, it interfered with his plans, why had she not consulted him? He would be arriving by boat on Saturday.

Saturday 11 June was very cold. Arthur Miles went to meet the boat but Vyvyan was nowhere to be seen. Miles consulted the passenger list: Vyvyan was not named. Instead, there was a message that he had been delayed and would arrive the following day. Eunice wanted to look as smart as possible for the reunion and with growing nerves went shopping. There was so little money in her purse and she was so unused to buying clothes for herself that she did not know where to begin. After wandering around the shops worrying about how to look her best, she settled for a pair of new shoes and took her hosts to the pictures at the Paramount theatre.

The next morning, while Eunice was still in bed, she heard his voice in the house. Before she could get up, he had come into her room. Her first thought as he came towards the bed was that he had grown stout.

That evening she attended Vyvyan's lecture at the New Century Hall. Vyvyan stayed in bed all the following day until it was time for him to set off for his occult class in the evening.

Vyvyan then announced that he had found somewhere else to stay. They would not live at the same address. Time had mended nothing; they were as awkwardly matched as ever. He took rooms in Nairn Street with Miss Routledge, a member of his congregation and rented a private office in Willis Street. He assured her that she could visit him whenever she wished but she could not live with him. Eunice continued dutifully writing up her diary, but loyal as ever to childhood restraint, now reinforced by New Thought theories of positive thinking, she recorded nothing in her diary about the renewed separation from her husband. She hoped that if it went unacknowledged the problem would wither away, that actually allowing herself to think or write about it would in some alchemical way cause its recrudescence.

When Vyvyan fell in love with Bella, he had convinced himself that he and Eunice were permanently apart. To his wife he had been sending money regularly and sometimes advice: why not learn shorthand and typing, he had suggested, perhaps thinking this would make her more independent of him. To Bella (who had passed her shorthand exams) he gave a ring. Then it had seemed simple. Eunice's arrival made matters more complicated. As if that were not enough, Olive Young had travelled down from Christchurch to be with him. Eunice met her in the office one afternoon but decided she was a 'very nice girl'.

Mr Fabling found himself faced with yet another moral crisis: Mrs Deacon had arrived but it was clear that she was not living with her husband in the usual way. He went to consult the New Zealand president W.C. Nation, who happened to be an admirer of Vyvyan's work. Nation proposed a compromise: post Deacon to Auckland where he already had a following, he suggested, such a course of action was in keeping with the original contract. Mrs Pedlar and Susannah Harris were due for an appearance in Wellington: when Vyvyan went to Auckland, these two mediums could visit the Wellington congregation.

Vyvyan would not co-operate with the plan. He did not wish to leave and would set up on his own if forced to resign from the Kent Terrace Spiritualist Church. He would still, though, want to be allied to the National Association of Spiritualists, he assured them.

Vyvyan asked Mr Nation and Mr Fabling separately what they would do in his place: they would resign, they assured him solemnly. On 7 August 1921 Vyvyan wrote out and signed his resignation which they received with formal regret. It was all done politely enough and Vyvyan was allowed to take the service on the following Sunday so that he could address his congregation. He explained that it was time for him to move on but urged them to stay faithful to the church; a change of leadership, he assured them, would be a positive thing. He would still be close at hand. Mrs Pedlar was given a contract to the end of the year and Susannah Harris would follow. Vyvyan continued to work as a herbalist and healer from premises in Willis Street and held lectures in the concert chamber of the Town Hall of Wellington.

It was only a week since the Spiritualist newsletter *Message of Life* had carried an enthusiastic account of Vyvyan's work in the 1 August issue.

When he celebrated his twenty-sixth birthday two days after his resignation, Vyvyan took both Eunice and Bella to dinner at the Commercial Hotel. It was like Miss Key all over again: an intruder was being made into a part of the family. Vyvyan then left to take his occult class, leaving the two women to be taken care of by a third, Miss Adams. She was a milliner and a devout supporter of Vyvyan, ready to support and contribute to any of his plans. Since Vyvyan seemed settled in Wellington, she established herself in business there, in Cuba Street.

On Bella's birthday, also in August, there were again celebrations. She, Vyvyan and Eunice returned to the Commercial Hotel and then ended the evening at the office. The following day it was the turn of Olive Young, nicknamed 'Leone' because of her birth sign Leo.

When Vyvyan resigned from Kent Terrace Spiritualist Church, a good number of what had been his congregation continued to go to his lectures and to consult him at Willis Street. One of them, a healer called Laurence Pope, paid Vyvyan fifty pounds for training in oratory and occultism, money that was used to set up the business in Willis Street.

Now that he was no longer employed by the Spiritualist church, Vyvyan needed once again to ensure that he made the most of the publicity that was available to him. He hit on the idea of opening a reading room and on 10 August a column in the local paper announced its existence. 'The reading provided comprises the best of books and periodicals' readers were assured. 'There is some Spiritualist litera-ture... on sale but it is not pressed on those who go there, nor is propaganda anywhere in evidence.'

On the Saturday following his resignation Vyvyan made sure the papers knew of his new course of lectures as well as the new reading room. He put the best possible gloss on his having left the Spiritualist church that had previously been employing him and, as in the past, he cited his being related to Robert Browning.

Mr Vyvyan H.R. Deacon, who is a cousin of the late poet Robert Browning and a son of Dr Cornelius Deacon of Croydon near London, is commencing a series of lectures in the concert chamber of the Town Hall on Sunday evenings. Mr Deacon came to New Zealand under special arrangements with the Worcester Street Spiritualists' Church, Christchurch as a forerunner to Sir Arthur Conan Doyle. Owing to the success of his work in New Zealand, Mr Deacon has been persuaded to take up residence permanently in Wellington and intends to continue his lectures indefinitely. He has formed a body of truth-seekers under the name of The Church Universal and in connection with his work has opened the Truth Centre at 80 Willis Street, Wellington, where are rest and reading rooms open, free of charge.

The Sunday lecture of 14 August made the local papers, which reported an audience of some 200 people. The subject of the lecture was 'The Ladder of Lives'. Seven lectures were advertised for the near future, with the announcement that the lectures would be followed by demonstrations of the power of the mind over the body in which young men from the audience showed how the muscles could be flexed by concentration, in illustration of what Vyvyan had been saying about fakirs.

Vyvyan lectured on reincarnation, rebirth and the evolution of the soul. After that he spoke on personal magnetism.

91

The Master Key to Attainment. Power of Voice and Eye-Attention to Details – a Retaining and Scattering Mind – Cleanliness – Breathing – Exercise – How to Obtain Magnetic Personality. – The lecture will be followed by demonstrations of the existence of Personal Magnetism.

The demonstrations were essential in drawing the crowds as they lent a certain fairground touch to the events. Vyvyan and Eunice took a Sunday school and Eunice played the piano for the hymns. Eunice meanwhile minded the office and dined with Vyvyan and Bella. On the Sunday 28 August, after attending the church at the Town Hall she remained home all day and wrote in her diary, begging her 'higher self' to comfort her. The next day after they had worked together in the office, Vyvyan went out to dinner, not taking her. 'I am so lonely and long for a confessor, a comforter,' she recorded in a rare admission of despair. The press reported Vyvyan's lecture had been on 'life's problems'.

By now a kind of normality had established itself. Eunice even seemed quite to enjoy Bella's company; meanwhile she was becoming close to Laurence Pope. He and Eunice ran the Sunday school together, gradually becoming friends. Sometimes the four of them, Vyvyan and Bella, Eunice and Laurence would all go out together for the evening.

Sunday 4 September was the day of Laurence's 'dedication'. The local paper announced that at the Church Universal meeting in the Town Hall concert chamber Mr Vyvyan H.R. Deacon would lecture on 'Nature's Law of Justice' and added that 'At the 11 am service... Mr Deacon will speak on the Reality of Things Eternal... the service will be one of especial Devotion to the Holy Spirit at which a Brother will be dedicated to the Cause of Truth and Consecrated therein.' Eunice spent the following Wednesday evening with Laurence, writing 'Congratulated Laurence. Had supper in William Street after lecture'. The diary entry is enigmatically decorated with a star, as if to mark an event of importance.

Shortly after this Eunice, in secret from Vyvyan, began to take violin lessons. She had a twenty-first birthday in October but it was a miserable day. She recorded the event, stubbornly assuring her diary that 'All is well.'

Meanwhile Vyvyan and Bella's relationship continued. Mrs Stables had written about Vyvyan to leading Spiritualists in Australia and to the Press in both Australia and New Zealand. She tried to interfere with a meeting which was to be chaired by Vyvyan, writing to warn

Dr Seton who would be conducting it. Julia Seton knew Vyvyan of old, though, and ignored the warning letter. It was not the first time Mrs Stables had acted this way.

Vyvyan's following was such that the Church Universal warranted its own catechism. Official application was made for the 36 page book compiled by Vyvyan for use in his Church Universal. On 8 October 1921 the Patent Office of New Zealand registered the copyright of a Literary work. The catechism, using a mixture of everyday and Biblical language, reflected the New Thought style of Sister Veni. The papers in October were kept informed of growing membership and the new church's ambitions. There would be 'sick visitations, prison and asylum visits, distribution of literature and finding employment for those in need of work... walking tours, picnic parties, socials, dances, drama, literary and debating societies.' Then public events suddenly tailed off; Bella hastily moved away from Wellington and went to stay with relatives. She was pregnant.

Vyvyan fled back to the Worthington family in Christchurch with whom he had stayed eighteen months before when he had arrived in New Zealand full of confidence. Eunice would not hear of a divorce. She did not suspect that Bella was pregnant.

Vyvyan decided that he had to accept that he was married to Eunice and that any attempt to live with Bella would doom his work as a Spiritualist lecturer. After Christmas they took a furnished house at 89 Main Street in a suburb of Wellington. It was a house large enough to hold meetings in and to accommodate lodgers rather on the lines of the Ivycliffe establishment. 'O God! how I love him - even if he were the devil himself I could not help it,' Eunice recorded. After all the turmoil, she decided that she needed a holiday and would visit Christchurch.

The newly-arrived Susannah Harris conducted a séance in their front room but the results were not good. Eunice excused this, attributing it to the medium's being upset by the continual squabbling at Kent Terrace Spiritualist Church. She was very kind to Eunice and donated the whole of the evening's proceedings of £4.4s.0d to Eunice for her journey. Vyvyan wanted to borrow the money as he was in financial difficulties but Eunice was afraid he would be unable to repay it before her sailing date planned for the following Friday. She lent him half.

Susannah Harris telephoned for Eunice to do some typing for her, so Eunice called into the office one afternoon and took down some reports of her travels in the astral body. On the eve of her departure for Christchurch, Eunice typed out the reports, delivering them to Revd Harris who was lecturing that night at Kent Terrace Spiritualist Church.

When Miss Adams returned from Auckland, Eunice went to the Union Company to book a berth for the night. Mr Field took her and her luggage to the boat in the evening. Vyvyan brought her violin and Miss Adams went to the wharf to see her off. Sybil was upset at being separated from her father again.

At Christchurch station they were met by Veni Worthington, the eldest of the four Worthington daughters, who took them to their home in the Cashmere Hills with a view of Christchurch that Eunice loved. After she unpacked they went sightseeing in the afternoon and saw St Elms and the church where Vyvyan had lectured in his first days in New Zealand.

Returning to Wellington brought Eunice back to a life where nothing was certain. They had no plans, no idea what to do next. Now that he was no longer paid by the Spiritualist church, Vyvyan was not succeeding in earning a living. Casting around for something to do, she went to an Esperanto class. Then, missing a period, she realised that she was pregnant.

Somehow the news forced them to make a decision and they began to make plans to return to Sydney where the rumours of scandal would not have reached. Vyvyan gave Bella a little money, promising her that he would certainly send her any money he could and reassuring himself that in any case she had an allowance which would ensure that she would not go hungry. News came that Annie Besant was soon to visit the Theosophical Society in Sydney. Eunice and Vyvyan were both excited by this and decided to renew their membership.

On 5 April Miss Adam called. She had decided that she would follow Vyvyan to Sydney and had wound up her millinery business and bought her ticket.

Chapter Five

One sometimes gets the impression that the mere words
Socialism' and 'Communism' draw towards them with
magnetic force every fruit-juice drinker, nudist, sandal-
wearer, sex-maniac, Quaker, 'Nature Cure' quack, pacifist
and feminist in England.

George Orwell, *The Road to Wigan Pier*

HEN THE *MANUKA* docked on Easter Monday 1922, it
brought Vyvyan and Eunice back a married couple who
had undergone nearly two years separation. While Vyvyan had found life away from his wife liberating and
had lived out the Thelemic creed of 'Do what thou wilt shall be the
whole of the Law', Eunice had continued to feel herself tied to her
husband, to be unable to imagine a life apart from him, while at the
same time to be still unable to express herself. The rigorous, confining,
church upbringing she had received as a minister's daughter continued
to govern her every action. Sexually inhibited and emotionally confined, she found it difficult to tell herself about what she felt, wanted
or feared, let alone communicate any of this to her large, loud husband.

In Sydney they found continuing excitement about New Thought
and Theosophy but also factionalism. Visits by Annie Besant, Dr
Seton, Krishnamurti or Leadbeater were constantly expected and their
followers would meet and speculate about who would attract what
size of audience, about which one would prove to be the great world
teacher, the one to whom all the others would ultimately pay homage.

From 7 Glen Street, Milson's Point, where Eunice and Vyvyan were
staying with a Mrs Black for the first two weeks after their return, they
went to the Theosophical Society, only to find a disharmony that
matched that in their own relationship. Audiences that had gathered
to hear the same teacher would be covertly riven by factionalism. As
Eunice and Vyvyan had not paid up their membership fees while in

New Zealand, they were seen by some as intruders, while others, filled with suspicion, regarded them as belonging to 'the other side' in one or other of the internal disputes in the society. On 23 April they went to King's Hall to hear Jinarajadasa on the history of the Theosophical Society, illustrated by lantern slides. Krishnamurti, his brother and Annie Besant were supposed to be visiting Leadbeater; people were speculating who would follow which leader. Eunice recorded on this occasion:

Did not see Krishnamurti or his brother. Bishop Leadbeater is ill. Annie Besant is expected after all, at no distant date... Dr Seton of the New Thoughtists...is expected very soon.

When Annie Besant did arrive, a reception was held in her honour at King's Hall on Thursday 11 May. Vyvyan and Eunice went up with Leadbeater and spoke to Dr Besant who made a powerful impression on Eunice, with her cropped white hair and skin tanned from her time in India, where she had been elected president of the Indian National Congress and dedicated herself to the cause of home rule. Annie Besant always stressed the need for scrupulous attention to personal hygiene when congregating in a crowd, so that the risk of picking up adverse vibrations would be minimised. One small mark of the effect she had on them was that Eunice now became the only one to cut Vyvyan's hair, as he decided not to take on the magnetism of a hairdresser who tends so many different types of person.

Vyvyan had a long, private conversation with Leadbeater, after which the latter greeted Eunice so effusively she thought he must have mistaken her for someone else. She wondered whether his obvious joy was as a result of Vyvyan's talk with him or the excitement of being reunited with Annie Besant. Eunice and Vyvyan went to mass in the Liberal Catholic church the following Sunday and there was an unusually good attendance, even though Annie Besant's presence had not been announced. The seventy-five year old woman preached a sermon leaving no doubt in anyone's mind that she favoured Leadbeater as much as ever.

The close links between the Theosophical Society and the Liberal Catholic Church continued to be strong. Krishnamurti himself never liked the services: he was bored by the ritual 'with all those prayers and bobbing up and down, the robes etc'. But George Arundale, who became president of the society on Annie Besant's death in 1933, was enthusiastic and decided to become a bishop himself.

At Fuller's Theatre that night the doors were closed at 6.35 pm because the place was packed though the lecture was not due to begin until 7.15 pm. Annie Besant spoke for nearly two hours on 'Britain and India' with a power of oratory that Eunice never forgot.

On Wednesday 17 May 1922 Vyvyan and Eunice went to hear Annie Besant speak at the King's Hall to members only on 'The Troubles of the Theosophical Society and the Liberal Catholic Church'. The trouble in Eunice and Vyvyan's case was that as they had not paid their subscriptions (Vyvyan's name had been taken off the books while he was in New Zealand) the stewards at the door refused them entry, until Leadbeater personally came and ushered them in. On Sunday 28 May in the evening they went to hear their friend Mr Martyn speak on the same topic, again to a full hall.

The Theosophical Society in Sydney, Eunice noted, had divided itself between the original Lodge, now calling itself the Independent Lodge, with the philanthropic Martyn, who had built the I.O.O.F. building, re-elected as President, and the Blavatsky Lodge, to which those who favoured Leadbeater gravitated. One key point of contention was the relationship with the Liberal Catholic Church, which had prompted a kind of 'back to Blavatsky' movement, among those who felt that the original independent vision of the society had been obscured by this condominium with Christian ritual. A second cause of dissention, which was also centred on Leadbeater, were the continuing allegations of his sexual involvement with young men and boys. Martyn had condemned Leadbeater and urged his expulsion. When Mrs Besant proved stubbornly loyal to her old friend, Martyn sought to force her to resign as President of the Society. His hostility to Leadbeater dated from when the latter had been his guest. Leadbeater had warmly urged Martyn and his wife to sleep in separate beds but had then been seen by Mrs Martyn taking their son naked into his own bed. In 1922 there was a police investigation of Leadbeater's conduct, during which statements were taken from Krishnamurti and his brother Nityananda; in March of that year Wedgwood had resigned from the society. No action was taken against Leadbeater by the authorities, on the grounds that there was insufficient proof to bring charges, but he remained under suspicion and under surveillance. With so much adverse publicity, Vyvyan, now more confident in his own ability to conduct séances, began to distance himself from Leadbeater.

Vyvyan was learning how to conduct direct voice séances. They remained desperately poor: unless he was paid for a specific meeting, there was nothing to live on. He had begun using aluminium trumpets which were supposedly the passive recipients of sounds created on the psychic plane. The trumpets act almost as a symbol of an enduring aspect of Vyvyan's life, that of the hollow mouthpiece, the role he first played on Broadstairs sands. All his life Vyvyan kept the same two trumpets (named Hosanna and Harmony), a long collapsible one in three parts which could be fitted in a small bag and another in one piece which took up more room.

Horace Leaf, the Spiritualist sponsored by Sir Arthur Conan Doyle, arrived in Sydney. A fellow of the Royal Geographical Society, he practised as a clairvoyant, psychometrist and healer himself. Leaf travelled widely, interviewed many mediums and sought to root out frauds. He approached the materialisation medium, Charles Bailey, to whom Eunice had passed responsibility for Vyvyan's occult class, to report on a séance under test conditions. Bailey had the reputation for producing live fish and birds at his séances and on one occasion a live 18 inch shovel-nosed shark was said to have been brought in; his patron, Thomas Welton Stanford, created a museum of Bailey's apports. Bailey, however, refused to submit himself to a search. Disappointed, Leaf then turned to Vyvyan.

> Our sitting with Mr Vyvyan Deacon was much more satisfactory, although we expected much less than when we sat with Bailey. Mr Deacon has recently developed trumpet mediumship, although he was well-known throughout the Commonwealth and the Dominion as a capable speaker and clairvoyant. Twenty-eight people were present at the séance and three aluminium trumpets were used. Judging from the conversations between the voices in the trumpets and the various sitters, a good deal of evidential matter was coming through. The extraordinary thing about my experience was that a brother of mine living in the United States of America purported to communicate with me, giving his correct name and referring correctly to a very special fact about himself in a voice and manner strikingly characteristic of him. He stated that he was alive and suffering from a fever, that he had been brought to the séance by 'Ronald Beecham,' a deceased friend whom he had known in Los Angeles, California.

Mr Leaf goes on to say that this was possible as his brother lived for years in that city. He wrote to America, hoping for confirmation immediately after the séance and learned later that he was indeed alive at the time of the séance.

The number of sitters accepted for a direct voice sitting by Vyvyan in Sydney appears high: there are frequent recordings of twenty-three to twenty-eight people arriving to sit in a front living room. This is far more than usual and Spiritualists would regard such numbers as a dangerous strain on the medium. It may be taken that the need for such number is a reflection of Vyvyan's poverty and the need to make each séance pay as well as possible. No fee was specified but a brass bowl was put out for donations, usually this was to pay for refreshments; Vyvyan was known to return money put down as payment for sittings.

Like most direct voice mediums, that is those who are believed able to produce in a darkened room the voices of the dead friends and relations of those present, Vyvyan followed a certain pattern in his séances. An Irish voice, 'Larry', acted as a master of ceremonies, introducing other visitors. Irish voices, like Cockney voices and American Indians, Chinese, Eskimos and Hindus, all tend to frequent the séance with their accented or imperfect English.

On Saturday 2 September a reporter came because of a letter from one of the regular sitters saying that at the séance he might solve the so-called 'Ryde mystery', a newspaper cause célèbre of the time. After the séance the reporter admitted that his brief had been to mock and condemn but he was so convinced by the event that he could not. The following Tuesday a long detailed account appeared in the *Sun*, under the headings 'A Night with the Dead':

> Ghostly voices coming through tin trumpets; conversations between persons and supposedly departed relatives and friends; uncanny elevations of the trumpets in the air; rattling of articles of furniture and violent vibrations of the walls and ceiling; gentle pats from strange hands.
>
> These were some of the weird and, if the senses could be relied on, supernormal happenings in a North Sydney home...
>
> The occasion was a 'trumpet' séance which differs from the ordinary Spiritualistic séance in that it is claimed that the voice of the disembodied entity comes direct through the trumpet instead of through the body of a medium.

The well-known Spiritualist W.T. Stead, the late Baron Rothschild and the dead relatives of various sitters, spoke during the séance which lasted over two hours. The reporter was startled when from one of the trumpets, came a voice announcing the Christian name and surname of a departed colleague. He answered and the voice eagerly asked after a number of friends. A question was indeed asked about the noises heard in Ryde and as an answer to this Vyvyan went into a trance and a cultured voice spoke through him denying that the voices were paranormal but hinting that they were unable to tell everything.

When the voices grew weaker, the séance closed. The sitters sang the doxology, during which the walls and the floor shook as if violently agitated, the chairs rattled and the trumpets collapsed with a resounding clang to the floor. The lights were turned up; the reporter left.

As Vyvyan developed his psychic career, his weight increased and Eunice noticed that the habit of lounging in bed became more and more marked. He seemed to be in poorer health. Séances continued to be crowded but although Horace Leaf seemed impressed by his experience in a crowded meeting, results were sometimes not good because there were simply too many people. Vyvyan very rarely turned people away; one evening they had eight people waiting in one room for a second séance while eight others had to be turned away.

In a bright and happy mood despite a dishearteningly small audience, he lectured on the 'Key to Health, Wealth and Joy'; Eunice played the hymns. The next day he denied feeling unwell and in the evening twenty-one people turned up for a séance in their small front room. Eunice was busy ironing elsewhere when, after one and a half hours, someone came to tell her that Vyvyan had been in a trance for over an hour and that they had been unable to rouse him. She arranged for him to be carried to his bed and brought him round with vinegar bandages to his head and hot water bottle to his feet.

The next day although looking weak he held another séance which ten or eleven people attended; a collection was made and Vyvyan received a guinea.

Vyvyan had a sore throat over the next few days; when Eunice came back from the pictures she found one Mrs Donell massaging his throat and commented, 'Impudent and imprudent I thought it'.

Money was still short and Vyvyan borrowed where he could and pawned typewriter, desk, book-shelves and books, partly to send funds to Bella. Eunice, who did not believe in either borrowing or lending, hated the whole business. She found a letter Vyvyan had written to Bella and her jealousy sprang up all over again. Bella's baby was born on

Friday 9 June and was named Paul Vyvyan; Eunice entered it in her diary, mournfully but without comments. as 'P. born today'.

On 9 August Vyvyan did not celebrate his twenty-seventh birthday or have any presents because they were too poor. They lived in fear of their landlady. Eunice attempted to befriend Mrs Shaw as a defence policy. She tended to become angry when the rent was late. Eunice accompanied her singing on the piano and showed her how to crochet, all in the attempt either to distract her from the subject of rent or, by becoming 'friends', to make it more embarrassing for her to demand payment.

In his *The Comforter* Vyvyan wrote of about what he called 'the science of truth': his concern here is with the laws that govern life, attempting to show that the universe is coherent, that things make sense. It is as usual an optimistic philosophy and its Christian vocabulary and attitude of mind over matter makes it a text Eunice could have agreed with happily. Vyvyan was certainly closely involved with the O.T.O. by now (influenced by Crowley's writings, to which he had been introduced by Frank Bennett and Sister Veni, he had been living according to his understanding of the Law of Thelema) but when trying to express himself, when writing or lecturing, it was always to the language of the New Testament, with which he had been brought up, that he turned. Later in life, when he and Crowley had become friends, the self-proclaimed Baphomet would call him, half mockingly, half admiringly, the 'Christ-child'.

There is many a man today whose life and thought are of the most deeply religious character, who is anathematised by those who ought to know better, as infidel and heathen. These things ought not so to be, and will not under the light of the brotherhood of man...

This Science of Truth is not magnetism, will-power, faith- cure, spiritism, or any form of mesmerism under a new name. It is a formulation of the laws governing life; the understanding of the power of mind over matter; the proof of a sequential procedure from premise to conclusion, clenched and made secure by demonstration.

Learn the truth... that spirit has power to regulate, or free, because the motor power resides in spirit, and because spirit represents substantiality instead of the contrary, and you have at command the means for mastering all conditions of sense, falsely imposed under false law - the law of ignorance. It is man's birthright to be well, happy, harmonious. This condition of well-being he can gain and keep. A knowledge of Spiritual law is the talisman whereby the disorder, the discontent, the unhappiness of life, as generally lived under the old form, may become so vivified under the new thought as to show forth as healthfulness and glad certainty.

What religious or philosophical teaching - except that given by Christ - has ever shown us how to govern the material phases of life so as to bring them into subordination to the spiritual law of life, gaining thereby perfect results, with a thrill of conscious satisfaction never before known?

If the Science of Truth offers to a sad and suffering humanity the fruits of goodness, gladness, healthfulness... are not its teachings everywhere demanded? From what other source can a fuller more satisfying supply of practical benefit be derived?

Vyvyan held O.T.O meetings in the 'Abbey', the house which he had named after Crowley's Abbey at Cefalù. Rosa and Kathleen Walsh, two sisters who had joined Vyvyan's classes before he went on to New Zealand, called regularly as did Mrs Turner from New Zealand; and Susannah Harris from time to time wrote one of her incomparable letters:

Maney thanks for your letter mrs turner feels oful bad I got a latter from them she is very anguish to here from you I wish you would wright to her She is a good friend to you I am glade to here that Mr Decan is dowing well and that you all ar well I seen Dr Seton She is a fine person and sailed on the Niagra for USA tall Mr Decan to wright to I wish to corespond with both of you am plesed to here that your Sibil is well hope all will be well and (illegible) well I am here in New Plymouth hope you all are in your work and that the Church universil will be a Success I for my pard wish you the bast of Success give Mrs Champerland my bost wishes and my love to you all

Later that month Vyvyan and Eunice came into contact with the writings of Mary Baker Eddy, the nineteenth-century American founder of Christian Science. They both liked its practical tone and its optimistic conviction that spiritual health created physical health. Vyvyan had already embraced Rosicrucianism, Theosophy, herbalism, Spiritualism and the sexual magic of the O.T.O. as well as the Church Universal. Christian Science was another influence to absorb.

On Thursday 7 September Eunice and Vyvyan read a surprising article in the Sun referring to Ivycliffe and its residents past and present, an exaggerated account by their friend Meatheringham, although the article appeared anonymously. The headlines were: 'Our Commune; Chidley's disciples; birth, death and nuts, by one of them'. It was a very readable, imaginative romance of their past friends with whom they had shared their life there.

When Chidley died some of his followers decided to start a Commune. They would privately live the life of semi-nudity, fruit and nuts. The leader of the movement took a large old house with beautiful gardens near Berry's Bay, North Sydney.

Everybody was enthusiastic. In fact some were so enthusiastic that after the first week they forgot to pay their rent, so the Archdeacon threw them out.'

Inmates were described as 'writers, poets, philosophers and pagans, some were married and some were not.' The most famous, Diogenes, was described as 'a professor of something or other down on his luck; who had to be banned from the communal table for eating more than his fair share, and anyway he was a bad payer.' He peddled music from door to door to earn a living and accidentally called on a woman friend, who was shocked as she thought he was 'something big' up at the University.

The article went on to describe two Russian residents who were famous for their continual feuds, swearing death and violence on one another only to be discovered later embracing each other over borscht in an ecstasy of reconciliation.

A baby had been born in the commune and it was suggested that the members had soon put it onto the regulation diet of fruit and nuts, thus causing the baby's immediate death. There was a romance between a poet and a girl who came to one of the farewell parties for an inmate dressed as a Greek Goddess (this was May Schott). The poet (this could have been intended to mean Meatheringham or Vyvyan, for they both liked May and Vyvyan left Ivyccliffe on unfriendly terms with Meatheringham as a result) wrote poems to her and they were discovered together by the boat-house. The girl's parents were shocked and angry and hastily took her away. The article also recalled the death of John Brigden, making the macabre joke that the commune had heard the sound of his skull crack when he fell on some stone steps.

Vyvyan had a letter in answer to 'Our Commune' published in the *Sun*. Adopting the respectable, even pompous, tone that he occasionally found useful, he objected

> strongly to the unkind insinuation contained in the heading of Our Commune, which implied that Chidley did evil which still survives, while all his good deeds are dead. It is not accurate that when Chidley died some of his followers decided to start a Commune. No such thing ever happened. One of Chidley's followers took a house and others rented rooms there. It is incorrect that after the first week some forgot to pay the rent. The sentence 'Some were married and some were not,' contains an insinuation which I regret, as my wife and I were the only married folk there; the rest were single, except for one family who stayed there for a short while. Diogenes was a courteous gentleman with a B.A. degree. Another regrettable slur is cast by your correspondent when speaking of the advent of the baby. It is not correct that the baby died at the 'Commune' - it died of gastritis six months after leaving... Old John did not die at the Commune, but in hospital, and it is also quite incorrect that 'we sheltered all and refused none,' for the Archdeacon was then, and still is, very strict as to who is allowed to enter the Commune.

On Monday 6 November an excited Vyvyan rushed home with the news that he had been invited to stand as a candidate for the Majority Labor Party in South Sydney. Mr Catts, the party leader, knowing his financial position, assured him campaign funds would be provided. The man who would have been the candidate had fallen ill and Vyvyan had accepted the unexpected invitation with enthusiasm.

In the *Daily Telegraph* a week and a half later photographs of all the candidates appeared and there was Vyvyan, looking suitably dignified.

Vyvyan H.R. Deacon will be remembered as a champion of the late Mr Chidley, dress and sex reformer. Mr Deacon is a very bright young man, enthusiastic to fight hard 'in the cause of the people.' He is an advocate of the 44-hour week for workers and says he is afire with zeal to restore the people's movement to its former cleanliness of conduct. Realising the utter impossibility of cleaning up the Australian Labor Party from within he has thrown himself into the Majority Labor Party, and now he only wants the public to give careful attention to his party's constructive policy as (he says) he knows full well that the people's opinion can be safely trusted to decide rightly on December 16.

On Wednesday 22 November in the Sydney Morning Herald Vyvyan's picture appears in larger form, and readers anxious to be reassured about the candidate's racial purity had their worries laid to rest:

Mr Vyvyan H.R. Deacon, the Majority Australian Labour Party candidate for South Sydney is British born and of wholly British stock. He is a young man, and is an advocate of the 44-hour week for workers.

During the poorly organised, underfunded campaign, Vyvyan proved to lack real enthusiasm for the basic work of politics. Eunice

105

noted that he was not sufficiently interested really to involve himself; 'why must he always bring God into his politics?' Eunice wrote. He spoke at public meetings (his mother went along to hear him) but there was never really any doubt that he would not win. Amid all the novelty of the electioneering, I was born on Friday 1 December. It was only after several days that Vyvyan opened a miniature edition of Tennyson's *Idylls of the King* and chose from it the names Elaine Vivien.

For Vyvyan and Eunice, sexual incompatibility continued to be a problem. They slept in different rooms. He continued to find the lack of sexual expression in his marriage a constant encouragement to have affairs. Vyvyan, feeling justified by the teachings of the O.T.O., believed he had the right to sleep with other women, that this ought to be nothing improper. Eunice, on the other hand, still found the fact that he now drank alcohol sufficiently shocking. The young women who came to his lectures and classes to gaze adoringly at him were thus a constant invitation. In New Zealand, Bella had been one of these, and coming back to Sydney, he found that Kathleen and Rosa had remained friendly with Eunice through the years, largely because they always wanted to have news of him. To Eunice they seemed to be her own friends. It was some time before she realised that their invitations to go swimming were planned in order to watch for her refusals: they hoped by this means to work out the pattern of her menstrual cycle, watch for periods and choose them as the moment to flirt with Vyvyan, believing that this would be when he was most likely to be deprived of sex and therefore open to suggestions.

On Sunday 14 January 1923 Vyvyan gave a lecture entitled 'The Rosicrucians, their Rites and Mysteries', a title taken from a once famous book by Hargrave Jennings. The report on the lecture, headed 'The Rosicrucians - Does Mysterious Order Still Exist?', quoted liberally from Vyvyan's lecture.

> 'In the early days the Christians were graded to accord with their possession of Spiritual Gifts. Our Lord Jesus Christ Himself said to certain disciples, "Unto you it is given to know the Mysteries of the Kingdom of God, but to these others I speak in parables;" and later we find St Paul asserting that he "speaks wisdom among them that are Perfect," and that he gives "milk to babes" but reserves "Strong meat for men"...
>
> The existence of a special mode of training and a secret advanced teaching for those who were "ready", called "The Mysteries of Jesus"

is well enough known to advanced Christian Scholarship. By some it is claimed that these precious teachings, including the ability, like St Paul, to travel in one's Soul-body, are still in existence, and an historic tradition tells of an order which throughout the Christian era has preserved this esoteric Christianity.'

Vyvyan continued by describing the pamphlet *The Fame of the Fraternity of the Meritorious Order of the Rosy Cross*, whose publication in 1614 had initiated the Rosicrucian controversy, and then talked about the history of the rosary.

'Soon after the first Bishops of the Church were created (all holy men "knowing the Kingdom", and participants of the "Mysteries of Jesus"), the necessity arose to cope with a growing Christendom , by creating more bishops to look after the Church. Rosicrucian Bishops were alleged to have displayed in their churches the Cross with seven roses hanging thereon, representing to the uninitiated, a prayer to each of the Angels of the Seven Churches to pour out their vials for Our Lord's swift return. The newer members of the Church, not knowing there was another and inner meaning, began to add roses and prayers for their various endeavours and thus was created for usage in Christendom that spiritual aid known as the Rosary, that is according to the Rosicrucian legend.'

The lecture ended with the statement that whenever a Rosicrucian manifesto had been issued to the public, 'it has called upon all to turn to the Divine, and by fasting and prayer to seek Spiritual aid.'

In April 1923 Eunice received another letter from Susannah Harris:

deare ans I was to Wellington and attended the convanson - we had quite an excited time nerely all new oficers Champress Prasodand both from Hamilton Mr Wiliams Sectary from Auckland and Mr Rice trasure from Auckland See you see quite a change - why dont you answer my latter I seen so many of your old friends I seen Nura Mager She was saying she often thinks of you and of the birthday pardy and that Miss Adams gave you Such a nice perl nacklas and said she coultin got you anything purer for you than that they all spoke so well of you I remember you showed me the nacklas and Harmoney tried to pass it for you and you said you wore luckier sinse they all sand thare love to you and Harmoney sais Kiss litel Sivel for her and the baby.

I must stop it is mail time I wish to get it off on this steamer.

All this time Vyvyan continued to move in a vaguely bohemian circle, where friends inevitably painted or wrote. He himself published

107

an article at this time on the art of his friend Norman Lindsay. It is a characteristic piece, full of the attempt to voice large abstractions and coloured by eschatological notions.

Let us discuss the art of Norman Lindsay, and his place in the modern world, without us sheltering behind Coleridge as an excuse. Let us away with all excuses; they are for cowards, not for warriors. In Norman Lindsay's pictures 'there is only one idea,' says Mr Henderson. It certainly would be an interesting piece of self-revelation, to hear in plain English just what one idea is, from Mr Henderson's point of view... that there is but one idea emphasised in Norman Lindsay, is very good insight into his human nature, and shows his genius in philosophy as well as art. For all philosophy and art are in the last analysis but a seeking for the underlying unity. Man has ever felt that somewhere there is the key to the universe, knowing which, all else is known. And maybe Lindsay has found the key.

This turning from dreamy Utopia to the establishment of true beauty on earth, this understanding of the meaning of the body and being true to the earth, will cause a better and healthier-minded race to be born, will usher in the next great civilisation which will grow out of this dying civilisation. This is Norman Lindsay's message, and what he means to numberless Australians. He is the soul of the new humanity, which is otherwise hidden in Australia's womb.

Tis the spirit of Australia that speaks so distinctly in Norman Lindsay's work, just as it spoke through Henry Lawson or Bernard Ingleby. Let me close with Ingleby's 'Chant of the New Men'.

Bernard Ingleby being another of the circle that Vyvyan belonged to, Vyvyan's dropping his friend's name is a piece of cheerfully bold oneupmanship, since few of his readers would have heard of Ingleby but they must all have been left thinking they ought to have done.

At the end of February 1924, the Melbourne Spiritualist Society wrote to Vyvyan and contracted him to work there as a lecturer and medium. He quickly packed and set off, leaving Eunice to follow a fortnight later: it was the old pattern.

Chapter Six

He had not only put him into the condition known as deep
trance and extended his insensible body by neck and feet
across the backs of two chairs, but had actually sat down on
the rigid form as on a bench, without making it yield. The
sight of this unholy figure in a frock-coat squatted on the
stiff body was horrible and incredible.

Thomas Mann, Mario and the Magician

ONCE AGAIN, Vyvyan found himself standing on a station
platform waiting for his wife. It was Saturday 15 March
1924 and he had hired a cab and brought a colleague from
the Spiritualist church, Dr Dunn, to help with the luggage.
As the train steamed in promptly at 2.30, Eunice felt filled with hope.
Melbourne was another new beginning and she felt that this time they
would be able to make a life together without the crises and dissensions
of the past repeating themselves. The two men loaded up the cab and
they went to Casa d'Espana, 73 Rathdown Street, Carlton.

Eunice was introduced to Vyvyan's new circle. There were regular
at-homes where Dr Dunn used to sing and Vyvyan recited. It was not
long before she was encouraged to sing and chose 'My Task', a piece
she had often performed. To her surprise, one of the women afterwards remarked in her hearing 'Yes, her voice is quite good for
someone who obviously hasn't had any training.' This was Dulcie
Cherry, whose voice had some professional training and who had
already begun to be attracted to Vyvyan.

One problem was that at some of these gatherings there would be
alcohol and Eunice remained steadfast in her opposition to strong
drink. She always declared herself too tired to go out with Vyvyan to
socialise whenever there was the risk of alcohol. Temperance had been
part of her upbringing and she could not abandon it.

There were always people calling for tea. Someone would need putting up for the night. A playreading would develop and Vyvyan would pass round copies of *Lady Windermere's Fan*, or the banned Paris edition of *Salomé*, for the 'Rise and Fall of Oscar Wilde' was one of his standard lecture topics. Sybil and I usually recited rhymes of our own making or poems from the Coles' anthologies.

As well as his talk on Oscar Wilde, which Miss Cherry (Eunice noted) attended, Vyvyan lectured on the Egyptian Mysteries and Greek Mysteries and the God of Spiritualism.

On 29 March Vyvyan brought home a friend from Sydney, whom Eunice had never met. Ian Dickson, a cartoonist whose work had appeared in the *Daily Graphic*, became a frequent visitor and left a thick sketching book as a gift. He drew one profile of Vyvyan in charcoal, with a dark background, gazing down profoundly into a crystal ball; Eunice had it framed.

In recognition of the visit of Mr and Mrs Vyvyan Deacon, the Melbourne Progressive Spiritualistic Lyceum organised a social evening on Thursday 3 April 1924, with an orchestra and dancing. Eunice bought an evening dress and spent all day getting ready. Vyvyan held a healing meeting that afternoon and then in the evening they found themselves at something which was perhaps the happiest moment of their lives together. They were cheered. They were popular. They were praised. It was a glimpse of what might be, of what could be achieved. Eunice wrote in her diary that Vyvyan could do so much 'if only he would be true to the people', by which she partly meant his not drinking alcohol and his not missing appointments.

At first things were promising. In May they began buying a house for the first time. The deposit on the bungalow was £200 and they paid the balance in the form of a weekly rent of £2.5s.0d. The money was forwarded by Mrs Benson, a Sydney medium who was devoted to Vyvyan. This was 'the Abbey, Collegium ad Spiritum Sanctum' at 99 Hoddle Street, West Richmond.

I remember the sound of my first pair of white shoes (bought by Mrs Benson) as I ran on the bare slatted floor of the new house. I remember being caught up in the arms of an enormous woman and smelling sweat from her armpits as she hugged me. I remember being taken away in a steam train and kneeling to look out of a window, putting my fingers on the window-sill and the window slamming down on one hand; I remember someone putting the whole of my small hand in her mouth. Someone sang to me

Lula, lula, lula, lula bye-ay
You want the moon to play with
the stars to run away with
they'll come if you don't cry
Lula, lula, lula, lula bye.

I was wrapped in a big warm brown rug, lifted up with strong hands and carried. I had whooping cough.

On the last day of the month things were sufficiently sorted out for them to have a house-warming there. It should all have gone well but afterwards Eunice simply wrote in her diary, in characteristic reticence 'D.C. Episode'. Dulcie Cherry had made an undisguised attempt to seduce Vyvyan. It didn't work though and after May 1924 there was no more contact with her.

Eunice nevertheless left her husband and they lived apart again, communicating by letter. In one Vyvyan mentions his discovery of Nietzsche's letters. 'I enjoyed reading my book of Nietzsche's letters, which I find contains some absolutely wonderful and most gloriously beautiful passages, revealing the growth of Nietzsche's mind until it fully reveals its grandeur in maturity.'

During Eunice's absence, Gustav Pillig painted Vyvyan's portrait in oils, signed, and dated 1924. Significantly, Vyvyan's Pan ring is clearly to be seen on his *right* hand ring finger. This ring was a mystery. Set into its solid Italian gold was an emblem featuring the full figure of the God Pan formed from minute mosaic fragments, tan-coloured against a jet black background. Only a magnifying glass could reveal the God's green eye. It was Vyvyan's most crucial symbol of attachment to the Pan cult, which had first flowered during his friendship with Norman Lindsay before the 1914-18 war. It echoed the 'Pan' thread running through his mother's links with the Browning circle, and with Machen and Blackwood, Golden Dawn associates whose numinous tales featured irruptions of Pan.

A journalist came to one of the meetings at the Abbey and was found trying to hide a sword from the ceremony under his coat to take away. Perhaps annoyed at being caught, he wrote an article attacking Vyvyan's work as a medium. In reply, Vyvyan wrote a letter to the editor:

My attention has been called to the account of a so-called exposure of Direct Voice Mediumship which has just been published in *Smith's Weekly*.

I must crave your space, and briefly state what actually occurred.

During the process of the séance in question, a young man, who had previously attended a séance, and who was present on this night accompanied by another young man, suddenly in the middle of a Direct Voice Communication, turned an electric torch full on into the Circle. I remember seeing the light flash, thereafter all was oblivion to me until I returned to consciousness some time later to find myself being resuscitated by some of the Sitters who informed me what had occurred. They told me that immediately the light flashed out they saw the trumpet fall to the ground. The two young men responsible for the incident said something about Spiritualism being all a fraud and immediately left. When I had sufficiently regained consciousness to realise what had occurred, I asked that the light be extinguished. I was in great pain. Immediately the light was out, Larry's voice was heard speaking from the various points of the Circle testifying to the reality of the Phenomena, and asking if everyone was satisfied in the genuineness thereof.

I might mention that two gentlemen present whose names and addresses are in my possession, and who will, I am sure, testify to the truth of this statement, held *both my hands* while Larry's and other Spirit Voices were speaking. However, I felt very faint and ill, and realised the necessity of immediately retiring to bed, first deputing one of the Sitters to obtain the names and addresses of everyone present.

The next morning, Tuesday, I was in great pain and actually passed a little blood, which rather frightened me. During the morning the dark young man responsible for this most unfortunate accident had the audacity to call upon me. When my wife informed me who it was, I naturally thought he had come to apologise, and said I would see him for a few minutes. When he entered the room I was naturally at a very high tension, and asked him what he meant by doing such a dastardly thing, and was he not heartily ashamed of himself? He protested his ignorance of the possibility of any dangerous results from this procedure, and stated that he had come to see me because, although sceptical, his last night's experience had made him feel there must be something in Spiritualism that he did not understand. His apparent earnestness, I candidly admit, deceived me. I never dreamt or suspected for a moment that he was not sincere or had any ulterior evil motive.

Had I suspected his sincerity I certainly would not have granted him an interview. But my zeal, ill and weak though I was, to share with him the glorious Truth of Spiritual Knowledge, led me inno-cently to tell him of my various experiences, little dreaming that he was a newspaper man sufficiently engulfed in depravity as to be capable of writing such a garbled and untruthfully distorted account of my conversation with him.

The editor added a note to the letter testifying to Vyvyan's genuineness.

Despite his enjoying some moderate success, Vyvyan became down-cast. 'No one knows,' he wrote to Eunice, 'how lonely I am.' But he assured her 'we are on the verge of good things.' Convinced of his own supremely important and unique role, he was frustrated at the lack of recognition and in one letter to his wife listed those among his heroes whom he felt would have best understood his situation. It is a list that would have seemed less surprising then.

> There are so few who know me, hardly any who realise just what I am. Wilde and Nietzsche and Frank Harris would be able to sympathise and understand – but here there is no-one. We must make a supreme effort to leave Australia – how ashamed Australia will be when at last she learns that I lived and toiled here, not unknown, God knows that would be reprehensible enough – but known, and ridiculed, laughed and jeered at – just because they lack the necessary ability to know.

Naturally attracted to performance, Vyvyan began touring, not as an actor but as a conjurer's assistant. Eunice was disappointed that he was earning his living in so undignified a way but Vyvyan was happy responding to the crowd. He wrote admiringly of Dr Mac's tricks.

> His Hypnotic Show is the thing that takes – that and his conjuring. I can do *all* his tricks *better* than he can now, and the Hypnotic turn I could improve in many ways. His mind reading – the most wonderful thing he does – I cannot do – but although it is so very wonderful – it does not catch the general public like conjuring and Hypnotism.

Dr Mac would put him easily in a trance and then plunge a red hot needle through his cheek. He would lay Vyvyan down with his neck on one bar and his ankles resting on another and then show that he could himself stand on Vyvyan's rigid, unsupported frame like on some human pontoon bridge. Between acts he could make the audience laugh and would improvise. In Dr Mac Vyvyan seems to have found yet another of his admired older men. Despite considering that he could do many of the conjurer's tricks better himself, he never attempted to start his own show.

It upset Eunice to know he was working as a magician's stooge and hypnotist's puppet, to have the magician stand on her husband's rigid body. But although Vyvyan was lonely on the road with Dr Mac and the show did not bring in a great deal of money, he was very happy in that kind of life. By November 1924 they were back together at the Abbey but still in debt. After the freedom of being away from the Spiritualist platform he found it tedious beyond words to return to the Abbey and become involved once more in the old, familiar programme of healing. He found the people he was surrounded by dull and grumbled at the lack of intellectual and literary and artistic company.

Vyvyan was becoming more seriously interested in Crowley and kept in close touch with Frank Bennett. That month Bennett's wife and children left for Britain and he himself came to stay a few days at the Abbey. On his return to Sydney he sent them a newspaper cutting from *Smith's Weekly*. Headed 'Sydney's Temple of Love: will it be built at Roseville? First High Priest in our midst!', the report interviewed the supposed high priest.

> Bennett looked a man of about 50. In his boarding-house front room he affected a corduroy smoking jacket and a strong pipe... He said, 'Ours is a higher branch of Freemasonry. That order has only 33 degrees. We go much further than that. For instance, I am a 96 degree man... All of us when we are sufficiently advanced can be our own priests... I have been with Crowley since I was 27 and I'm no chicken now. I first met him in 1905 and spent some time with him in Sicily, France and Germany. I am not a Christian. I have no time for Christians.'

The strong pipe was probably full of 'perique', a blend soaked in rum which Crowley favoured; later Vyvyan too started smoking it.

Bennett's theme was men becoming gods. He said in the interview that a couple of years previously a police sergeant had come to see him, thinking Bennett was a fraud. Having met him, the man became entirely convinced and was now a priest himself with his own temple. In a reflection which perhaps stemmed from his visit to Crowley at Cefalù, Bennett declared that 'Once a student has realised what he can do by cultivating the subconscious self, new sensations are forever open to him.'

When the reporter asked if he would take him as a student, Bennett asked him if he had ever studied Theosophy. The reporter admitted he had not and Bennett said 'Then I'm afraid you would not make a good student.'

Meantime the clergy are compared most unfavourably with business men. While members of the Stock Exchange and bookmakers are elevated to a higher hierarchy still... the neophyte is seriously enjoined to 'experiment with' strong drink and other temptations, ostensibly to 'discover the extent of his power to resist them.' He can then say to the pure all things are pure.

Commenting that Bennett was employed on the Blue Fish outfall, the reporter observed that his was 'certainly a fine religion for anyone working on a sewer.'

In a leaflet he published that year on mental healing, Vyvyan took as his theme the familiar one of the ability of the mind to control the body, quoting Darwin on the traces left on the human face by emotions and the character traits displayed in gait. A letter that reached him at this time shows the effect he could himself have on clients' lives:

I attended two of the trumpet séances one of which will *ever live in my memory* in as much as it put me in touch with my *Father*. I often think of it as a sacred occasion... I have gone through a severe struggle as far as this life is concerned. But the revelation of another and a better life seems to have put new heart into me and I am determined now to look forward to better days both *Spiritually* and materially and strange to say that with this determination there is come the almost *Positive Assurance*, that what I want I shall get.

It is because I got such help from the Trumpet séance, coming as it did just as that moment, that I was anxious to enquire if you were still holding the séance.

I am a stranger to you but wish you God's Blessing and hope I shall live to see the day when 'A Gift' such as you are blessed with will ultimately be valued by poor humanity at large.

Vyvyan was invited to speak on the wireless in October 1925 and his picture, again looking suitably solemn, appeared in *The Listener In*, which carried an article as a trailer for the programme. He remembered some advice Lewis Waller gave to a young and rather inexperienced actress:

'Do you know my dear, even today, after all these years of constant acting, I am always nervous when I first walk on.' He then went on to explain that the person who was absolutely insensitive never made the best performer, and that the more highly-strung and sensitive person, if they felt a nervous strain, and yet mastered it sufficiently to conceal it, yet conveyed a subtle something to the audience, a tentative magnetism that compelled attention and sympathy...

So many people who are toiling day by day to earn their daily bread are quite unable to spare the energy and time necessary to read at all widely of modern literature... the modern Russians Chekhov, Dostoyevsky, Gorki and Tolstoy... Balzac or Strindberg, Housman and Ibsen... But to sit back and listen, while some lover of good literature reads the words of some of our word wizards, and to hear the living words repeated with life, feeling and understanding; ah! that is something the weary toiler may enjoy to his lasting benefit... this is work that requires and deserves the utmost help the Government of a country can afford, and so let us hope that in the future whatever party is in power, will extend a helping hand to aid the education of the people by means of extended wireless operations.

We left the Abbey in September 1926 and, after staying with friends called McKenzie, Eunice brought us to stay at an isolated shack at Tallangatta, where Vyvyan was already lodging. Mrs Moran lived there with her two sons; their motorbikes would set the birds shrieking. The slatted wooden house was raised on stilts to be away from snakes. When snakes were found, they were killed and their dead bodies gingerly hung over the fence until after sunset as we thought the venom would remain alive in the bodies until then. As a child I was fascinated by snakes and iguanas (also believed by us to be venomous) and used to go searching for them. While we were there Sibyl had toothache; she was taken the long journey by horse and cart to the dentist who removed the wrong tooth.

Whenever money was particularly short or Eunice was angry with Vyvyan for his obvious interest in another woman, she would go to work as housekeeper for the Mackenzies at Geelong. For Christmas Eunice took us to the sheep ranch at Geelong, where we could run with the sheep through fields with yellow billy-buttons growing thick as clover near the billabongs. Then in January they found a shop in the road where Eunice's mother ran a sweetshop. It was dirty but in good repair.

Eunice painted the shop white with some paint from her mother and as always, she had long oak planks delivered, sawed them up and lined the rooms with bookshelves. Vyvyan went to a warehouse and bought 17s 9d worth of stock for the shop. He began to hold séances again and Mrs Tulloch always arrived early, smelling of face-powder, and would sit tatting as she waited for everything to be ready.

116

Vyvyan and Eunice were still sleeping apart. Her bed, mine and Sybil's were all crowded into the same small room, together with orange-boxes, stacked up, filled with clothes and draped with a heavy mauve curtain to form a wardrobe. One night the curtain caught in the candle flame and the orange-boxes were suddenly in flames. I opened the door and tried fanning the flames, thinking this would blow them out. Vyvyan and Eunice were not in the house; it was the neighbours, who were keeping an eye on the place, who called the fire brigade.

The years passed like a dream with little to mark them. One Sunday in March 1927 we went to hear the visiting Bishop of London, Winnington Ingram, preach to a packed St Paul's Cathedral, Melbourne. We were all impressed by the amplifiers that were in position to help relay the sermon. That Easter the Duke and Duchess of York, later King George VI and Queen Elizabeth came to the city and Eunice joined the crowds to see them. She was trying to get a license to use the shop as a café. While she was cheering the royal couple, an inspector from city hall visited and refused her a license on the basis that there were already other tea-rooms in the area and the building was too old. With all her money spent on stock, she could not afford to accept such a decision and went to the City Hall to get permission to sell food over the counter.

Vyvyan, performing in Port Melbourne in May, sent Eunice a copy of Crowley's 'Hymn to Pan' and was surprised at her not acknowledging receipt of it. Left alone by Vyvyan yet again, Eunice found herself becoming involved with another man. This was Jim Morrison. She tore two weeks from her diary in a characteristic effort to rid herself of the attraction and once again she decided to make a new beginning. On Wednesday 13 July a medium called Mrs Plum told them about a vacant house in Prahan. It was small, clean and quiet. They took it.

Chapter Seven

All these people came to Gatsby's house in the summer.
F. Scott Fitzgerald, *The Great Gatsby*

THE TALL SLATTED GATE opened into a fenced garden, filled with Madonna lilies, geraniums and fuschias. Two steps led up to a wooden verandah; inside 'Thelema', the first door on the right was marked Private and it was here that Vyvyan held consultations. One day I told Alan Trethowan, our neighbours' son, to be quiet because Jesus was in the front room: I had recognised him from the picture hanging in Vyvyan's consulting room. The visitor was a young poet, the only person they knew with long hair and a beard in a world of clean-shaven, close-cropped men.

One room ran the full width of the house and was large enough for couples to dance. It had musical instruments hung round its walls: a xylophone, ukuleles, two violins and a Hawaiian guitar. A window overlooked the side verandah where a tarantula built a web. Vyvyan's room was next to the kitchen. At one end of the room there was a small dispensary with the blue-glass bottles, the pestle and mortar, the avoirdupois scales with round brass weights, and huge jars of herbs and pellets. The most memorable of the pellets were gold and the size of golf-balls. I was waiting for someone to be prescribed this so that I could see one swallowed.

The mirror over my mother's dressing table, made of planks laid across orange boxes, reflected the red dots of lighted joss-sticks, like fire-flies in the black of night. From the end of Sybil's bed I could look out of the side window at the praying mantis swaying on the fence. Beyond the fence lived Mrs Wray who never smiled; her baby had died and we were told not to ask about it.

It was a house of meditation and prayer, of philosophic discussions, Gilbert and Sullivan and music hall songs. To this house, with its peach tree in the back yard, came the odd people that Vyvyan used to collect from cafés, séances and the audiences of his lectures, so that there was always someone new to show us telepathy or magic, experiments in sending vibrations, cracking glasses and hearing harmonics from an unheld violin after concentration.

Born near Essen, Gustaf Pillig studied sculpture in Düsseldorf and migrated to Sydney in 1913. He settled in Melbourne after being commissioned to decorate the Regent Theatre. He had occasional moods of black despair: one sudden departure from Sydney had given rise to rumours of suicide. He came to listen to Vyvyan's lectures, having first heard him speak in the bohemian cafés; he painted his portrait in 1924.

Marietta, a professional studio portrait photographer, was his exact opposite. Born in Sweden, a member of the Malgren family who emigrated to Melbourne at the end of the last century, Marietta married Eunice's violin teacher Stanley Gibson, who followed Vyvyan to New Zealand and used magical cyphers in his letters. Her studio was in Austral Buildings, 117 Collins Street, Melbourne and her husband gave lessons and sometimes arranged concerts there.

I saw John H. Booth on two occasions. His voice was deep and booming. Booth, who had acted with Henry Irving, coached me in reciting 'When Polly puts her apron on' which he wrote out for me, urging me to emphasise the plosives and round my vowels.

James Bunn had known Sister Veni in the early Sydney days. He worked as a ship's steward and published his own poetry. The address given on one of his 1919 *Song of Liberty* pamphlets was the New Thought boarding house Non-Pareil, in Merriwa Street, Katoomba. Tall and thin, his knees gave the appearance of being about to pierce his dark pin-striped trouser-leg. He published *The Mystic Mantle: or The Demon Spider and the Angel Fly* in 1913. He often used to visit Thelema and recite comic verse.

Godfrey Ashwin wrote poetry and like all the others appeared to have no day-time work. He used to take me to the Botanical Gardens, always wearing the same old overcoat and carrying a leather suitcase in which he kept apples and candied honey in grease-proof paper. He ate the apple alternately with chunks of candied honey, and occasionally proffered me a piece impaled on the end of a stained pen-knife. He took me to feed the black swans and wrote poems to all the members of the family.

Bomberg was still following Vyvyan, coming from nowhere and going nowhere, doing nothing but strange things and always alone. He used to walk round and round our sitting room, obsessively repeating the same nonsense rhymes.

Jim Morrison and his wife Lena lived at St Kilda, a tram-ride or long walk from home. Jim was rather keen on Eunice and they used to quote Crowley's *Hymn to Pan* to one another; she was always careful to remain good friends with his wife. We had Christmas dinner with them in the Australian summer heat on St Kilda beach. Eunice brought her ukulele, which was small enough for her to carry with her, and sat on the sands playing. One day the shark bell went while we were in the water: the life-savers rescued an eighteen-year-old girl from the jaws of the shark but not before one of her legs had been ripped off. The next day we were in the queue to see the dead shark at a penny a time; the funds raised were to go towards the cost of providing the victim with an artificial limb.

The entrance to Luna Park was a clown's mouth. Often we would wander round just looking but sometimes Vyvyan would have some money and treat us to the ghost train, or we might be paid for by Mrs Tulloch, who looked like Queen Mary and lived in Majestic Mansions with her white pomeranian, Petty.

I liked Mr Morrison at first. Sometimes taking us round Luna Park he would bring a handful of change out of his pocket and pay for us to ride on the big dipper. But when his nine-year-old daughter Patsy told me that in winter he used to hold her under a cold shower every day because it was character-building, I went off him.

Towards the end of 1926, Vyvyan made plans to open up a commune at Tallangatta, based on Chidlean principles and run on the lines of Crowley's Abbey at Cefalù. He asked the Crookes family to join. Mr Crookes was a tall respectable-looking Englishman but his wife was French. The four children all spoke both languages but I could never understand the youngest because he mixed English and French words together in sentences. At their house at Cockatoo, Victoria we ran about the bush naked, watching kookaburras catching snakes. We were never sent to bed: we just fell asleep where we were.

Bernhard Ingleby ran the Ingleby Advertising Company; often drunk he used to recite his own verses in a gutsy, husky voice. Jack Somers was an artist whom Eunice banned from time to time because he habitually became shot with cocaine. Another artist called MacInnes gave us some of his pictures.

Anthony McSwenny was a smart schoolboy in short grey trousers and oily straight hair. He would never go to bed without kissing his mother's feet. He gave me a silver three-penny-bit.

Jack Allingham ran a cafe in Smith Street, Fitzroy; he knew our friend Les Buddle. He knew Vyvyan in the early Sydney days and developed a gift for spiritual healing. Jean Livingstone walked with callipers and was always surrounded by young men. Ethel Newman was an actress who looked like Evelyn Laye, a slightly wilting English rose. She was always hungry when she arrived, although she pretended she had just eaten.

Hazelhurst College, Chapel Street, near Leggatt's ballroom dancing school, was run by two spinster sisters, Miss Annie and Miss May Wright. In the single hall, three trestle tables to the left were supervised by Miss Annie who took the young children. The three trestle-tables to the right, where the older pupils sat, were supervised by Miss May. Vyvyan's friend Mr Weber taught Eurhythmics there and the school had a name for elocution. For the school concert the first form did movements with large wooden hoops garlanded with flowers and ribbons. When we had finished I realised there was an audience and went to the front of the stage peering through my hoop to see if I recognised any of the people there until someone came on the stage to lead me off.

The sisters used the cane. When I stuck my foot out into the aisle while trying to write the loops in my copy-book, Miss Annie gave me smart rap with her cane. When Max Quinn who was five arrived at school with three new pens in his blazer pocket Miss Annie asked him where he got them. He said his father had given them to him but she accused him of lying and he was ordered to stand in front of her, sideways to the front of the class so we could all see her administer several strokes of the thin yellow cane to his outstretched hand.

I used to go up to the grocer's shop in Commercial Road where the lady called me Queenie and sold me a huge paper bag of broken assorted biscuits for a half-penny. We played hopscotch in the street drawing the squares with chalk on the pavement of Athol Street and using a fine wooden 'Taw'.

There were few Chinese in Australia since immigration was restricted but there was one old Chinese vendor who used to call. Sometimes we bought jars of ginger from him. If we had no money we would give him a cup of china tea. Because we liked him, Eunice wanted to take a picture of him with her Brownie box camera but he picked up his wares and fled.

One day I opened the door to two small girls carrying a box of home-made candy for sale. Their English accent suggested they had not been in Australia for long. Times were hard and families looked for every possible means of earning a little money. Eunice could not send them away without buying anything from them, so we scoured the house for our last pennies and half pennies and bought some candy for our night's supper.

Even though they had very little money, Vyvyan still found the means to go to the theatre. He saw Moscovitch in *Trilby*, in which a girl falls under the spell of the hypnotist Svengali who is able to release the beautiful voice that had been hidden in her. Vyvyan was fascinated by George du Maurier's tale, he may have perceived analogies with some of his elocutionary procedures. Mrs Hawkins, an Anthroposophist, bought Eunice a season ticket to attend Alice Crowther's lecture recitals at the Queen's Hall at the beginning of August and odd tickets for concerts.

For Vyvyan's thirty-second birthday Eunice bought him an hexagonal brass tobacco-jar. It was lined with lead and in it Vyvyan could keep his Perique. He also received a new single bed, some anonymous food parcels and seven shillings.

On Tuesday 15 November 1927 Eunice's grandmother died. She had been to see *For the Term of his Natural Life* and collapsed on leaving the picture house. After the funeral the family sat in the kitchen talking about Grandma's life. I wanted to know how she would see me now her eyes were buried.

When Eunice went to work at Geelong, Sybil and I stayed with Grandma Lois at 13 Mountain Street for a short time, where more than twenty cats lived in the back yard. Grandma thought Providence kept the number at that but Eunice's younger brother Timothy was responsible for quietly killing any surplus. Only a three-legged tortoiseshell was allowed into the house, where it had a favourite chair. When Uncle Tim came he brought his Hawaiian guitar.

In January the second conference of the Australian New Thought Alliance was held but the influence of Sister Veni was already waning in Australia and after the second conference the centre of activities was America where on 20 January 1924 James Pateman had already become ordained by Dr Albert C. Grier of the Church of Truth in

Cincinnati, a New Thought pioneer and the author of *The Spirit of Truth*. Dr Julia Seton, who was the godmother of the Pateman's third daughter Julia, had founded New Civilization City in Florida. Vyvyan kept in touch with Grace Aguilar who continued to practise New Thought and in 1928 was centred in the Manly School of Arts. Another link from former years was the Revd Lily Lingwood-Smith who had a successful spell in Britain until the end of 1924 when she returned to Australia to run the Order of Light Christian Spiritualist Church in Adelaide and Melbourne until 1930.

Vyvyan held Spiritualist meetings and services in Queen's Hall, Collins Street. Sybil and I put out the hymn-sheets, printed on large square white cardboard, and collected them afterwards. On 12 July 1928 he gave a well-publicised lecture on 'The Phenomena of Materialisation' in Collins Street. The theme of the lecture was that the impossible of today is the possible of tomorrow and Vyvyan was able to show slides of the scientific investigations of the eminent Munich physician Baron von Schrenck-Notzing. In October 1928, at the urging of Krishnamurti who had lost patience with Theosophist hierarchies and all talk of degrees of advancement and stages along the spiritual path, Annie Besant dissolved the Esoteric Section of the Theosophical Society. Despite this the esoteric meetings Vyvyan held on Tuesday evenings continued. (Annie Besant was in fact to reopen the section less than a year later.)

In October 1928 Vyvyan found himself in the papers twice. The first time was relatively trivial. He had been one of the organisers of a pyjama party, in the Willow Dance Hall, with dimmed lights, burning incense and Chinese lanterns. There was a jazz band and a general atmosphere of modest naughtinesss. *Smith's Weekly* ran a piece on this 'Night Out with the Pyjama Club', mentioning the presence of a 'thought apostle, large and resplendent in a dinner suit, surmounted by a flowing opera cape who... gathered a little group around him and they discussed German philosophy and where you can buy unexpurgated editions of the classics.'

The same day, Saturday 13 October 1928, in a paper called *Truth* another article appeared headlined: 'Vyvyan Deacon is a Fraud'. The headings referred to him as a 'humbug churchman who is subject to two spiritual influences, ethereal and bottled' and referred darkly to the contribution made by Mrs Benson towards the cost of the 'Abbey'.

For years charlatans, quacks and crooks who have made other States of the Commonwealth too hot to hold them, have scourged Melbourne with their presence... Vyvyan Deacon is one of these parasites. He describes himself as a Spiritualist, though he has been a herbalist, a layer on of hands and many other things. On Sunday afternoons he occupies the stool at one of the Spiritualist Churches in Prahran, where devout, sincere folk go searching for light... *Truth* first met the pastor three years ago, when he cut a sorry drunken figure at the Artists Ball. This paper renewed its acquaintance with him a week or so ago when he presided over a meeting of Spiritualists in a café in Swanson Street... Deacon was asked to leave the Theosophical Society of Sydney during Bishop Leadbeater's regime, about nine years ago, when he was accused of having attempted to induce an infirm old woman to part with £500 or 600.

Besides liking the ladies, queer costumes and beer, 'Pastor' Deacon has an eye to business on the side.

Until this article appeared, Vyvyan was enjoying a degree of success again: he was selling his herbal remedies, appearing on the Spiritualist platform and leading séances. But how could anyone book him now, as a trance and direct voice medium or to demonstrate psychometry and clairvoyance, with this kind of publicity dogging him?

James Chidley
Courtesy of the
Mitchell Library.

Dr Julia Seton, in 1912.

The Worthington family in Christchurch New Zealand.
Vyvyan is seated centre.

Left to right Arthur
Cushion (medium)
James Pateman
and Frank Bennett.
Sydney, Feb 1913.

Chapter Eight

The first thing we do, let's kill all the lawyers.
Shakespeare, *Henry VI* part two.

VYVYAN took legal advice and brought a case of libel: the
newspaper's reply was that a man with no reputation was
not entitled to damages. There was six months to wait
before the case could come to court and in the meantime
Vyvyan had to find the means of earning a living. He was in debt and
now the debts were growing. At the beginning of 1929 Mrs Little, an
old friend, found him work at Mildura, the fruit plantation where
shoes were lined with mulberry leaves, constantly renewed, to stop the
soles of the feet from burning.

Vyvyan's letter to Eunice gives some idea of his life at the time.

Beloved - Although I am dead beat I feel I must answer your last lovely
and so welcome letter. I was like you unable to say anything much over
the phone, although the sound of your voice was sweet music to my
ears. I have been very worried and out of work for 3 days through all
the sacks being full. I am now working on piece work ten shillings per
100 buckets and by going like mad I have only been able to do 80 per
day – so I am very sad and almost broken hearted. The work is awful
in the broiling merciless sun.

All day 110 in shade yesterday 108 today. I stink of sweat all day and
cannot eat in spite of hard work. My stomach turns at the horrid
workman's lunches (bread and jam etc.) and I vomit it all up again.

Mrs Tulloch annoys me asking if I give any readings or hold any
séances, – just imagine it!!!!! even if there were not 40 brutes in the
house – I work from 7.30 to 5.30 and have 6 miles journey to and from
work. Sometimes my heart pains horribly and I only wish it would burst
and be done with it. My only consolation is to imagine Uncle Tom on
the cotton fields or poor Wilde in jail! How I can sympathise I dare not
think. Mildura is 70 miles from another town so there is not much hope

of walking out of it. O the appalling worry of my horrid debts – they worry me in the few hours sleep I get. The men play poker next to my bed until 1 am – every morning I have to rise at 6 to get to work.

Then Mrs Tulloch (who is no longer *human*) has the confounded impudence to say she does not understand my letter.

I am a cad to worry you like this dear – but I have no-one else who even remotely understands. I must be more cheerful for your sake. I have no idea what is due to me tomorrow – but I must pay thirty shillings to Mrs Little whatever is over I will send you dear.

I sent Miss Lake a reading of a sort – it will have to do. I will attend to all other matters on Saturday and Sunday.

Throughout April and May bills were delivered and creditors called. When Vyvyan returned, my teacher Miss Annie visited to find out why the school fees were overdue; he took her to one side for a private chat. She had arrived looking belligerent; she departed with an expression of spiritual ecstasy, but without the fees.

On 4 June 1929 the young barrister Henry Minogue, who had been briefed by Vyvyan's solicitors, left two sheets of deep mauve paper sketching out the six issues on which plaintiff should be prepared to offer evidence. The reference to flower mediums is the result of a flower medium Mrs P. being then under suspicion of fraud: Minogue was anxious to distinguish Vyvyan from her.

The issues in this case are somewhat involved on account of the defendant's taking refuge in the 'rolled-up' plea – without specifying what are facts and what are comments the defendant's answer to the plaintiff's claim is that the comments are fair comment on a matter of public interest.

At the same time the matters chosen for interrogating the plaintiff are substantially the only matters in issue and the plaintiff must be ready with a rebutting case on all the issues.

1. Ethereal and bottled. The only instance in which it is alleged that the plaintiff was drunk are at the Artist's Ball and at the Pyjama Dance. Witnesses should be subpoenaed who were present at the Artist's Ball and can testify to Mr Deacon's sobriety. There is a photo in existence which I am informed would support him there. As to the Dance at Shaw's some persons should be called including Aitkin, Mrs Deacon and the reporter from *Smith's Weekly*. These can testify to Deacon's general conduct and to his sobriety. It might be advisable to call some witness or witnesses who have been in almost daily touch with Deacon

to prove that he is at most a mild drinker and can be described as of sober habits.

2. As to the question of Deacon being a fraud and a fake – Mr Johnson – a solicitor of Yarrow should if possible be called to give evidence of his own experience of Deacon. Mr Robert Sproull – a solicitor of Sydney could also give the evidence. I regard this evidence as being extremely valuable to plaintiff's case because without this Deacon is left to put his case having only his ipse dixit as to what he has accomplished. I think Deacon would undoubtedly win his case hands down if these two men could be brought to give evidence for him.

3. Witnesses might be in readiness also to testify re Spiritualists that have been so close to Deacon and have even had their hands on his throat and that Deacon should bring along with him any articles written by Sir Marshall Hall K.C. and Randall on Spiritualism and a list of prominent persons who have given an adherence to Spiritualist beliefs.

4. Mrs Deacon and plaintiff can testify that although he has at halls taken the chair or lectured where a woman has given flower readings he has never employed her or been otherwise than a spectator at such readings.

5. A full account of Mr Deacon's leaving Sydney, parting with his wife as on a definite and permanent break over his relations with Mrs Field should be prepared showing that it was not while at the Church that he became intimate with the latter but while he was lecturing at the Town Hall. He must insist that he has never been called Reverend or Pastor.

Emphatic denial must be given to the story of his saying women throw themselves at me. It isn't true because the only girl he had anything to do with was B. Mrs Field now.

Re financial matter Mr Deacon's denial is sufficient as to his alleged borrowings.

6. Some office bearer with the Theosophical Society in about 1919 (during Leadbeater régime) to prove that there was no scandal about £500 or £600 and that Deacon was not asked to leave.

7. As to Deacon having to leave Sydney it would be wise to have a witness like Mr Aitken of the said office Sydney who could come to Melbourne *if necessary* to rebut any proof that Deacon was forced to leave Sydney over entanglements with women in his class.

Mrs Field was Bella Sly, who had in 1925 married Cyril Field, an old friend of Vyvyan's. Vyvyan was hoping that there would be as little mention of her as possible. Given the kind of publicity that Wedgwood and particularly Leadbeater had enjoyed in the past, it was also important that their names be kept out of his trial. Even his host in New Zealand was dangerous company, for he had been in prison, probably for a sexual offence involving young women. During questioning Vyvyan declared that he knew nothing of the prison sentence and that Mr Worthington had not been present during his time in New Zealand. In fact, a photograph survives of Vyvyan and the Worthington family, including Mr Worthington, in a formal family portrait.

In the street where we lived, houses were built of siatted wood and because of the danger of fire, the laundry, with its huge boiling-copper, was in an outhouse in the yard. Eunice never threw anything away: cardboard boxes full of odds and ends were stacked up in the outhouse. Just at the time when the trial was starting a fire broke out there, a noisy blaze that I watched from the kitchen window. The fire brigade came: the crowd that gathered to stare grew so large that they burst through the back fence and did not retreat until the firemen turned the hoses on them. All the papers and documents that had been stored in the outhouse were lost in the fire.

The trial finally began on Monday 22 July 1929 and played to packed houses throughout the week, being fully reported in the daily press. Vyvyan, now in his early thirties, cut a striking figure in court: over six foot tall, dark-haired, pale-skinned and with eyes whose colour varied slightly, the left eye pale green and the right eye hazel, a trait that the ancient Egyptians particularly valued in the eyes of their sacred cats. He had prepared for the trial by fasting and by shaving his head. His theatrical voice in the Australian court was hypnotic. Eunice had a quiet voice and a shy manner. Each day she came to court in the cloche hat and short skirt that were then the fashion. There was no role she would have rather played than the loyal, devoted and true wife to Vyvyan; it was a key part in the drama.

The beginning of the defence case was reported in the *Herald*:

Charles William Bender appeared in the First Civil Court. He described a long interview he had with Deacon in September 1924 – the day after he had attended a séance on behalf of *Smith's Weekly* the previous evening.

Deacon suggested we should go for a walk into the country. He said,

'You are an earnest seeker after the truth.' Then I pulled out two affidavits and said, 'My friends and I have sworn two affidavits, alleging that you are getting money under false pretences.'

Deacon staggered back and said, 'Think of my wife and children. I have to keep them. Look at my hands. I couldn't go to work on the wharves.'

'Why!' he said, 'You don't know how I loathe it all. They really drove me to it' (meaning the members of his circle). 'They are as much to blame as I. I was really driven to resort to trickery.' He said he had as a boy of ten preached on the sands at Carstairs(sic), England. Out here, he joined the Congregational Church of St. James, Fitzroy. But there is no money in that, so he left it.

I said to Deacon, you had better give up this trickery or I will report you to the police. He said he would, adding, 'It is not worth the risk, I only get half the collection.'

As the defence was keen to put Vyvyan in as bad a light as possible, it was emphasised that he had visited Chinese restaurants; it was also suggested he had made a Chinese love potion for a girl, perhaps Eunice, possibly May Schott; he had organised the pyjama party; he was accused of improperly spending time with young girls in the congregation with which he had been associated and had practised hypnosis upon them. It was all reminiscent of the scandal in the Spiritualist church in New Zealand. As part of the prosecution case, Vyvyan made a statement to the court.

I first started publically as a medium in Melbourne. Before that I had experience in England as a boy. I gained a knowledge of herbs while I was working at Coles' Book Arcade. I was always interested in the study as my father was a physician and had studied the subject himself. When I was 17 I started as a herbalist.

I was married in January 1916 in the Congregational church, Victoria Parade. There are two children. My wife's father was Anglican Chinese minister at Bendigo. It is not a fact that I said I was taking her from her cruel parents. I went to Sydney in 1917. There I opened a small herbalist shop in Junction Street, North Sydney. At most I charged five shillings a week for treatment. Meanwhile I lectured at Spiritualist churches. I also acted as medium at séances at my own shop and went out to private homes. I made no charge for these séances. I was practising trance mediumship. I was then engaged to go to the Christchurch branch of the Spiritualist Church from which it was intended I should visit other branches. My wife did not accompany me to New Zealand. We were not on friendly terms. Just before this I had begun to smoke and drink and eat meat. Previously I had been a strict vegetarian and my wife was annoyed at the change. I continued to send her and my child Sybil £5 a fortnight. I was then getting between £5 and £6 week.

Never at any time have I bragged about my relations with women, or that they ran after me.

I have been to Chinese restaurants. Many people used to go to them. I have even seen members of the Bar there.

I have always said openly that I am not a teetotaller, and that I do not profess to be a saint. I am not bad, though.

At the Pyjama Party he had seen nothing improper. It had been a tame enough affair, the guests wearing pyjamas over ordinary clothes. Vyvyan also explained he could psychometrise, reading the soul of things: he could read the souls of flowers, he explained.

Mr Menzies, who would later become prime minister of Australia, questioned Vyvyan about the use of aluminium trumpets in séances and wanted to know how a man became a medium. 'It is a matter of establishing harmonious conditions. A man should sit frequently by himself,' Vyvyan told him. Mr Minogue asked about the role of particular spirits:

Did an Irishman named Larry speak at the séance Bender (a previous witness) attended?

Deacon: The voice of an Irishman named Larry is heard at almost every séance. He seems to be in charge of the exchange over there.

Mr Menzies: Does he answer 'Central' or 'Windsor' when you call him up?

Deacon: No. He sometimes laughs.

Mr Menzies then demanded to know whether Vyvyan believed in the ethical teaching of the New Testament: Vyvyan declared that he did. And yet he had been engaged in improper relations with a woman while acting as a public spokesman for Christ's teachings? Vyvyan disarmed this line of questioning by declaring 'I have always been ashamed of that.'

The Thursday papers carried news of Eunice's evidence. She denied ever seeing Vyvyan drunk: never more than merry, she insisted. She also denied – an important point – that he was a minister. She had been decently dressed at the pyjama party and her husband had behaved quite properly. She told the court how she had found a letter proving

Vyvyan had been unfaithful to her: she forgave him because she believed it partly her own fault.

Vincent Pantin described séances in Sydney conducted by Deacon:

> At one the voice of a man named Arthur Douglas Miller spoke to me. I did not remember him until he reminded me of a book I had lent him in London. Then I remembered him. He was killed in the Boer war. I have also conversed at these séances in German with spirits. German, I know, is beyond Deacon.
>
> At another, Mr Walter Gate, manager of the New South Wales State Savings Bank was present. The voice of a Dr McCarthy conversed with him.
>
> Once I held a test séance, holding Deacon's hands and knees. We were the only two present. A trumpet moved about the room and a voice spoke to us.

Kenneth James McLean, a journalist, said, 'At a séance I attended the voltage was something awful. Even chairs rocked as we sat on them.'

Ben Percival Johnson, a lawyer from Yarraville, was called to give evidence. He said he was interested in Spiritualism. He had attended one direct voice séance and five or six trance medium séances conducted by Vyvyan in Prahran.

> 'At the direct voice séance,' he said, 'I heard a voice purporting to come from my son say, "Dad, do you doubt any more?" I had doubted for a long time. During the séance I was touched on the head and knee.
>
> Mr Menzies: What were you 'touched for' before you went in?
>
> Johnson: Nothing at first, but I left fees of five shillings for each of my family who had attended.
>
> 'I have not made many enquiries into the direct voice séances,' he said, 'but by the other method I feel perfectly certain that the dead can communicate with us.'

Mr Johnson was the last witness called, and Mr Brennan, for the defendants, began summing up for the defence. His case was that Vyvyan had no character to defend, that the article in *Truth* was based on facts and contained fair comment, and that the case brought by Vyvyan was simply a ruse to gain the £5,000 damages.

Mr Justice Cussen, in his summing up, said that the defendant newspaper could not succeed unless it proved that all of the serious allegations made were true. A defendant in such circumstances might say, 'I truly state the facts, and my comments upon those facts are fair comment.'

The jury might conclude that it would not have made the comment so strong but if the comment was such as a reasonable man might make, that was sufficient for defendant's purpose. There could be no fair comment upon statements which were untrue. One of the statements made was that 'TRUTH first met Deacon at the Artists' Ball, where he cut a sorry drunken figure.' That was a statement of fact. Was there any evidence to support it? He could recall no such evidence. There was a suggestion in the article that as late as 1928, Deacon was of such a type that no investigator should bring a wife or sister to his séances. There was no evidence of any investigation of the kind having taken place. There was also a statement that Deacon left Sydney because of his entanglements with the women members of his flock. There was not a word of evidence that he had any entanglements in Sydney of any kind. Mr Justice Cussen's guidance to the jury was finally unmistakable:

> There is a considerable body of evidence about affairs with women in New Zealand, when plaintiff was a young man and separated from his wife. It is for you to say whether it is fair to suggest that years afterwards, when he was reconciled to his wife, there were still entanglements. There is some evidence to show that as far as witnesses could speak of him, his conduct towards women at that time was quite correct.
>
> Deacon has said that he never considered himself a minister, and that the word was used only to emphasise his so-called shortcomings. Counsel for the defendant company has asked you to assess damages, if you assess them at all, in farthings, and counsel for the plaintiff has asked that the verdict be in thousands of pounds. You need not take any notice of either of them in that respect. You will assess the damages entirely as you think fit.

The jury retired at 2.33 pm. For nearly two hours, during the hearing of another case, the court remained crowded with Spiritualists, friends and curious spectators. Vyvyan sat in the body of the court. At 4.20 pm the jury knocked. Immediately there was a stir. People hurried from all parts of the law courts to the First Civil Court.

Before the jury entered, Justice Sir Leo Cussen said: 'If there is any demonstration in the court, I shall take steps, to deal with those responsible. I hope I shall not need to do so.' Then he ordered a policeman to stand in the witness box from where he could survey the court. (Two days before, the spectators had clapped and stamped when a Spiritualist witness made a striking declaration in defence of Christian principles.)

132

The Warden's room, Greyfriars, Canterbury, where Vyvyan held seances in April 1933.

Eunice, in 1922.

Vyvyan, the last studio portrait taken in 1936.

The jury awarded Vyvyan £3,500 damages with costs. So ended what the newspapers called 'one of the most unusual cases tried in the civil courts'. Every day the gallery had been crowded. Rarely had a case caused so much laughter in court.

Outside Vyvyan was surrounded by an excited crowd of friends. Many colleagues hastened to congratulate Minogue, who had so successfully fought Vyvyan's case. Arm in arm with his wife, Vyvyan (hatless, as the newspapers noted was his custom) walked away smiling.

On Saturday 27 July the telegrams started to arrive. Some were full of congratulation, others envied the windfall. There was a letter of congratulation from Stanley Gibson, Eunice's violin teacher who married the photographer Marietta:

> Do what thou wilt shall be the whole of the Law.
>
> I must congratulate you on the way in which you passed through the trying ordeal of the past ten days. As a Nietzschean you withstood the tests in a magnificent manner, especially as the whole attack was made from the standpoint of Christian Morality, a Morality which has 2000 years authority and 90% of the heredity instinct of the Present day at the back of it. I suppose *Truth* will now do their utmost to secure a reduction of the damages awarded.
>
> Whether they succeed or not it does not affect the main issue. You have been absolutely vindicated: the matter of a paltry few hundred pounds is only secondary.
>
> Love is the Law. Love under Will.

Before long some Brownings presented themselves to Eunice, claiming kinship and, implicitly, money. As *Truth*, in its account of the trial proceedings, had further libelled Vyvyan, he again sought the protection of the law.

A week after the verdict, *Smith's Weekly* published an article on the outcome of the trial, observing:

> It was probable that an imputation (to prove which no attempt was made) concerning the alleged use by Deacon of a Chinese love potion containing unprintable ingredients, helped materially to load the damages. Deacon's cheerful and non-aggressive demeanour in the box, his kindly remarks to a witness for the defence, that although the latter had gone out of his way to injure him, he felt sorry for him when he saw his shocking physical condition, and also the exhibition of Mrs Deacon's loyalty to her supposed erring spouse must have contributed largely to the result.

The paper also noted that several of the jury were well on in years, suggesting that older men might be more inclined to believe in a contactable life after death than younger men for whom it was a less pressing issue.

When the award had been made, a stay of 14 days had been allowed, conditional upon *Truth* paying Vyvyan £750 within 14 days. Vyvyan made plans to visit Tasmania where New Thought and Spiritualism had been active for years. Then the State Full Court, headed by Chief Justice Sir William Irvine, ordered a retrial. Even the £750 interim payment was to be returned. Vyvyan decided to go ahead with his journey to Tasmania. It was a rough journey and Vyvyan was proud of the fact that he suffered no seasickness. On the way he made friends with a Brahmin from Kashmir. He found on his arrival at Launceston that a room in a cheap boarding house had been arranged for him. This was too like what he had so recently left at Mildura and he hastily arranged to move. He booked Mechanics' Hall for a lecture on 'Clairvoyance and Mental Healing', and the Kings Hall for the following Sunday night.

When he came home for Christmas, he was able to describe not only his lectures and séances but also being knocked down by a motorcycle. He had been asked to stay on but Eunice had again not joined him and this time he refused the invitation. All this time the discussions continued in and out of court. Vyvyan made no attempt to follow them.

A friend of Vyvyan's, the fair-haired and athletic Percy Reginald Stephensen, sent him a copy of Aleister Crowley's lecture on Gilles de Rais, which he had printed. This was the lecture famous for never having been delivered: the Oxford University Poetry Society had invited him to speak but the University authorities had banned the event. Vyvyan was interested to see that Crowley had quoted from Browning's 'Parleyings' in the preface. '*The Legend of Aleister Crowley* by P.R. Stephensen' was advertised on the back of the pamphlet as forthcoming: a copy of this too reached Vyvyan. Stephensen, the sub-editor of the *New Outlook*, appears in Huxley's *Point Counter Point* as 'Cuthbert Arkwright'.

It was June 1930 before an out of court settlement was agreed. Vyvyan's mother came from Sydney to look after the children while he and Eunice went to Tasmania.

When news came that Sir Arthur Conan Doyle had died on 7 July 1930, Vyvyan was in Hobart and was asked to give a talk on the radio about the dead man's life and work. Vyvyan was said at the time to be the first medium to give a broadcast on the wireless.

While in Tasmania, Vyvyan and Eunice went to a photographer. To their delight the picture marked the presence of Vyvyan's spirit guide. He wrote excitedly:

> On Monday last Eunice and I went to Robinson's the leading photographer here and we had our photos taken and last night to our amazement and great joy we found Dr Cheong's face imposed on one of my pictures. I was so glad and excited that I hardly slept all night.

The fact that the court case had brought in some money made Vyvyan feel that now at last he could escape Australia and go to London. In preparation Sybil and I were taken to Myers the department store. Eunice had always made all our clothes by hand: this was our first experience of clothes from a shop. The arrangements were made by Les Buddle, who had taken over Vyvyan's finances. There was enough for our fares, so long as Sybil was passed as a half-fare, which she was when the tickets were bought, though no longer by the time we sailed. On the *SS Jervis Bay* we had a small four-berth cabin and I was put in a top bunk with Vyvyan beneath me.

Chapter Nine

Dire dealings with the fiendish race
Had mark'd strange lines upon his face;
Vigil and fast had worn him grim
His eyesight dazzled seemed and dim...
                    Sir Walter Scott, *Marmion*

THE JOURNEY TO Britain took five and a half weeks. The cabin was cramped. Soon the whole family felt too ill to get up. We were all brought mugs of beef tea and thick water biscuits known as 'dog biscuits'. When we were up and about again, Sybil, now twelve, was not pleased to find herself eating at tea-time with the children. At first a compromise was to serve her the adult meal at the children's table: she ate the macaroni while the other children were given bread and jam. The second evening she sat at the adult table.

Vyvyan was soon busy organising entertainments. He held services, gave talks, performed monologues, conjuring or stage hypnotism as if at a music hall. At a fancy dress party Eunice stitched playing cards to her evening dress and hung empty gin bottles and cigarette packets on a string round her neck under the title, taken from a play in which Vyvyan's old friend Roy Redgrave had acted in 1913, 'The Road to Ruin'. Vyvyan, meanwhile, appeared in a nightdress made out of sheets, a pillow case folded to look like a bonnet and a borrowed dummy and bottle. It was as if, in their choice of costume, each of them was exorcising a personal ghost. If Eunice was acting out her shadow, her fear of everything to do with alcohol, tobacco and excess, Vyvyan, with his horror of being a mother's boy and yet his tendency to like being babied and looked after in practical matters by Eunice, was doing no less.

On deck there were games of quoits, tennis and a small square canvas swimming-pool in which to cool down when the sun became too hot. Stewards would bring round citrus fruit drinks and trays of green oranges. Two weeks passed before we saw land. Passing ships were always a great excitement; there were strange birds, flying fish and porpoises.

At Colombo bum-boats sailed up with traders and entertainers, all keen to make money. A magician turned coins into live newly-hatched chicks. I bought shell necklaces, small white elephants and buddhas and a pair of small china-faced dolls. When we went ashore Vyvyan left us eating and went to meet an occult contact, perhaps the guru he had first met when he had visited India before travelling to Australia. (He had photographs of both Ram Krishna Paramahansa and Vivekananda.) He was late back and we missed the ship. Greatly excited, we rushed along behind Vyvyan as he found a motor-boat and hired it. We set off after the departing ship, which was still easily in view, and when they spotted us they lowered ladders so that we could climb aboard. It seemed a great adventure but if we had been left in Ceylon, we would have been destitute.

At Port Said Vyvyan once again had contacts to make; we were left eating coloured sorbets flavoured with fruit and almond and watching boys diving for pennies.

In the Bay of Biscay we ran into a storm and the ship started to roll. Clamps were fitted to the furniture and we were tossed from one side to the other like marbles rattled in a tin. The decks were out of bounds: one man went outside and was swept overboard.

On a foggy 1 November 1930 we docked at Southampton and caught the boat train to London. A taxi took us to 336 Brixton Road, where a large man welcomed us. This was Uncle Neil, we were told. He turned out to be a man who always carried Fry's chocolate cream bars with him so I took to him very readily. Sybil and I were put in the ground-floor back room, where there was a settee on which we slept.

A couple of days after arrival we had a huge bonfire for our first Guy Fawkes party. Burning the Guy, was too reminiscent of St Joan and Jacques de Molay, the Templar martyr mentioned in the O.T.O. Gnostic Mass. These I knew from Shaw and from Browning's 'The Heretic's Tragedy', so I could not feel quite at ease, but then Vyvyan began to tell tales in the glow of the firelight.

We discovered the Brixton Road and all the surrounding picture houses, theatres, libraries, shops, arcades, markets; there was a 3d and 6d Woolworth's store and a railway arch. There was shopping on the dark afternoons, with Christmas lights and decorations. The Pavilion and Palladium had films, at the Empress a pantomime was coming and the Brixton Astoria was showing a double-bill and stage-show. A tram ride up the hill took us to Brockwell Park and there were also buses and trams to the Crystal Palace. Then suddenly we moved and did not see Uncle Neil again.

By December we were installed in 12 Kellett Road, almost opposite the huge white Lambeth Town Hall. The rooms were lit by gas-mantles, some of which had a pilot light requiring only a pull on small balanced chains to ignite and extinguish, others required lighting with a match. The mantles were frail, and sometimes crumbled. At Lambeth Library I went through first all Andrew Lang's coloured Fairy Tale Books and then Rider Haggard.

With an address for correspondence, Vyvyan was able to contact all his occult friends such as James Wedgwood, now living in Camberley, Surrey and suffering from syphilis, which he had contracted in the course of his homosexual activities. The disease had been diagnosed in Sydney when he went to a doctor complaining of a throat infection but he had rejected the diagnosis. Periods of insanity and lucidity alternated in his final years and he received treatment from the German analyst Georg Groddeck. His followers continued to take a close and respectful interest in his visions of angels and other worlds. Through Wedgwood Vyvyan heard about Bishop James of the Sanctuary, where we were later to become regular attenders.

He had links to develop with the Spiritualists – the Psychic Press, the Stead Bureau run by W.T. Stead's daughter Estelle, and the various Spiritualist churches. John Lewis, the editor of *Psychic News*, prepared an article about Vyvyan. The sub-editor, Gerald de Beaurepaire, had started life as a stage-hand at the Aldwych (he was a great admirer of the farceur Ben Travers) and had also worked with film scripts. Both Gerald and his mother Madame de Beaurepaire became trance mediums and had engagements on the Spiritualist platform. Gerald de Beaurepaire visited us from the beginning and remained Vyvyan's strongest admirer.

An article also appeared in the *Two Worlds* on 5 December 1930. It took the form of a letter from Tasmania regarding Vyvyan Deacon but did not advertise the medium's arrival in England:

> We have no organised church here, but we have established a few family circles. We have had several visits from Mr Vyvyan Deacon, a very remarkable medium from Melbourne. In December last we held a direct voice séance with him in my own home in Launceston, and the

voices were persistent for nearly four hours. Each sitter was spoken to by one of more of their own loved ones. Mr W.T. Stead came and spoke with great force, and his message was encouraging. One of our sitters, Mr Fred Parsons, had a very long conversation with his spirit father. He advised his son to go to Melbourne and open out in a new business, which would be a great success. He was followed by my own grandfather, who came and talked with me for quite a while, and was then interrupted by another voice which came and asked my grandfather if he would allow him to speak to his son Fred again on a matter of great importance. My grandfather immediately gave consent, when Mr Parsons' father told him not to go to Melbourne until March, as he had seen that it was in his mind to go at once. He then thanked my grandfather for permitting him to resume the conversation, and we continued our talking. It was a very remarkable thing to hear quite audibly the spirit people talking to one another. Mr Deacon visited us again in July of this year. The sitting was held in the house of Mr J. Hughes, of Launceston, in the presence of the Mayor (Mr R. Osborne). We had not been sitting five minutes when the voices commenced. Mr Deacon's chief control for the direct voice, 'Larry', told us they were going to do something out of the ordinary. Mr Deacon was then entranced by a spirit claiming to be Mr W.T. Stead, who asked Mr Hughes to sit opposite him and to hold both the medium's hands. While we sang a hymn a materialised hand came and touched Mr Hughes on the forehead twice, after which Mr Hughes' deceased father spoke to him through the trumpet in a strong, clear voice. In response to his request, we sang his favourite hymn, and his voice was heard above ours singing through the trumpet. Mr Osborne had a long conversation with his deceased wife, who spoke in a beautiful strong and vibrant voice. Mr Stead gave a very powerful discourse through Mr Deacon, and after that the voices still came.

It was very interesting to hear Mr Deacon's guide, 'Dr Cheong', who, while using Mr Deacon (in trance) continuously talked to 'Larry' (the Irishman) who was answering through the trumpet. They conversed with each other for several minutes while the sitters sat listening. We had very wonderful proof of life beyond death.

In the course of the proceedings Mr Deacon was asked to sit for some photographs by one of Launceston's leading photographic artists, in order to obtain studies for the studio. When one of the plates was developed and printed a face of a Chinese appeared very clearly beside Mr Deacon, and this was recognised as 'Dr Cheong', one of Mr Deacon's controls. It has caused quite a sensation in Launceston, as the photograph was taken in the ordinary course of business, and it has proved to many people that life after death is a fact. At Mr Deacon's request I forward you one of the photographs, which I am sure will interest you.

Vyvyan had a word with the woman in the box office at Brixton Theatre, saying that he was an actor temporarily 'resting' and would appreciate complimentary tickets. Eunice made soup from scraps. She used to buy pigeons at threepence each in the market and cook them gently with bacon rind. When Christmas came, we went out late on Christmas Eve and stayed until about 9 pm so that we could buy our turkey cheaply from among the ones left unsold. Like Chatterton, we seemed to live on air.

Uncle Neil died on Christmas Eve 1930, in Lambeth Hospital. Years later I found a photograph of Vyvyan's father and to my surprise recognised him as Uncle Neil. The death certificate confirmed that 'Uncle Neil' was indeed Cornelius William Deacon. Eunice, who at the time wrote to Vyvyan's mother, giving her the news of the death, told me that the meeting of father and son after so many years was very dramatic and had left the older man badly shaken. It could even have been this event which brought on his fatal heart attack.

An article headed 'The Medium who Thrashed a Newspaper' appeared in the *International Psychic Gazette* in January 1931, hailing the result of the Melbourne trial as a triumph; once again Vyvyan cited the fact of his being related to Robert Browning. The article ended with Deacon's intentions of staying in England for some time, lecturing in London and the provinces.

I feel I have still much work to do for Spiritualism to which I have dedicated my life, and I shall follow the guidance of my guides and inspirers wherever I go.

That Vyvyan was beginning to be noticed is indicated by an advertisement for a lecture he was giving to the Jewish Society for Psychic Research on 'Judaism and Supernormal Phenomena' on Sunday 18 January at Armitage Hall, 224 Great Portland Street. The society also announced that a 'series of Group Sittings with Mr Deacon is being arranged by Mr Victor, Caxton Hall, London.'

The February issue of the *International Psychic Gazette* featured an article by Vyvyan on 'A Séance with the Reflectograph'. W.T. Stead had predicted through a séance that through experiment communication at

THE INTERNATIONAL
PSYCHIC GAZETTE

No. 208. Vol. 19.   JANUARY, 1931.   PRICE SIXPENCE NET

The Medium Who Thrashed a Newspaper !
A RELATIVE OF ROBERT BROWNING.
THE STORY OF HIS LIFE, AS TOLD TO THE EDITOR.

ONE afternoon, early in December, a bluff and hearty gentleman, with a classical cast of features, called at the *I.P.G.* office, and introduced himself as Mr. Deacon of Australia. He mentioned at the outset that he was the medium who had been villainously slandered by an Australian newspaper called *Truth*, and who had been awarded £3,500 damages by the judge and jury who tried the case.

We recalled this *cause célèbre* at once, for we briefly reported it at the time in this *Gazette*, and it well deserves to rank as a landmark in the history of Spiritualism, for it marked the first occasion on which a wealthy newspaper was taught a sharp lesson that mediums, any more than other respectable citizens, cannot be injured with impunity. The days when the yellow press could enliven dull times by having "another go at the mediums," and by holding them up to contempt as frauds, tricksters, vultures, and what not, are passing, if they have not already passed. The Bill for their relief from police persecution has already passed its first reading in the House of Commons, and when that has fully become law they will no longer be cruelly harassed as vagrants and outcasts, as they had never any right to be. In fighting this iniquity in the law courts, no medium has ever achieved so great a triumph as Mr. Vivian H. R. Deacon.

A very interesting point worth mentioning is that Mr. Kelly, M.P., who introduced the Spiritualists' Relief Bill in the House of Commons, the Judge who tried Mr. Deacon's case in Australia, and the Junior Counsel who successfully fought for him, are all Roman Catholics. That fact should be noted and underlined with gratitude. It is difficult to understand why Protestant legislators and lawyers should have been so lax in clearing away the last remnants of religious disability oppressing a Protestant nation.

We had not talked to Mr. Deacon many minutes when he said, "Give me a piece of paper, I have to write." And thereupon he wrote automatically an acrostic, the nine lines of which began with the letters J-O-H-N-L-E-W-I-S. We asked him to add the author's name, and at once he added the initials, "E.W.W.", which we recognised as those of our old friend, Mr. E. W. Wallis, the late editor of *Light*, who used to write such acrostics, and whose son still writes them, claiming "it is a trick of the family !"

Next Mr. Deacon relapsed into trance, and after describing his inspirer, uttered a beautiful encouraging message from someone who claimed to have Sir Arthur Conan Doyle beside him, which message concluded with the words "William Crookes." The message was quite

characteristic of the great scientist, who was a valiant pioneer of Spiritualism, and who had personally given us his last public testimony that he believed in it to the end. The description given of him by the medium also fitted him perfectly.

We arranged to visit Mr. Deacon at his flat in Brixton one evening to get his story in detail, and the following is what he told us :—

EARLY DAYS AND FAMILY HISTORY.

I was born at Newbury, near Reading, England, in August, 1895, but the first fifteen years of my life were spent mostly at Broadstairs, in Kent. My father was a doctor, who died when I was very young, and after his death we went to Australia. My mother had married a farmer, and we lived in the bush until I went to Melbourne to begin my business career at Cole's Book Arcade.

My mother was a woman of some culture. Her maiden name was Elizabeth Browning. Her father was Reuben Browning, who was confidential clerk to Baron Rothschild for many years. Reuben Browning's brother was Robert Browning, the father of the eminent poet, so that my mother and the poet who wrote "Sludge the Medium" were cousins. I remember my mother telling me that she was once taken by her Aunt Sarah Ann to see the poet, somewhere in London. Robert Browning's father had married much earlier in life than my mother's father, so Robert was a man almost in middle age when she was still a little girl. She remembers his patting her on the head and speaking kindly to her.

VIVIAN H. R. DEACON.
Photo by Vaudry Robinson, Tasmania.

ROBERT BROWNING SAYS HE IS SORRY.

Since I became a Spiritualist a spirit, who purported to be Robert Browning, has several times spoken to me at the seances of various mediums. At one seance in Sydney some guide said through the entranced medium, "There is a man here with a beard ; he gives the name of Robert, and he says he is a relative of someone in the circle." I did not answer, for I never thought of Robert Browning coming to me. The guide said he was for the gentleman sitting opposite the medium. As I was in that place, I said, "Is it for me ? " and the guide answered, " Yes, he is Robert Browning." Now that name had not been uttered or even thought of till that moment. Then a much deeper voice spoke through the medium, in a hesitant manner, and apparently with some effort, saying, "I am so sorry ; I am so sorry." I said, "Are you Robert Browning ? " and he replied, " Yes, I am so sorry." I said, "What are you sorry about ?" He said, "About that poem." Now at that time I had not read the poem about "Sludge the Medium," and did not know to what he referred. Then the voice seemed to struggle to say something further, but died away.

"SLUDGE THE MEDIUM !"

"Many years afterwards, when I was at a seance in

séances would become easier. As an alternative to the usual aluminium trumpet a shastophone was designed by a Mr Ayling according to directions received from his spirit guide, an Egyptian named Shasta, after whom the instrument was named, and this had been used at the home of Mrs Hilton-Benson, the medium friend of Eunice and Vyvyan, in Sydney some five years previously. Vyvyan encountered the reflectograph, which was invented by George Jobson and B.K. Kirkby, in the company of John Lewis when a séance was held under the mediumship of Mrs L.E. Singleton in a room arranged like a chapel, which held a cabinet (usual in those days for materialisation mediums) and a reflectograph. Over the mantelpiece was a large metal frame, divided into glass squares, which, when illuminated, showed the alphabet in clear red letters; there were also Yes and No squares. The keys of the machine were so sensitive that a person blowing on a particular key would be sufficient to light up the corresponding letter over the mantelpiece. The keys were placed in front of the cabinet in which the medium was seated.

Becoming better known in Britain, Vyvyan took part in the 83rd Anniversary Celebration of Modern Spiritualism held at the Co-operative Hall, Manchester on the afternoon of Good Friday, 3 April 1931. There were hymns, a solo of 'There is a Green Hill Far Away', and Vyvyan spoke twice.

In May 1931 Maurice Barbanell in the 'London Notes' column of the *National Spiritualist* mentioned Vyvyan as a visiting medium who 'has been serving several churches in this area; they all comment on his very fine platform manner and the high standard of his psychic gifts'. At this time a bill was passing through parliament which would make mediumship illegal. Barbanell, the son of an atheist barber-dentist who became the editor of *Psychic News,* noted that according to such a law, 'every time that Sir Oliver Lodge or Professor Low have sat with a medium they have broken the law.'

John Lewis contributed an article to the *Two Worlds* on 'The mediumship of Vyvyan Deacon':

> One of the most recent Spiritualist propagandists to visit England from overseas... Vyvyan Deacon, a well-known Australian medium with a wide circle of experience. He is an excellent and convincing speaker and a brilliant and witty conversationalist. His mediumship is versatile. He is an inspirational and trance speaker, a clairvoyant and clairaudient and, in addition, possesses mediumship for physical phenomena...

The article, later reprinted on the front page of the American *Banner of Life*, was well-timed as it came out just before his first trip to Belfast, where he spoke to packed houses at 29 Rosemary Street, under the auspices of the local Spiritualist Alliance. In the morning he spoke of psychic development and emphasized that the main essentials to a serious and profitable study of modern Spiritualism were a strong will, a keen intelligence and an ardent desire.

In addition to the Spiritualists who organised his meetings, Vyvyan's contacts in Ireland included Stanley C.M. Foster, who was secretary of the Egyptian Club in London but whose family had originally come from Loughrea, County Galway, Æ (George Russell) and W.B. Yeats, whom he had first met in London in rooms above a shop in Museum Street. At Yeats's request he held a séance in the Abbey Theatre. He later mentioned he had met Æ in London, in the company of Watkins, the renowned esoteric bookseller of Cecil Court, and again when he visited the New Forest.

Throughout May Vyvyan was booked up for lectures at 35 Marsham Street, Westminster, on psychic faculties and their development, followed by psychometry. A leaflet announced that 'The Library has arranged for Mr Deacon to follow this series by a Course of 12 Lecture Lessons on General Occult Unfoldment and Psychic Development, with Demonstrations'. In July it was noted there would be a continuation of his Thursday lectures at 8 pm and that there would be a course of twelve lectures organised by the Borderland Library. In July he lectured on 'The Proof of the Existence of the Soul' at the Central Spiritualist Church at Brighton. In September, Hebden Bridge National Spiritualist Church advertised a set of lectures by 'the Great Australian medium Vyvyan Deacon'. The coming year's programme of lectures issued by the St Albans Society for Psychic Study was headed by Vyvyan's name. One member of the audience at the talks he gave to this society was a boy called Leslie Flint. He himself later became a famous direct voice medium, the author of a book called *Voices in the Dark*, and appeared on television when he declared that he had taped the voices of Elizabeth Barrett Browning and Robert Browning at one of his direct voice séances.

There were now so many engagements Vyvyan did not have time to deal with his own correspondence, so he hired a secretary.

Vyvyan often went to see Miss Stead and I would go with him. At one séance I was very embarrassed because W.T. Stead told his daughter to give me copies of his 'Books for the Bairns'. She was sure that none remained but later found some, together with Charles Lamb's *Tales from Shakespeare*, in the same edition for children. When I hesitated to accept them as they had been her father's books, she insisted saying that they must have materialised at her father's wishes.

In addition to the Stead Bureau there were engagements at the Richmond Spiritualist Church (the Free Church) in Surrey, and at the London Spiritual Mission 13 Pembridge Place. This last was a favourite with Vyvyan and because it had such a lovely atmosphere he took me with him and on one occasion asked for me to sit with him on the platform, believing that I too would one day speak from such a platform.

The London Spiritual Mission was founded by three brothers, Percy, Ernest and Glen Beard. Percy Beard, who had attended Susannah Harris's test séance, was vice-president of the Mission and lived for a number of years in the church house. The premises were originally the stables for Whiteley's Department Store. The Beard brothers, originally part of a home circle at the turn of the century, had been directed by the medium to find stables in the Bayswater area, buy them and build a Christian Spiritualist church there.

A testimonial now arrived from Edgar Tozer, president of the Society of Psychic and Occult Scientific Research in Melbourne 1915-1930 and one of Vyvyan's students. Although Vyvyan was receiving quite a lot of publicity, Tozer was highly regarded in Spiritualist circles

---

Kenton Spiritualist Church,
NORTHWICK PARK HALL.
Stations : Northwick Park (Met) and
Kenton (Bakerloo).

SUNDAY, JUNE 14TH, at 6-30,
MR. HAINES, Trance Addresses by
Three Controls.
TUESDAY, at 3, WOMEN'S MEETING.
THURSDAY, at 8, MR. VYVYAN DEACON
Clairvoyance.
SUNDAY, JUNE 21ST, MR. HORACE LEAF

Richmond Spiritualist Church,
(The Free Church),
Ormond Road, Richmond, Surrey.

SUNDAY, JUNE 20th,
At 7, **Miss HELEN SPIERS.**

WEDNESDAY, at 7-30,
Mrs. Nutland, Address and Clairvoyance.

SUNDAY, JUNE 27th,
Mr. VIVIAN DEACON.
Healing Service every WEDNESDAY, at 3.

Forest Hill Christian Spiritualist Church
BEADNELL RD., FOREST HILL, S.E.23

SUNDAY, JUNE 7TH, at 11-15, PUBLIC
CIRCLE.   At 3, LYCEUM.
At 7, MR. VYVYAN DEACON.
TUESDAY, at 3, MRS. PEARSON.
At 7-30, HEALING CIRCLE.
THURSDAY, at 8, PUBLIC CIRCLE.

Crouch End Spiritualist Society,
44, COLERIDGE RD., CROUCH END, N.8

SUNDAY, MAY 24TH, at 7,
MR. VYVYAN DEACON.
AFTER-CIRCLE follows Service.
THURSDAY, at 3, MRS. SUTTON.
At 8, MEMBER WORKERS.
SATURDAY, MAY 30TH, at 7-30, SOCIAL

and a reference from him was still welcome. Vyvyan was recommended both as a trance medium and as an inspirational speaker.

It was arranged that Sybil, Eunice and I should stay in Scotland with Mrs Miller, who had become an admirer of Vyvyan's mediumship. (She would sponsor talks and send him expenses. It was illegal to receive money for work as a medium.) We were met by her chauffeur at the Edinburgh coach station and driven to Peebles. Sybil and I were to be looked after by a governess and a Norwegian girl. Here we encountered for the first time the idiosyncrasies of upper middle class life. We had been to the theatre in Edinburgh one time. Cook had been instructed to leave food set out for us. Mrs Miller was left still hungry. Now, we knew there was more cold meat in the kitchen: Mrs Miller would not think of going in search of it for fear of what Cook would say the next day.

On 18 September 1931 Lady Doyle wrote to Vyvyan wanting to arrange a séance at her home at Bignell Wood and asking about costs if he were to come on a Saturday afternoon and stayed until Monday morning. Her letter carefully quotes the fare from Waterloo as being thirteen shillings and tenpence for a weekend ticket return, or if he were to come down just overnight, the ordinary return would be nineteen shillings and tenpence. She also wanted to know about a séance at Windlesham, a house at Crowborough in Sussex, where the weekend return fare would be six shillings and fivepence and the ordinary return would be nine shillings and tenpence. As an afterthought she wondered about a séance at her flat at Victoria in London.

This letter was quickly followed by another, again full of arrangements about trains:

> There is a train which leaves Waterloo at 9.35 arriving S'ston West 11.50. Then we could have lunch, and give you time for a little rest, have tea and then a stroll in the forest which is looking lovely at present. The return train on Monday morning is 11.18 arriving Waterloo at 12.50.

On 1 October Jean Conan Doyle wrote from Windlesham on behalf of a friend in Australia who was asking for the name of a nearby medium.

Vyvyan made several trips to Lady Doyle and part of the experience was always that he was late leaving to catch his train back to London, so that her son Dennis, a racing driver, would cheerfully take him to the

145

station at over 90 mph, a terrifying speed on those country roads.

At the end of November Vyvyan was working in the north of England and Scotland, touring with his usual programme of lectures, séances and clairvoyance. The atmosphere of the traditional service was always retained and hymns such as 'God be with you will we meet again' continued to be favourites. His letters to Eunice at this time were typed on white paper with a green ribbon and signed in green ink. The initial V of his signature opened and closed with an exaggerated loop, similar to the insignia of the Secret Seal of Solomon in A.E. Waite's *The Book of Ceremonial Magic*. The signature is also notable for its being an inversion of Crowley's characteristic style. Where Vyvyan began with a flaccid, characteristically passive, phallus symbol, Crowley started with a tumescent, perhaps exaggeratedly active, A for Aleister. The two men, who were soon to meet, appeared diametrically opposed even to the first capital letter of their signatures.

The British College of Psychic Science, 15 Queen's Gate, London, advertised in Light that Vyvyan Deacon would give an address and demonstration of clairvoyance on Friday 23 October 1931 at 8 pm. In the same issue Vyvyan announced:

> Mr Vyvyan Deacon is at home on Wednesday at 3 pm. Lectures, Psychometry, Trance, Afternoon Tea 2/6. Applications for Private Sittings and places in Trance Circle at 111a, Alexandra Road, NW8. Telephone Maida Vale 6772. There is still a vacancy in Developing Circle and applications are also invited Winter Session.

During the spring of 1932 we rented a ground floor flat at 66 Clapham Road. Trams rattled by all night from Stockwell to the Elephant and Castle.

That summer Vyvyan was always out. If not leading a séance or speaking in Ryde, Ilford, Letchworth, the Stead Bureau, the Marylebone Spiritualists' Association, Mrs Egerton's Circle and private sittings, then there were people to meet at such literary and bohemian haunts as the Café Royal, the Cheshire Cheese (home of W.B. Yeats's Rhymer's Club) and the Fitzroy Tavern. If I was out of school, he would take me with him. On the top of a tram to Stoke Newington I asked him about reincarnation: if I had two or more, which one would I return as to speak at a séance? Sometimes, when I heard him lecture, I would recognise part of our conversation, turning up as part of his address.

In the *International Psychic Gazette* of June 1932 there was an article by David Bedbrook, headed 'Lost Airmen's Trumpet Manifestation'. Bedbrook had sat with Vyvyan on 18 April 1932. After his brother, killed in the war, had given his right name and spoken there was another visitor:

Captain Hinchcliffe, whom I knew personally. He made his presence known by introducing the noise of an aeroplane engine into the room which gradually increased in volume until it was... as though the engine were in the room... my business brings me into contact... with various types of aircraft, and consequently I am in a position to know an aeroengine when it is operating on half contact. It is a noise physically impossible to simulate by any human organism, because the rhythm would be broken, and this noise was kept up without a break for close upon twenty minutes. The vibration caused the whole room to shake, and ornaments, pictures, etc. to rock.

Captain Hinchcliffe said that he had created the noise on a memory, after the medium had requested the noise to stop.

In reply to a test question I discreetly put as to where we had last met, the Captain very promptly replied, 'Rue de Rivoli, Paris'. This was correct. I dined with him in 1921 in a hotel there, the last time I actually saw him, when he was chief pilot for the Daimler Airways – a company in operation prior to the formation of Imperial Airways.

Sir Sefton Brancker also spoke... strangely enough he was a co-passenger with me on a maiden flight over the Channel from France to England – his voice was typical of the voice so well remembered...

Frankis Evans senior anaesthetist at St Bartholomew's Hospital, London and former president of the Anaesthetists Section Royal College of Surgeons, later remembered sitting regularly with Vyvyan at about this time:

I heard Dutch spoken by a communicator there and one of the sitters spoke fluent Cantonese to the Chinese guide and there ensued quite a long conversation. Finally both guide and sitter changed to Mandarin and carried on a conversation in that language. Sir Sefton Brancker of R100 airship fame used to speak to my hostess...

It was there that my mother gave me a code word we had arranged together before she died. The celluloid trumpet poised itself opposite me and then I heard whispered three words 'Frankis... Mother.. dear', and the trumpet fell to the ground, recovered itself and repeated the

147

procedure once more. I had been introduced as 'Mr Smith' and no one knew my real name except my friend who introduced me.

Another connection with aviation was Bill Lancaster. Mrs Lancaster was a friend who had taken us to her box at the Albert Hall on Remembrance Day the previous year. But during that summer of 1932 she used to visit us regularly in Clapham Road, complaining bitterly about her family and all that was happening to it. Her son, Bill, had separated from his wife and flown off to Australia with his girlfriend. Later, on a trip to America, he found himself charged with murder when a friend shot himself using Bill's gun. In August a Not Guilty verdict was reached. We saw Bill when he returned to Britain later in the year; he was already planning another long flight. In April 1933 he set off to try to break the record flying over the Sahara to Cape Town. He was never seen alive again. Vyvyan told his distraught mother that Bill's message from 'the other side' was that he had died instantly. Vyvyan commented to us at the time that this was naturally the only message Bill would have sent. It was not until 1972 that the plane was found and in it his diary, showing that in fact he took eight days to die.

Aviators Jim Mollison and his wife Amy Johnson were among the guests at the Twenty-third Foyles Literary Luncheon, held at Grosvenor House on 15 September 1932. The Chairman was Mr Charles B. Cochran and Arthur Rackham (whom Vyvyan later got to know) and J. Beresford respectively proposed and replied to the toast. Other guests included the novelist Rose Macaulay, the translator Scott Moncrieff, Naomi Royde-Smith, wife of the actor Ernest Milton, an Old Vic regular – and a certain Vyvyan Deacon. E.F. Benson's account of the spirit of Cardinal Newman, speaking at a Spiritualist séance and giving the blessing as 'Benedictine' was one of the anecdotes. (It was one which was also in Vyvyan's repertoire.) But the event attracted particular attention because of the presence of a very different individual, for on that occasion the speaker was to be Aleister Crowley.

Crowley was the object of great interest, though his talk on 'The Philosophy of Magick' was a disappointment to many. 'For a man who has been described as brilliant Mr Crowley's speech was not intelligent. It was hardly intelligible,' was the verdict of one journalist. Rose Macaulay hoped he would not 'turn himself into a goat'. This was the first occasion that Vyvyan had heard Crowley speak, though they had long had friends in common. Vyvyan had begun reading Crowley's books years before and Crowley had studied newspaper reports of Vyvyan's libel trial keenly. The previous year the articles in the psychic newspapers that accompanied Vyvyan's arrival in Britain had been drawn to Crowley's attention. He was in need of money and Vyvyan's successful libel suit suggested a course of action. He performed certain rituals and when in January 1933 he saw in the window of a bookseller a notice alleging that his *Diary of a Drug Fiend* had been withdrawn from publication after 'an attack in the sensational press', Crowley sued for libel and won. He was awarded £50 and costs.

Further magick yielded a second attempt. Crowley sued Constable, publisher of *Laughing Torso*, the autobiography of his long-standing friend Nina Hamnett who had hinted that there was black magic at Crowley's abbey at Cefalù and that the disappearance of a cat was suspicious. On 10 April 1934 the case for libel opened: this time, though, the verdict was for the defendant. Still, the case brought benefits of a kind. It brought notoriety, on which he could dine out, and therefore publicity for his books.

Born twenty years earlier than Vyvyan, Crowley was the child of strict Plymouth Brethren parents. As a child, he had crucified a frog and the macabre seemed always to attract him. Where he set out with the motto *Perdurabo* to overthrow and outrage, Vyvyan chose as his motto the almost papal *Vicarius Filii Dei* (vicar of the son of God) and always retained a strongly conventional side to his nature. On the copyright page of his Bible, Vyvyan notes how this motto had the value 666 when the values of the Roman numerals contained in the three words was added up (this was known to nineteenth-century Protestant propagandists against the papacy) and wrote after: 'Here is wisdom. Let him that hath understanding count the number of the Beast! for it is the number of a man; and his number is six hundred three score and six. Revelations 13:18.' Crowley, who adopted the name of the Great Beast and signed letters '666' on a similarly gematrial basis, was educated at Malvern College and Cambridge. He claimed a knowledge of several languages and studied the classics, the cabbala and also eastern religion and magic from original sources. He believed in the will, in actively seeking to make things happen. Vyvyan had no orthodox education and never having had an arithmetic lesson, could not even manage more than the very simplest multiplication. He was by contrast a person to whom things simply happened. Such passivity may have made him a disasterous manager of his own finances but it made him an excellent medium.

Chapter Ten

Farewell, Brothers most dear, in the name of those whom you
sincerely honour. Farewell, I say, and farewell again; favour me
and approach me (I implore and entreat you by your assurance
and because of the ignorance of the age in the true and pure
Philosophy); be mindful of me and your promises.

Robert Fludd, *Tractatus Apologeticus*

FROM THE EARLY THIRTIES Vyvyan acted as the medium for an
Anglican Spiritualist group. Revd Arthur Sharpe, who had
been Vicar General in Sarawak, had been invited to participate
in a committee investigating the 'Communion of Saints', meeting at All Souls, in Langham Place, London. One day Sharpe, who had
become the chairman of the committee and would later chronicle the
affair in his book *The Spirit Saith*, was telephoned by the Revd
Maurice Elliott, Vicar of St Peter's, Cricklewood and author of *The
Psychic Life of Jesus*, to say that the late Archbishop Davidson had
spoken through Vyvyan, urging the importance of mankind knowing
the truth of what happened after death. From this committee, and this
event, developed a circle which sat every Thursday evening in a back
room near London Bridge. Vyvyan was the regular medium and the
sitting was always lit only by a red light. Meetings included Captain
Michael J. Hunter, a Conservative Member of Parliament, and his wife
(herself a medium), a doctor from Charing Cross Hospital, a theological student, a churchwarden, two priests and two men who worked in
the City. One of the latter was Stanley Barber, a fish merchant; he used
to have baskets of fish delivered to us. During one meeting, at which
Mrs Hunter was the medium, the sitters were unnerved to hear
themselves being addressed by the Virgin Mary. At another Archbishop Davidson suggested that an Anglican order be formed to
investigate Spiritualism and that Vyvyan be used as a medium for a
séance close to where the late Archbishop had lived. So in April 1933

the circle met in a small room in Greyfriars, Canterbury, close to the Cathedral, bringing Vyvyan back to the part of the world where he had grown up. The meetings were attended by Mr Lander, a Justice of the Peace and the president of the Spiritualist Society. The Archbishop spoke there through Vyvyan's mediumship and at further meetings at London Bridge, continuing to urge that an order should be formed, to be called the Order for the Preparation for Communion of Souls. Sometimes Eunice, Sybil or I would go with Vyvyan to the now regular meetings at the Lady Chapel of St Stephen's. We were always called for by the limousine of one of the members of the circle. One evening towards the end of 1933, during a businessmen's meeting attended by eight men, including Maurice Elliott, Vyvyan rose to his feet and announced in a voice of immense strength 'Charles Edward Gore'. One witness remembered being impressed by the power of the voice, wondering if people out in the road would hear it and start filing in to hear the speaker. Bishop Gore had been a churchman opposed to the work of Spiritualists. Vyvyan, as Gore, told the circle that he

151

had been brought by the Revd G. Vale Owen, whom in life he had always regarded as a misled eccentric. He regretted his opposition to Spiritualism and now wished to address his fellow clergy to make good his past errors by letting them know what he had missed.

Vyvyan was popular with Captain Hunter of the London Bridge circle and in July 1933 he went as a guest to Stoke Hall in Derbyshire, from where he wrote to Eunice of how unnerving it was to be attended by Todd, an old manservant. When Todd unpacked Vyvyan's bags and went off with his suit, feeling it needed pressing, Vyvyan was left with a choice of wearing either formal evening wear or pyjamas. Mrs Hunter was the means by which Vyvyan was given a job with the Unicorn Press, publisher of occultist writers since the end of the nineteenth century. This was a sinecure with the intention of providing him with some regular income, since being paid for working as a medium was illegal.

The Bishop of London, Winnington Ingram, was in contact with the group and wanted to sit with Vyvyan, though he always kept his association with it strictly secret; he and Earl Grey attended private séances at Stoke Hall. Mrs Hunter was responsible for inviting senior diplomats and members of the clergy. Donald, later Lord, Soper was always closely interested. After a séance one evening, Eunice told me that I must never, never reveal whom I had met there. I was puzzled because I had not recognised him, but it was the Prince of Wales.

The group also met at the Hunter's London home in Portman Square and it was here that Vyvyan met the enigmatic author Walter Harrington Crawfurd Price, who worked in Intelligence as well as being a widely travelled journalist. There were also sittings at Rockingham Hall, hosted by Lady Seymour. In addition a secret 'businessmen's circle' met weekly, attended by smartly dressed, well-to-do men; the members regarded confidentiality as crucially important. In 1935 we met Wedgwood at a séance at Miss Niven's house near St Stephen's in Hampstead and he chatted with Eunice about Sydney. His presence at this Anglican gathering indicates the way in which, through the Spiritualist network, very different people and groups used to meet, for when young, Wedgwood had been associated with a number of Anglo-Catholic movements and had only abandoned early plans to train for the ministry on being converted to Theosophy by hearing two lectures in York by Annie Besant. Even when ill, he continued to come up to London to attend the businessmen's circle and meetings associated with plans for the Order.

In 1935 the Commission of the Order of Preparation for the Communion of Souls was issued, containing the resolution to protect those with gifts of mediumship and prepare those who wanted to participate in Spiritualist circles. The Order, it was hoped would bring back into the church those who it was felt were attending séances instead of services. Vyvyan's membership card of the order, dated 18 March 1935 and signed by Maurice Elliott, bore the motto 'All things are yours in Christ' and declared 'As a member of the above Order, you bear witness to your belief that the gifts of the Spirit were promised to the Faithful in perpetuity, and you will do all in your power to assist and encourage the exercise of these gifts in the name of our Lord Jesus Christ.' At this time Vyvyan embarked on a purifying three month fast and shaved his head, as he had done at the time of his trial in Australia. He was later able to draw both Gerald de Beaurepaire and Leslie Flint into the Order, to carry on when he himself withdrew.

By September 1935 we had moved from the flat in Clapham Road to a house in Lorn Road, Stockwell, London: our first house since 'Thelema' in Melbourne. We were able to manage this because two Swedish Spiritualists, Mme Mandahl and Carl Carlesson, had arranged for Vyvyan to visit Sweden for a series of direct voice séances and had paid half the fee in advance. The house had four storeys, though the top storey held only two gabled attic rooms. A narrow flight of stairs led steeply to the tiny square landing my bedroom and a bathroom.

In December 1935 Vyvyan found himself acting as the medium for a circle at Mrs Egerton's flat in Earls Court. Geraldine Cummins, a well-known medium engaged in automatic writing (and the author of a book about it), had been trying, by use of automatic writing, to find out what had become of Colonel P.H. Fawcett, who, together with his son and a friend had been missing in the Brazilian jungle for ten years. Reports had just appeared in the press that a body had been found, possibly that of the missing Colonel. During the séance Vyvyan came out with the information that the body was not that of Colonel Fawcett, that he was not in the spirit world but still alive, being held by an Indian tribe and well cared for.

One night, on 30 November 1936, I stared out of the bathroom window soon after 7.30 pm and saw a reddened sky which grew more and more dramatic as the hours passed. The Crystal Palace, where Vyvyan had taken me, and where Robert Browning had attended concerts, burned all that night. On another occasion I woke to find my father holding a large sausage on a fork under my nose. He had let the smell of the cooked sausage wake me. I took the fork and he crept away, leaving me to munch in the cold dark room. Once Vyvyan and Aleister Crowley woke me to share a feast of the steak puddings they called 'babies' heads'. I told people at school about this and the staff were nervous to hear that I had been sharing a 'babys' head' with someone regarded as the reincarnation of Gilles de Rais. I also began to write to my school friends with the opening 'Do what thou wilt shall be the whole of the Law' and taught them to do the same. At the end of each term, we had to submit a list of our reading. My first list started with Oscar Wilde and went on through Annie Besant and books on Indian philosophy to Baudelaire's *Fleurs du Mal*. The teachers watched me with increasing unease.

Ours was a house crowded with books. Books on the Christian Mysteries and the early Gnostics, the complete Crowley collection to date, two dark blue volumes of Frazer's *Golden Bough*, the rarest banned books from Paris and first editions of Blake. There were manuscripts on vellum: medieval medical books, material relating to the Templars, to Hippocrates, Celsus, Paracelsus, Pythagoras; a copy of James Branch Cabell's *Jurgen*, which had been lavishly praised in his *Confessions* by Crowley who believed that his own version of the Gnostic Mass had formed the basis of part of the book; and rare books on magic were all within reach of Vyvyan in his study, together with his favourite volumes of Wilde and the German philosophers.

In the drawing room were the complete works of Dickens and Macaulay's *History of England*, Coles, Jerome K. Jerome, Conan Doyle, Annie Besant, Leadbeater, books on Yoga, *The Song Celestial* and *Light of Asia*, the *Rubáiyát of Omar Khayyám*, Matthew Arnold, Browning, Shelley, Keats, Byron, Spenser, Shakespeare, Shaw, Huxley, Charles Morgan, Dunne, author of *An Experiment with Time*, Chesterton, Frank Harris and D.H. Lawrence. A special bookshelf was reserved for the fine plate books on Renaissance art and modern art and sculpture, another for the works of Chidley, Havelock Ellis, Culpepper, medical and herbal books. On the stairway were books on arts and crafts, short stories and essays and books for bedtime.

On Vyvyan's desk stood a heavy ceremonial head of Pan, which is now in the possession of Leadbeater's biographer Gregory Tillett. Close by was the small skull of a Peruvian boy from centuries ago, which a woman friend called 'Byll' Barton had brought back for him. Other ornaments in the room were a pipe-rack, with an assortment of every conceivable shape of pipe, clay, meerschaum, petersham and long-stemmed pipes almost like hookahs; figurines including one or two Pillig figurines from Melbourne; sets of ash-trays; Star of David candlesticks; a finely plaited black and white cat-o'-nine-tails with thongs at the end of each tassel; Egyptian figures in bronze or alabaster and an eastern bald, plump cross-legged god of plenty made of cherry-wood with ivory eyes. One night the god appeared to laugh out loud and rock and with loud cracks and snaps, and while we watched, his belly split like Freud's sideboard. No amount of oiling and first aid ever sealed the cracks but he was polished and placed on a folded rosewood card-table in the hall. It may not have been unconnected with Vyvyan's friend Crowley's prankish sense of humour. For the latter had once been photographed as Fo-Hi the Chinese god of Joy and Laughter whose god form he had assumed.

His journey to Sweden was hard for Vyvyan, who found being alone in a non-English speaking country disconcerting. On one occasion, not knowing the word to look for, he could not find a lavatory. When he came upon a door marked 'Dam', there seemed a useful association with water and on going in he found it was indeed a lavatory. He closed the door of a cubicle and immediately the sound of female voices arose. 'Dam' had of course nothing to do with water: this was a ladies' lavatory. He was forced to remain hidden until silence suggested it was safe to make his escape.

Nevertheless, the séances went well and Vyvyan wrote enthusiastically describing the response he had received. A Swedish magazine published an article describing one evening. The whole event was something of a novelty and the article, for which Paul Beard found a translator, puzzled over whether the vibrations felt were the result of passing traffic and whether the medium was empowered not by spirits but by telepathy.

> Ten to twelve people attended. Participants always sit in a circle, holding hands to make a link. In the middle of the floor is a plate of water and two trumpets. The water is to concentrate the power from the other side... the medium was a fat, middle-aged gentleman, big brown eyes and not very congenial. There was nothing fanatical about him. He appeared to be a good man. The lights were turned off for total darkness.
> He prayed in English and a Swedish lady said the Lord's Prayer and

we all joined in. Somebody played softly on the piano and the medium fell into a trance.

There was some deep breathing; at the same time whisperings in the air – the medium's guide. He starts to speak to those there, organising them. He tells them it is not necessary to sit with joined hands. They could free them and place them palms upwards on their laps.

The guide appeared humorous. Then the wonder started. Sir Arthur Conan Doyle spoke about his visit to Sweden. He said he was a believer in Spiritualism long before the First World War, not when he was a senile old man! Similarly Oliver Lodge was not old when he started to believe.

Other spirits there included W.T. Stead, a very well-known newspaper man who did a lot for Spiritualism in England. Swedenborg was there and spoke to his descendant. He gave good advice. It was strange the people who couldn't speak English in their life-time now could speak perfect English. When the medium got used to his new environment, the spirits could be made to speak in their own language. This was too advanced for Mr Deacon's visit to Sweden this time. Mr Carlesson went to the United States and visited séances there and his sister who was on the Other Side, came and spoke her native language. It is some materialisation which occurs in the voice organ.

When spirits finished their talk, Mr Deacon's guide started, a Chinese called Cheong who speaks when the medium is in trance. He started with a little speech in Chinese, and afterwards in what is called 'pidgin' English. It was really interesting the Cheong talk, in that he addressed everyone and gave them special advice and individual messages. Every sitter heard something. He knows something about them. There was no lack of good will or love coming out of the mouth of the medium. Ladies who have been married and want to marry again received permission to do so, from their husbands on the other side. Always the personal things seem correct.

Carl Carlesson wrote about Vyvyan's visit to Sweden in *Psychic News*, 5 October 1935. He had recently been in America, where he had been instrumental in obtaining the release of Mrs Cook, a medium arrested for fortune-telling following an investigation by escapologist Houdini.

On his return from Sweden, Vyvyan was invited to speak in Bournemouth. He and Eunice set off together early on the Saturday morning but a little later Eunice returned and went to bed. She had been boarding a tram when it pulled away and she slipped and was dragged some distance before she let go. Vyvyan had gone on alone. Sybil had to admit that she had arranged for friends to come to a party. Eunice did not like to ask her to cancel it. All that evening young people in party dresses and smart clothes ran merrily about the house, in and out of Eunice's room. In the end she told me to call the doctor. Dr Moulin Feroze was Persian and teased me that my open-toed sandals would be dangerous for my health as they would allow germs to enter between my toes. After seeing Eunice he called me up and asked for hot water and clean towels. It was just the strain to her arm, she continued to insist. Later our friend Byll told me that Eunice had in fact miscarried, perhaps aborted, a male foetus.

Vyvyan never even learned that Eunice had been pregnant. But his letter from Bournemouth reveals his concern about Eunice's health:

> I have been so anxious about you, although everyone here has assured me that they feel you will be alright. I'm afraid I spent rather a restless night. I rose at 6 am and walked to the big Roman Catholic Church of the Sacred Heart in Bournemouth where I stayed for 7 o'clock Mass and prayed for you.
>
> I walked back here and had several cups of tea with Mr and Mrs Curtis. They are both very sweet and kind in every way. I have had every attention and I am sure you would have enjoyed your stay here if only you had been well enough to come.
>
> However, of course, it was impossible under the circumstances – but you must come down and recuperate later. I will telephone immediately after my evening work is done tonight to learn how you are. If thoughts can help, you have been greatly helped as everyone here is constantly sending out thoughts for your recovery.

Vyvyan never got out of bed before midday, or later if he had difficulty finishing the *Morning Post* crossword. There was a telephone by the bed so that if he was really baffled, he could ring for help. (We always had the *Morning Post* delivered, because Vyvyan's maternal grandfather Reuben Browning used to contribute articles to it as 'Brutus Brittanicus'.)

Then Vyvyan would let out a stream of abuse and obscenity, as if to get rid of the poison of the day all in one long outpouring before moving to the bathroom. From there would come the sound of his singing 'Today I feel so happy'. In the hot weather he would come down naked. Breakfast would be waiting for him on the scrubbed wooden table covered with white table cloth; even eating a snack in the kitchen we now had damask table napkins and silver napkin-rings. At the beginning of a meal he would line up his collection of

157

condiments: French and German mustards, celery salt, cayenne pepper, paprika, oil and vinegar, Worcester Sauce, soy sauce, tomato ketchup, anchovy sauce, all preferably in novel containers. Vyvyan would arrange them and rearrange them all through the meal. At the end there was a ritual of folding his napkin.

Before going to lecture, Vyvyan would rest alone in a room, then bath, shave closely, rub Pond's cold cream into his inordinately white skin until his face was smooth as though it had never needed a shave. If he had to appear on a stage in a large hall with a spot-light he used theatrical make-up, with No.9 grease-paint base (as did his friend Bishop James) but for the smaller Spiritualist churches in night light, he would use Morny's 'Chaminade' dusting powder from a square white cardboard box with an elaborately decorated label.

Sometimes the Rachel powder was decanted into a peach-coloured, celluloid, art-nouveau box with a black lid. He would finish off with a suggestion of rouge from the small round box of 'Bourgeois' rouge sold complete with puff. Finally a vigorous brushing of his hair with a set of monogrammed ebony brushes, he would stand under the brightest light, hold his cheeks close to it and ask, 'All right? Too much rouge?' The final act was swinging on his velvet-collared cape and calling for his stick. He would have his favourite pipe with him and two or three books tucked under his arm.

If there was nowhere else to go, the White Horse, just around the corner, was always delighted to see him. The landlord and customers would buy him drinks. He was always asked to perform monologues but most requests were for him to tell fortunes with cards. Vyvyan always carried his own set, with red hearts, white diamonds, green clubs and orange spades on a black background but he was willing to be passed a new pack of cards, which he quietly arranged while speaking. He never pretended to me that there was any real magic in knowing what cards were in people's hands: it was a parlour game to him. He would deal the cards and start. He would say 'That is denoted by the five of clubs' or 'the ace of diamonds' or whatever card he extracted from their hands but really using reading the cards was a mask for reading the person.

When unexpected guests came, if we had the money Eunice would send me round to the cooked meat shop to buy a quarter of sliced cooked pork, or ham at nine pence a quarter. At the butcher's I would not be charged for some 'scraps for the dog', bones cut from the long thin chops of best end of neck of lamb. These had long strips of meat which we used to put on a toasting fork and hold in the open glowing coals of the diningroom grate. Once it was Countess Pahlin, who attended private sittings with Vyvyan, who arrived unexpectedly. Much to Eunice's shame Vyvyan then came home with a tramp who had been busking the Brixton Astoria cinema queue. When Sybil brought some friends back from St Michael's church youth club, I was sent out to buy meat scraps and French bread. The countess, the tramp and the girls all settled to toasting food in the glowing embers.

We used to go to Tring in Hertfordshire, getting up at 5 am to reach Euston in time for the workmen's train to Tring which cost one shilling and fivepence return. Dr Maud Westrup sometimes joined us. Witchlike, with a hooked nose, pointed chin and wispy grey hair, she was dressed entirely in black. She was the author of two books on Egyptian symbology. As we walked along Vyvyan, in Coleridgean fashion changed his position with that of Maud Westrup on either side of me as they changed topics of conversation.

We visited Nell Gwyn's house, where some of her clothes were then still hanging in a wardrobe, and we would end up at Stanley Lief's place. He ran Champneys, an avantgarde health farm, on the principles of Chidley. We used to go to the Champney open days, with Morris dancing and Indian dancing too. It was at that time that I was introduced to Nehru. He invited me to a Congress of Faiths banquet at Caxton Hall, where he looked after me as I attended unaccompanied.

Lief was a Spiritualist, involved in séances with Vyvyan, and an inveterate gambler. Once Vyvyan correctly predicted an outsider, not a horse Stanley Lief backed, would win. He was so excited at Vyvyan's prediction he implored Vyvyan to predict the winner of another race. Vyvyan refused, saying that psychic gifts were not to be used in that way. However he did say the names had just come to him and he wrote them down, posting them and addressing to Stanley Lief. Leif received them the next morning and they were again correct. He could not resist telling everybody and Vyvyan was inundated with requests for tips, but after this he always refused.

Vyvyan sometimes used to go to other people's séances. He and Eunice attended a séance given by Mrs Lilian Lilly, a materialisation medium, at her home near Vauxhall Bridge Road. Eunice saw her grandmother materialise in front of her, clearly recognisable. The next morning Vyvyan gave me a silver cross, with the words 'Pro Ecclesia

Dei' encircling the centre, which was, he said, an apport which St Thérèse of Lisieux had handed to Vyvyan. I was told it had belonged to her and was dematerialised from France and re-materialised for me. Mrs Lilly was killed during the war. She had been living on a boat in the Portsmouth area and driving herself up to London for engagements. Her Red Indian guide was reputed to have sat on the bonnet of her car to protect her on the long busy Portsmouth Road. One evening in London she was warned by her guide, in the hearing of the sitters, not to return to Portsmouth that night but to stay in London. She disregarded this instruction, believing it to be safer out of London. She was killed outright in an accident.

Vyvyan always used ten shilling notes as bookmarks. When we wanted money to go to the West End, we would look through the books until we found a note. On one particular evening, my parents were already in evening dress (Vyvyan, influenced by Leadbeater, always dressed for dinner) but we could not find any money. Vyvyan telephoned his friend Godfrey Tearle who was appearing in a play and was offered complimentary tickets. We were invited backstage and were guests at a party in the dressing-room. When we started to leave, Godfrey offered to call us a taxi. Vyvyan told him that it was such a beautiful evening we would walk to the embankment and pick up one from there: in fact we walked all the way home, having not even a penny for a tram.

Through the late Lady Doyle, Vyvyan had received many invitations. At the beginning of 1936, he started visiting Gilbert Mahon, a painter and a quiet, kindly gentleman. Before Spiritualist or other esoteric meetings, Gilbert Mahon would be working on a picture while talking to Vyvyan, who would light a pipe and relax in a chair. Once he took some photographs of Vyvyan there and from them worked up a portrait of him in an easy chair with chin sunk on chest and with his deep-bowled short pipe in his hand. The portrait was selected for the eighth exhibition of the London Portrait Society at New Burlington Galleries where it was admired by Crowley, Augustus John and Sickert. Mahon presented the portrait to Eunice as a gift. Eunice, who was not happy it showed Vyvyan with a pipe, a rumpled suit and unkempt hair, was not delighted and after Vyvyan's death she destroyed the portrait, allowing it to be thought it was a victim of the Blitz. And, although Pillig's picture with the Pan ring survived, it was kept rolled up, because it had been painted while Eunice was away – and he did not look 'tidy' on that one, either.

In the dining room was a picture of Vyvyan which Eunice did like, the small charcoal sketch of him with a crystal ball which Ian Dickson had given them in Australia. There were also two Augustus John sketches of Crowley, a Nina Hamnett sketch on a rough page of paper of Breton sailors at a bar and water-colours by various Irish artists. In the dining room was kept the russet gourd with a black stopper on a green cord which Augustus John had used for carrying water when painting in the country.

Byll came to stay and went to the annual Forest Hill Christian Spiritualist Church garden party at Round Hill House, Dartmouth Road. I was in my first long skirt, made of cheap yellow satin and bought for one shilling and eleven pence from Brixton market, and I danced with my father, who was very light on his feet.

One evening Byll was looking after me while everyone else was out. She told me stories of Peru and her friend, whom she had met while teaching in Peru and who was rector of a church in Cumberland. We played cards until it grew dark. She suggested we could use the Ouija board but instead we sat at a small table with our palms turned upwards. When the table tilted violently I assumed she was teasing until she said 'Stop mucking about', thinking I was responsible. Suddenly someone called out 'John'. It sounded just as though it was in the room but I thought it must have come from the street. At the same time a bright light the size of a human aura lit up the wall behind Byll and I said it must be children in the street calling out and shining a torch in the room. She pretended she did not know what I was talking about as she had not heard anything and did not see a light. The voice continued to call out 'John' and I saw what looked like a shrouded figure in the same bright light behind her. I asked her to turn and look at it: 'That's enough,' she said, 'you're getting too highly strung.' She put on the light and we went down to the kitchen to find something to eat and read a funny story.

When Byll came round a few days later, I was sent upstairs. Byll, Vyvyan and Eunice stood and whispered together and I heard my name mentioned. My father called me and asked me what I had heard and seen the day Byll sat with me. I was then told that, although the rector was a good friend, Byll had become engaged to his brother John, a missionary in West Africa. She had now had a telegram to say that he had been murdered by tribesmen on the very day that I had seen the light and heard the name John called.

We did not see Byll for several weeks after that but when we did she seemed her old self again and we used to go to Speakers' Corner to heckle Donald Soper, with whom Byll had worked and whom I knew through Vyvyan's work, or to see Prince Monolulu, decorated with feathers, who used to wave chits about yelling, 'I gotta horse, I gotta horse!', offering to tell fortunes and predict winners. We used to wander in Hyde Park and St James's Park to see the old British Israelite man who used to feed the birds by letting them take the bread 'pap' he had prepared from between his lips. Then we would visit the Cumberland Hotel for tea.

Aleister Crowley visited us on my father's forty-first birthday, 9 August 1936. I was thirteen and my yard-long plaits had been cut. I was sent to answer the gentle knock at the door to admit a short elderly man with thinning hair and a round face. His eyes seemed colourless in the dimming light. He was dressed in a hopsack suit: Vyvyan had a similar one made in green from Crowley's tailor.

In a gentle voice, slightly nasal from asthma and cocaine, he asked 'Is the little lady in?' We sat in the study, while Eunice cooked dinner. I asked Crowley to write in my autograph book and his characteristically odd signature joined those of the Bishop of Sydney, who had signed earlier in the year on 9 February, Crawfurd Price, Charles Laughton, who was a friend of Vyvyan's, Frank Pettingell (who appeared in the film of *Hobson's Choice*), and Julia Seton. Vyvyan encouraged me to show Crowley the copies I had done of Beardsley's illustrations to *Fleurs du Mal*. He was later so pleased with my illustrations for his *Salomé* that he gave me a painting of his own called 'Scarlet Woman'. This was in gloriously bright orange, yellow, red and green with thick black outlines. Eunice did not like his crude style. Crowley did a portrait of her after a picnic in poster paint as a present for Vyvyan's forty-second birthday; Eunice did not like it but at least she did not destroy it. She gave it to me.

I took 'Scarlet Woman' to school, where I used to do posters for the current events board, and I was ordered to put it in the wastepaper basket. With Crowley's encouragement I spent more time drawing. I also followed Browning's example, trying to write so finely it could only be read with a magnifying glass, and copied two of the psalms on pages not much larger than a sixpence.

I did a painting for Crowley of John the Baptist's head on a dish carried by Salomé but I made the skull (copied from the Peruvian one) visible, with the head lightly suggested round it. Then I added red paint at the base of the skull. I knew Vyvyan and Crowley would approve and I hoped Eunice would praise me. But when I showed her the picture she hit me and called me a wicked girl with hideous evil thoughts. (Still true to New Thought principles, she believed in banishing anything unpleasant or ugly.) She ordered me to sit still on a chair until she gave me permission to move. This was not what I had been brought up to expect and I fled screaming, furious at having been hit.

The next morning I went to tell Vyvyan I was running away. He asked what I was going to do and where would I sleep. He suggested that if I thought about it I might prefer to carry on with school. He told me also that he had not much longer to be with me, so he would like very much for me to be at home. He had nothing to leave me but the knowledge that was in all the books in the house and the secret that Robert Browning was a Rosicrucian. I went to school.

Eunice always got on well with Crowley, who noted in his diary that she was 'charming.' (It is a curious point to note that when young, Crowley's mother had been called 'the little Chinese girl' at school because of her appearance.) She reminded him that she had written to him from Tallangatta to invite him to stay there when Vyvyan had planned to open up an Abbey similar to Cefalù. The day after Crowley's visit Vyvyan and another friend called Edomi called on him, although Crowley took a dim view of Edomi's behaviour with Pearl and vice versa. Just over a week later Eunice and Vyvyan visited Crowley for dinner and Eunice reported the strange behaviour of Pearl: from her description it sounded as though she brought herself to orgasm, having taken a mixture of alcohol and other drugs. Crowley himself wrote of her 'kicking, moaning, muttering.'

Crowley had begun the study of astrology on entering the Order of the Golden Dawn in 1898, maintaining his interest until in 1917 he quarrelled with Evangeline Adams, with whom he was collaborating on books about the subject. He intended to stop writing on astrology altogether but his interest did not disappear, for he wrote wanting to know Vyvyan's exact time of birth to do a chart for him. Vyvyan replied, quoting a passage from Crowley's Liber *LXV* which celebrates floating 'in the infinite Abyss' in a way which suggests both repudiation of ambition and also surrender to death:

Do what thou wilt shall be the whole of the Law. Unfortunately there was such a turmoil and ruddy blush ere my departure from the City of

Dreadful Night that I could not drop you a line. I tried twice to get you on the phone - in vain!

I will be here for a few days and letters will find me here. We hope that things are clearing for yourself and the 'Pearl of Great price'! I have written to my Mother to ascertain the hour of my last birth on this fretsome orb! Whence? Whither? Is there not joy ineffable in this aimless winging?

On my return to London I will telephone 'Hollook' when perhaps we can arrange another meeting. Love is the Law, love under will.

After doing Vyvyan's astrological chart, he then did charts for Bishop James and Pietro Rambelli, whom Vyvyan introduced to him.

Aleister Crowley was struck by the fact that Vyvyan was related to Robert Browning, for Browning was a poet he held in high esteem. He was the first to recognise a dark side to the poet whom the Victorians had considered such a prophet of optimism. Crowley's 'Aceldama - A Place to Bury Strangers In' certainly shows the influence of 'Childe Roland to the Dark Tower came':

> I contemplate myself in that dim sphere
> Whose hollow centre I am standing at
> With burning eyes intent to penetrate
> The black circumstance...

In the Epilogue the image of loose hair enclosing the lover as in a lair echoes the actions of Browning's Pauline. Crowley observes:

> Browning attained, I think, when Evelyn Hope
> Gave no response to his requickening kiss,
> In the brief moment when exceeding bliss
> Joined to her sweet passed soul his soul its scope.

In 1905 Crowley had printed a poem entitled *Rosa Inferni*, with an original illustration by Rodin, which he introduced with a verse from Browning's 'The Heretic's Tragedy', one of three poems Crowley knew Browning had composed in Paris 'as in a dream.'

> Ha ha! John plucketh now at his rose
> To rid himself of a sorrow at heart.
> Lo, – petal on petal, fierce rays unclose;
> Anther on anther, sharp spikes outstart;
> And with blood for dew, the bosom boils;
> And a gust of sulphur is all its smell.

> And lo, he is horribly in the toils
> Of a coal-black giant flower of hell!

Similarly Crowley chose extracts from Browning's 'Parleyings, Faust and His Friends' to introduce his banned lecture on *Gilles de Rais*:

FIRST FRIEND
Dost surmise
What struck me at first blush , Our Beghards, Waldenses,
Jeronimites, Hussites – does one show his head,
Spout Heresy now? Not a priest in his senses
Deigns answer mere speech, but piles faggots instead,
Refines as by fire, and, him silenced, all's said.

Whereas if in future I pen an opuscule
Defying retort, as of old when rash tongues
Were easy to tame – straight some knave of the Hussite School
Prints answer forsooth! Stop invisible lungs?
The barrel of blasphemy broached once, who bungs?

SECOND FRIEND
Does my sermon, next Easter, meet fitting acceptance?
Each captious disputative boy has his quirk
'An cuique credendum sit?' Well the Church kept 'ans'
In order till Faust set his engine at work!
What truth will come flying from Jew, Moor and Turk.

When, goosequill, thy reign o'er the world is abolished?
Goose – ominous name! With a goose woe began:
Quoth Huss – which means 'goose' in his idiom unpolished -
Ye shall find quench your fire!

Fust.

I foresee such a man.

Vyvyan had always known actors and been linked to the theatre. Encouraged by him I began to go regularly to the Old Vic. In September 1936 I fell in love with the young actor playing Ferdinand in *Love's Labours Lost*. At the stage door I collected his autograph and I was also able to buy a photograph of him for sixpence. When Vyvyan saw this he was surprised and asked what I was doing with a picture of his old friend Roy Redgrave. I wrote to Michael Redgrave and he replied confirming that yes, Roy Redgrave had been his father. The following January, I watched Michael Redgrave play Laertes to Olivier's Hamlet. During curtain calls, Olivier announced that Laertes had a daughter: this was Vanessa Redgrave.

Many people in the theatre were Spiritualists. Through Lilian Baylis, who lived round the corner from us and was a close friend of his, Vyvyan met several of the actors from the Old Vic. Nancy Price ran the People's Theatre at the Playhouse on the Embankment and the first time Vyvyan took me to meet her she had a parrot on her shoulder. Through her I had an invitation to a theatrical luncheon in Park Lane. Beverley Nichols was one of the guests and I sat opposite Godfrey Wynn, who talked to me about the Peace Pledge Union. When my napkin dropped from my lap I slipped down after it and found myself seated on the floor with my knees pressed against Mr Wynn's legs. I emerged about a minute later to see a very red-faced Mr Wynn and several surprised people staring, wondering what I had been doing under the table to the blushing Mr Wynn.

Nancy Price encouraged me to attend meetings connected with the British Drama League and the Playhouse. Diana Wynyard and Edith Evans lectured and Peter Ustinov, then a handsome and versatile young man, gave talks on theatre, ballet and himself. I was particularly interested in Edith Evans after seeing her with Michael Redgrave in *As You Like It*. She was much older than he was and her features were very distorted when you saw them close to but in one lecture, after pointing out her worst features, she told us that when, as Helen of Troy, she declared 'I am the most beautiful woman...' there was not a sound in the audience by way of dissent. Flora Robson's face could look quite disagreeable in a photograph, yet that face too radiated beauty from its unusual features. I used to go to Edith Sitwell's poetry readings and her manicured hands, decorated with heavy rings, acted as a moving frame for her extraordinary, thickly made-up face. Watching these different people, I used to think they were an illustration of Vyvyan's teachings about projection of personality and beauty.

Bishop James, whom Vyvyan had met through the dying Wedgwood, held services in the Sanctuary Hall, 23 Basil Street, immediately behind Harrods, in Knightsbridge. Alice Bailey, an occultist and metaphysician, spoke there and Vyvyan was invited by Bishop James to lecture at the Sanctuary from time to time. We sometimes saw

Christmas Humphreys, the Buddhist, in the congregation there. Crowley and Gerald Yorke started to come to the Sanctuary after being taken there by Vyvyan, who introduced Crowley to Bishop James. Vyvyan, as Frater Memnon, Custodian of the Sanctuary, Sole Vice Regent for the Supreme and Holy King for England, Iona and all the Britons, held a meeting of the Christian Mystics of the Rosy Cross on Monday 21st September, 1936. The title commencing 'Supreme and Holy King' is similar to one of Crowley's own 'dignities'

In December 1936 Ngaio Marsh's *Death in Ecstasy* was published. It contained at the beginning a plan giving the layout the 'House of the Sacred Flame' in which the novel was set, a layout which appeared strikingly like that of the Sanctuary.

Practices at the House of the Sacred Flame also recalled those of the Sanctuary. There was a neophyte class on Wednesday evenings. The communion wine came from Harrods. The doors were locked during a ceremony: one of the most frequent references to the Sanctuary in the press was to the fact that the doors were locked.

A visitor's 'attention was arrested by a solitary voice of great beauty. The Revd Jasper Garnette had mounted the pulpit.' It appeared to the visitor as though the eyes of the preacher were on him alone and the sermon had an hypnotic effect. There was a hymn to 'Pan, the God-in-all': Crowley, who had written a famous 'Hymn to Pan', had been introduced to the Sanctuary by Vyvyan that year. Vyvyan still wore his Pan ring, but now on the ring finger of his *left* hand. (See last picture taken by Alexander Corbett, 1936.) At this time he refreshed his own Pan spirit by meeting both Algernon Blackwood and Arthur Machen.

The novel even suggested that Marsh not only knew the place and had witnessed services, but that she had seen Vyvyan. The villain was Mr Ogden, like Vyvyan a cigar smoker. He was 'rather fat and inclined to be flabby, but almost incredibly clean, as though he used all the deodorants, mouth washes, soaps and lotions recommended... The only irregularities in Mr Ogden were his eyes, which were skewbald – one light blue and one brown.' At the end Mr Ogden's idiom gave him away as being, not American but 'undiluted Sydney!' Now, Vyvyan did not speak with an Australian accent but Mr Ogden's coming from Sydney seems too much of a coincidence.

I wrote to Ngaio Marsh under my married name, so she would not know I was Vyvyan's daughter, telling her that because of my familiarity with Bishop James and the Sanctuary I felt she could not possibly have written some parts of the book from hearsay. She wrote in reply:

In answer to your question I am familiar with the exterior of the Sanctuary which was over the way from a flat I took in London some years ago. Friends of mine, Mr and Mrs Jack Atkinson, used to occasionally attend services there and on one occasion, when staying with them in London, I went with them. That is the full extent of my acquaintanceship with the Sanctuary but I do remember that in writing *Death In Ecstasy* I was influenced by this solitary visit. I had no personal interest in the church nor did I ever come across anybody connected with it. I am sorry to have to give you such a dull answer and am glad that you enjoyed *Death In Ecstasy* which was one of the earliest of my books.

During August Vyvyan was helping Crowley to raise money for the publication of the latter's works. Vyvyan, if paid cash for an engagement, would visit Crowley with a bottle of whisky or some tobacco and whenever he saw him at the Café Royal he would stand him a drink. Sometimes he would be in the company of Nina Hamnett, though she preferred the Fitzroy Tavern. I would often be with Vyvyan as he went from Watkins' bookshop in Cecil Court to a restaurant in Wardour Street, taking me to Marks, Beaumont's the ballet and theatrical bookshop and Zwemmers. As I was a child, I had to stand outside the Fitzroy Tavern and a lemonade would be brought to me. Vyvyan would leave messages for friends with the proprietor Mr Kleinfeld.

After meeting at the Café Royal they would go with Walter Sickert and Augustus John to the home of Beatrice Stewart the Chelsea model. Unlike Betty May, who was slight and modelled for Epstein, Beatrice Stewart was large and fair with her hair parted in the middle, draped over her ears and tied at the back. She wore flowing garments and flat-heeled shoes.

Eunice and Vyvyan went to dinner with Crowley several times that winter. Crowley noted in his diary for 15 January 1937: 'Party (with Morton Smith and Eve Manning) continued. Vyvyan Deacon's Great Act, Frank Lewis in conference with Bracewell.' Nine days later he wrote: 'The Deacons to dinner. He has offered his aid to Franco; to be dropped on Madrid, and crush all resistance.' (By the end of 1937 fewer people in this circle would be joking about Franco, Mussolini or Hitler, for this was the year that the O.T.O. and other German occult orders were banned and a leading member of the O.T.O. called

168

Traenkel (Frater Uranus) was put in a concentration camp.) Eunice used to tell me what went on, how Pearl did this or Ruby did that and I recall her telling me about Ethel Mannin, the author of *South of Samarkand*. After dinner she used to open a box of matches, stand a match at each corner and stare at the box until everybody watched her in silence. She announced, 'The streets of Samarkand by day!'. Then she lit the matches so there were four little flames and then announced solemnly 'The streets of Samarkand by night!' whereupon everyone was convulsed with laughter, simply because they failed to see anything really funny in this act.

Shortly after Crowley's reference to Vyvyan and Franco, during February 1937 Vyvyan went to Tangier and stayed with Crawfurd Price and his wife, who had a villa there and who knew Vyvyan through the Unicorn Press. Like the journeys to Glastonbury and Llanthony, this was undertaken with the intention of establishing a link in the nature of Christian mysticism. Mr Crawfurd Price had travelled throughout North Africa. He had been special correspondent for the *Daily Telegraph* in Turkey and correspondent for *The Times* covering the Middle East 1911-1914 and then as a war correspondent covering the Turkish army during the First Balkan War. He held the Order of the Crown of Romania and was a Commander of the (Greek) Order of the Redeemer.

On Wednesday 10 March 1937 Vyvyan went out and remained out all night with Crowley. (In his diary Crowley wrote ('Christchild 4. All night with Deacon & Simpson the chef.') He came home at about six in the morning and I could hear Vyvyan's voice from the bedroom under mine. His speech was laboured and monosyllabic. Still under the influence of the drugs he had been taking with Crowley, he held a knife in front of Eunice and recited words of sacrifice. She responded by slowly placing her hand on the knife and repeating his words. While Vyvyan looked puzzled, she took the knife away from him and he went to bed. The next time an evening with Crowley was arranged, Eunice got up before he came home and went to Covent Garden 'to see the market'. Vyvyan came in and went quietly to bed. Years later Sybil and I asked Eunice why she did not leave Vyvyan: 'He was our bread and butter, he brought the money in for our keep', she told us with unusual asperity.

In the summer of 1937 Vyvyan weighed twenty-two stone. (Mediums are famous for running to fat.) He went on periodic total fasts of up to three months, taking in nothing but liquids. In June he went on such a diet in order to returned to his customary eighteen stone but he still kept his engagements. He also occupied himself in the usual way with correspondence and telephone calls.

Then on 19 July 1937 Vyvyan collapsed in the street, striking his head on the kerb. I was told he had tripped while getting out of a taxi, which would suggest it was the early hours of the morning, perhaps on his way home from a night with Crowley. Had they been drinking together? The combination of fasting and drinking would certainly have been enough to cause him to collapse. He was found unconscious and taken to King's College Hospital, Denmark Hill where he was diagnosed as having (like Paracelsus) a fractured skull. He lay unconscious for three days. When he opened his eyes he demanded his clothes and discharged himself against advice. At home he modified his fast to a light diet. By the end of August Eunice had to alter all his clothes. His face grew more ethereal looking and his powers seemed greater.

Contact with Crowley continued and despite Vyvyan's lack of money, Crowley still seemed able to borrow from him. As his friend Arthur Day appeared prosperous, Vyvyan took him to the Café Royal and introduced him to Crowley, who was looking for someone to sponsor his *Equinox of the Gods*. Day was in his thirties and curiously unmemorable. His voice had no accent and no particular pitch. He was of average height and build, with dark hair and small moustache. Vyvyan also met Ethel Archer at this time and she and Arthur Day visited us together. Crowley recorded in his diary that 'Deacon and Day' would do 'big things'.

Crowley had started taking an interest in the Sanctuary and Bishop James and he persuaded Gerald Yorke to attend services. Crowley and Vyvyan were meanwhile conducting secret negotiations as though in some partnership, possibly in connection with Crawfurd-Price, the secret service and Franco. During August Bishop James had gone on holiday to the Middle East, leaving the Sanctuary closed, but on his return, 3 September 1937 Bishop James and Vyvyan had lunch at the Café Royal with Crowley. The latter had criticised the Bishop's pronunciation of various words but Vyvyan sensed he was impressed by the Bishop's knowledge of Christian mysticism. For Crowley's benefit Bishop James answered Vyvyan's questions on '93', Crowley's thelemic doctrine and their place in the teachings of the Sanctuary. Bishop James apologised for his poor knowledge of Sanskrit.

A week later Vyvyan visited Crowley with a half-bottle of whisky and the following day Vyvyan and I went to the Sanctuary service. That Sunday the congregation sat waiting to see the Bishop after his holiday in Greece. Looking tanned he made his entrance through the door on the left of the broad altar and led the procession around the congregation and up the central aisle. As the acolytes followed, a tall, blond curly-headed new boy was noticed, walking solemnly behind the Bishop, his eyes raised only to acknowledge the statues in passing. Vyvyan whispered 'He has brought back a young Greek God.' This was Derek Aylward, a young English actor who was introduced to the Sanctuary by his singing teacher Muriel Terry when he was twelve. He continued singing until his voice broke. He became an acolyte in 1937 and continued there until the Sanctuary finally closed it doors and the Bishop retired. He inherited the episcopal throne. Another of the acolytes, a good-looking, tall fair-headed boy with a motor-bike was Sybil's boyfriend Brian. They were engaged and went on holiday in St Ives in Cornwall where they stayed in a cottage close to the artist Alfred Wallis. (In June 1938, Bishop James conducted their marriage at the Sanctuary.)

Crowley attended the Wednesday evening service on 15 September at 6.15 pm and noted enigmatically 'The Sanctuary. Looked very good prospects.' The following day Ethel Archer, Arthur Day, Crowley and other friends brought by Vyvyan met above Atlantis, the occult bookshop, launching the attempt to get the publication of *The Equinox of the Gods* off the ground. On Saturday 18 September Crowley wrote in his diary that 'Roberts says he thinks Day O.K. Deacon-Day will do bigger plan. Day wrote offering £50 towards AL' (AL being *The Book of the Law*).

Vyvyan visited him the evening before his birthday with some whisky and being unable to meet him on the actual day, Tuesday 12 October, sent a telegram:

CROWLEY 11 MANOR PLACE W2 = DO WHAT THOU WILT SHALL BE THE WHOLE OF THE LAW MANY HAPPY RETURNS OF THE DAY LOVE IS THE LAW LOVE UNDER WILL = DEACON

The pun of the returns of Day was not lost on Crowley.

On the day after his birthday, as it was a Wednesday, Crowley attended the evening meeting at the Sanctuary and thought that Bishop James was 'Talking pure A.C.' On Tuesday 19 October Crowley recorded vengefully the death of the judge who had put an end to his libel suit against

171

Constable: 'Drunken blackguard Swift dead.' For those who believed Crowley could curse to good effect, this was a powerful proof.

Horace Algernon Sheridan-Bickers, who admired Alice Bailey, was a close friend of Vyvyan and Eunice. (He proposed to Eunice after Vyvyan's death.) He had written a number of plays and been a special correspondent for several newspapers. He was the founder member of a literary and debating society in Torquay, where he retired. He introduced the actress 'Elizabeth Fox' (real name Jane Wolfe) to Crowley's works and she later joined Crowley's Abbey in Cefalù. In his *Confessions* Crowley mocked Sheridan-Bickers under the pseudonyms 'Gnaggs' and 'Dartnell'. He suggested that Sherry suspected his wife of infidelity, including flirting with Crowley. Finally 'Sherry' lay in wait and beat up a man who came out of the flats where they lived, spending that night in a state of terror in case he had killed the man. The papers the following day reported an unprovoked assault on someone who had been spending the evening with Professor and Mrs P: he had assaulted a complete stranger. When the marriage finally broke up, Sherry turned out to have another woman to go to.

Crowley described visiting the divorced wife when she was living in Paddington. The first time he went only the daughter Sheila was at home and Crowley said he 'had never seen a girl so perfectly evil'. He called the following day when Betty was there. She persuaded Crowley to stay with her until she left for Cefalù as 'he was ill and in need of loving care.' Crowley carried out some experiments with her. She came up with the word 'thighs' for the autumnal equinox. He interpreted the word through Hebrew and magical formulae, consulted 'The Holy Books and in the Yi King for an interpretation of the word' and was very content with the results.

On 19 December 1936 the novelist and well-known Spiritualist Violet Tweedale, who had been a member of the Golden Dawn and had known Vyvyan's mother, died. In the autumn of 1937, Vyvyan was asked to speak in Torquay at a meeting where Alice Bailey would take the chair. Alice Bailey was born in Manchester in 1880 and had attempted suicide as a child. A convert to Theosophy, she and her husband Foster Bailey left the Society believing it to be dominated by the Esoteric Section. They founded the Arcane School which itself split into several groups on her death in 1949. The topic was to be 'The Cosmic Christ', the title of one of the dead woman's books. Sheridan-Bickers wrote enthusiastically:

To hear two such speakers as Alice Bailey and Vyvyan Deacon on such a subject as 'The Cosmic Christ' is an opportunity too good for anyone to miss, who is interested in the eternal quest for spiritual truth and beauty; which all who remember in gratitude the unsparing philanthropic and social work of Mrs Tweedale in Torquay, especially in the League of Help, of which she was the founder and president, will delight to embrace this chance of joining in the beautiful and most appropriate voluntary tribute to her memory... Mr Vyvyan Deacon insisted on coming from London to have, as he called it, the honour of giving this lecture on Mrs Tweedale's 'magnum opus', though barely yet recovered from his recent very severe accident. He is a kinsman of Robert Browning, his mother – Elizabeth Browning – being first cousin to the great poet. Mr Deacon has lectured as one of the best-known exponents of Spiritualism, not only in various European countries, but throughout Australia and New Zealand. In Stockholm - though knowing no Swedish – he was able to receive messages in Swedish, while his address had to be interpreted by Carl Carlesson, the translator of W.T. Stead, Sir Conan Doyle and Dennis Bradley.

Pengelly Hall was full and the following day Sherry wrote of a 'masterly analysis by Mr Vyvyan Deacon':

The lecturer quoted from the dedication and foreword in the 'Cosmic Christ' in which the author referred to the statement of the Archbishop of Canterbury in 1929, that the foundations of Christianity were being undermined, the public outlook being dominated by the marvellous success and range of the material civilisation which science had built up... The lecturer urged the audience to reflect on the meaning of the three years ministry and to reflect whether they and the incarnation... were the sole manifestations of Christ on earth... Might it not be true that the Christ spirit was eternal, backwards as well as forwards... Violet Tweedale in her book pointed to a conception of the Cosmic Christ which remained unaffected by any scientific discovery made, in other words, a cosmic being which has been guiding the human race since its inception. She pointed out that there were two distinct elements in the character of Christ and she believed that they were latent in all mankind – the divine being which is the eternal Christ and the human being which was the personal Christ.

Crowley was at the Sanctuary again that Sunday. He commented that 'James stated practically all my teaching: even quoted 93 as the "Word of the Great Master"'. He and Vyvyan lunched afterwards at the Café Royal; Crowley was planning on writing to Bishop James (in fact the following day the bishop wrote to him) for Crowley was keen to understand him better. He noted in his diary 'James – Symbol R. message' and planned to call at 11 am the following morning but he overslept due to an asthma attack at four in the morning. The next Sunday Crowley attended the Sanctuary again, complaining of James's preaching 'Freewill'. On Monday 8 November, dissatisfied with the sermon, Crowley wrote to Bishop James about freewill and sent him a copy of his *Magick*. All this time plans were still in progress for a working relationship with Arthur Day and Crowley noted in his diary that 'Deacon has hopes of Day'. In the event Day must have proved harder to persuade than expected for when he wrote to the bishop, Crowley also had to send a 'despairing appeal to Day' which resulted in '£1 for *Equinox of the Gods*' finally arriving the next morning.

When he took Gerald Yorke to the Sanctuary the following Wednesday, James commented on a passage of Crowley's letter, mispronouncing some Sanskrit the latter had quoted there ('Visvaru pada vshana, which beat him'), much to Crowley's satisfaction. (It was one of the bishop's habits to direct a part of his sermon to an individual whom he saw in the congregation; when he saw Vyvyan he would refer in parenthesis to Spiritualism, of which he disapproved.)

Vyvyan, who had been ignoring the fact that he had sustained a fractured skull a few months previously, again collapsed in the street and hurt his shoulder. The doctor who attended him, mistaking a fracture for a dislocation, pulled on the arm and Vyvyan became unconscious. He was taken into St Giles' Hospital, Camberwell. Sybil, her fiancé Brian and I visited him, hurrying past the flower-seller and his stall outside the hospital gates, and into the stark building of corridors and clinical rooms smelling of disinfectant. Vyvyan looked exactly as he did at home, in his blue and white homemade pyjamas. Eunice visited him dutifully to bring him things he needed, such as clean laundry, but no more than that. In the last two years, since his friendship with Crowley, she had become more estranged from him.

Lilian Baylis died while he was in St Giles. She used to love to talk about the old days, the great Shakespearean actors, and about God. I have heard her described as a fearsome character but she was a dear, and very fond of Vyvyan. People call her a Cockney but I always believed her accent to be South African. I had spent a day in the country at Box Hill with Vyvyan and Lilian Baylis. I played with children and two dogs in a converted railway carriage while Vyvyan and Lilian had what Vyvyan explained was a 'private consultation' in a nearby hut.

When Vyvyan came home from hospital, Eunice made up a bed on the settee facing the window in his study. There he had all his books at arms' length. His pipe-rack and tobacco-jar were also in reach though I do not remember his smoking at this time. There was no money and no noise. There were no Christmas presents. I travelled with Mr Martin from the Oval on the top of a bus to Hyde Park Corner and walked with him to the Sanctuary for Midnight Mass on Christmas Eve. As well as being the caretaker at the Sanctuary, Martin worked as the supervisor of a Boys' Club in Stockwell. I saw an attractive dark blue plaited leather stranded belt in a shop in Brixton and I must have mentioned it to Vyvyan, because he sent me to his suit draped over a chair in the study, telling me that in the pocket I would find one half-crown. It was all the money we had. I spent it.

On Christmas Day we left Vyvyan at home and went for lunch at a house whose small garden led from the dining room patio doors directly down to a mooring by the river. Mrs Archer was our hostess and Arthur Day was with us. It was somewhere like Thames Ditton. Beside each plate there was a beautifully dressed shepherdess or crinolined lady, attached to the most beautiful Christmas crackers I have ever seen. Mine had a small china face, an orange brimmed picture hat and full skirt.

Vyvyan's hair was beginning to thin a little on the crown. He loved to have hair looking clean, sleek and healthy. I used to brush it for him with his twinset brushes. He had an electric comb, which was fashionable at the time, and although it seems crude in retrospect it was then the latest thing. It was formed by a double row of wavy metal teeth about an inch and a half long, on a handle about five inches in length; there was a battery in the handle. When combed through the hair it would give a tingling sensation which was supposed to act as a stimulus to the scalp. He read a book while I stood behind him, drawing the hair back in slow rhythmic sweeps of the comb for half an hour or so. Then he asked me to practise the piano, which he could hear through the dividing doors.

I played the *Maiden's Prayer*, which Eunice had learned from music at the Pateman's in 1918 and which I had learned by hearing Eunice play it, the *Doll's Tea Party* and selections from the *Peer Gynt* Suite.

We had seen the play at the Old Vic with Sybil Thorndyke and William Devlin. Vyvyan begged me to play scales, not arpeggios nor exercises but pure and simple scales. He sat there with his eyes closed.

On the 6 January 1938 Crowley was still wondering what he should do about Day:

> Get after him.
> 1. Emphasize need of assistance.
> 2. Appeal frankly.
> 3. Show him as picked man.
> 4. Don't funk.

The following morning Arthur Day replied: 'Friendly but uncomprehending.' Still keen to raise money, Crowley recorded that he 'Got ten shillings from Deacon', which was probably a ten shilling note found in a book. On Friday 14 January Vyvyan visited Crowley and had a very good talk. The latter noted that 'Deacon showed aura of light and became adolescent.' On 18 January he was with Vyvyan briefly in the afternoon. 'He is very sick and sore.' He visited again the next day. 'Tea with Christ-child.' Vyvyan was readmitted to hospital. He was still talking about going to Paris where he was expected on 19 February.

On 15 February Crowley wrote to Vyvyan. It was the last letter Vyvyan received in hospital.

> Care Frater
> Do what thou wilt shall be the whole of the Law. I am glad you are getting on well. It's a strain, of course, but it may do you good in the long run. Enforced rest ought to be a holiday; and you can do a lot yourself to make it that, and something better.
>
> To begin with, the Snake Ananda goes on eating his tail, and doesn't give a hoot for any of us.
>
> Try for the Trance of Indifference, then don't forget that rest in bed restores the unconscious forces, of whose well-being we are never much aware; we can only gauge them by results. It is not as if you were ill, and taxing those forces.
>
> So it is really a very good chance to meditate undisturbed. If you stick to it, you will find quite unexpectedly, as is its funny little way, illumination of some quite new order comes to you.
>
> I got some excellent results when I was only 10% alive with remittent

malarial fever. The experience was, in fact, the basis of a very large body of Work which comes as one of the best things in my life.

So be patient with physical, and ardent towards spiritual, affairs.

I have got Day back to the point of answering letters promptly. So there's a light at the end of the tunnel.

Love is the law, love under will

Fraternally 666

At 8 am on Saturday 19 February 1938 there was a loud bang on the front door. From my bed I heard Eunice go to the door. I could hear crying. Eunice and Sybil had their arms round each other and Eunice had a telegram in her hand. She put her arm round me, and the three of us went into a huddle. The tears automatically came to my eyes although I still did not know any cause. I heard Eunice say, 'Daddy's died' as she showed me a telegram which read 'Vyvyan Deacon passed away peacefully in his sleep 4 am.' This was the day he was to be discharged, and she had been up late the night before packing a suitcase so that my father could go straight to Paris after she had collected him from the hospital. I don't know what his business was in Paris. Vyvyan knew people there; he had always had the banned books sent to Australia from there, Wilde, James Joyce, D.H. Lawrence, Aubrey Beardsley. There was always a mystery involving Paris. Something to do with Satie, Debussy, Jean Cocteau, Eliphas Levi, William Shergold Browning who worked for the Rothschild Bank in Paris and why Robert Browning wrote 'Childe Roland to the Dark Tower Came' and the 'Heretic's Tragedy' in Paris.

We went to the cremation. I do not remember seeing or speaking to anyone. There was nothing to suggest my father was in any way connected with the occasion. Someone said the ashes were to be scattered on the rosebeds. Later we went to a cinema; Gary Cooper was in the film. In the evening Sybil went out.

When Eunice had collected the things from the hospital, everyone told her my father had spent his last days singing, reciting Shakespeare, telling fortunes and writing rhymed acrostics for people's names. She found that his Pan ring and silver-topped dark wood stick had gone missing: were they given to a significant visitor to the hospital?

Crowley was not at the crematorium but as soon as he heard of Vyvyan's death he and Pearl both wrote. Eunice replied briefly:

I do thank you for your very kind offer of help, and would have telephoned you the next morning, but could not find your telephone number anywhere; you omitted it from your letter.

I appreciate your thought but really there is nothing that you could help me in at present.

All arrangements have been made for Cremation... Had letter from Pearl shall write her later.

Crowley was himself unwell at this time. On 28 February 1938 he wrote to his friend Elmer Gertz that he had 'Been ill for about a week!' In his diary two months later on Tuesday 15 April 1938 Crowley wrote:

Vyvyan Deacon came in about 7 am. Taller, thinner, paler than in life. Dressed in white suit of 'flannels'. Seemed to want to speak, but I heard nothing.

Index

'Dr Cheong' 135, 139, 156
'Hymn to Pan' 59, 117, 167, 120
'Larry' 99, 139, 130
'Playing with Fire' 80

Abbey, the 110, 111, 114, 116, 143
Abbey Theatre 143
Aiwass 48
Arundale, Francesca 36
Arundale, George 36, 96
Astrology 35, 163
At the Feet of the Master 22, 58, 74

Baden-Powell, Henrietta Grace 9
Baden-Powell, Lord 9, 13
Bailey, Alice 59, 117, 166, 167, 172,
 173
Baker Eddy, Mary 16, 103
Barbanell, Maurice 142
Baylis, Lilian 166, 174, 175
Beaurepaire, Gerald de 138, 153
Bennett, Frank 9, 28, 29, 33, 41-44,
 53, 54, 56, 59, 60, 74, 83, 101, 114
Besant, Annie 12-14, 18, 22, 23, 35-
 37, 41, 46, 54, 94-97, 123, 152,
 154
Bethany Rooms, the 28
Blackwood, Algernon 1, 111, 167
Blavatsky, Helena Petrovna 2, 12,
 18, 58, 68, 97
Bomberg 22, 43, 52, 120
Broadstairs 4-6, 8, 9, 98
Browning, Robert 1-2, 5, 13, 14,
 65, 91, 140, 143, 154, 163-164,
 173, 177
Bunn, James 33, 63, 119

Café Royal 146, 168, 170, 174
Canterbury 5, 9, 18, 151, 173
Carlesson, Carl 153, 156, 173
Cefalù 102, 114, 120, 149, 163, 172
Celibacy 20, 46
Chaldea 68
Chidley, William 16, 28, 31, 32, 34,
 48, 50, 59, 103-105, 154, 159
Christchurch 2, 66, 67, 83, 85, 88,
 89, 91, 93, 94, 129
Christian Mystics of the Rosy Cross
 43, 45, 47, 49, 52, 67, 167
Conan Doyle, Jean 80, 145
Conan Doyle, Sir Arthur 45, 63, 67,
 79-81, 91, 98, 134, 145, 154, 156,
 173
Cooper, Joseph 27
Corelli, Marie 19, 21
Crawfurd Price, Walter Harrington
 152, 162, 169
Crester-Wilson, E. 33, 49
Crowley, Aleister 1, 3, 18, 19, 28-30,
 33, 35, 39, 41-46, 48, 55, 56, 59,
 62, 67, 68, 73, 101, 102, 114, 117,
 120, 134, 146, 148, 149, 154, 155,
 160-165, 167, 168, 169-172, 174,
 176-178
Crowther, Alice 122

Daniell, Mrs 13, 75
Deacon, Cornelius William 1, 3, 67,
 137, 140
Deacon, Elizabeth 2, 5
Deacon, Eunice 10-13, 15, 16, 19-30,
 32, 39, 40, 43, 46-57, 59, 60, 62-65,
 67, 73-75, 80-83, 85, 88-90, 92-98,

100, 101, 103, 105-111, 113, 116, 117, 119-122, 125, 128-130, 133-136, 140, 142, 145, 146, 151, 152, 156-163, 168-170, 172, 174-177
Direct Voice Mediumship 124, 143
Doyle, Lady 145, 160
Dr Mac 113
du Maurier, George 122

Eddy, Mary Baker 103
Egypt 21, 39, 68
Ellis, Henry Havelock 32, 154
Esoteric Section 18, 20, 24, 39, 46, 47, 49, 51, 123, 172

Fabling, Mr 87-90
Fox, Elizabeth see Wolfe, Jane
Field, Mrs (see also Bella Sly) 127, 128
Frater Memnon 21, 68, 167
Freemasonry 1, 2, 35, 36, 44, 58, 68, 114

Gladstone, William Ewart 2
Golden Dawn 1, 2, 20, 35, 42, 43, 111, 163, 172

Hamburger, Michael 29
Hamnett, Nina 149, 161, 168
Harris, Frank 63, 113, 154
Harris, Susannah 75, 90, 93, 102, 107, 144
Hartmann, Franz 58, 68
Heroin 29, 30
Homosexuality 18
Houdini, Harry 19, 156
Hunter, Captain 73, 150, 152

Independent Order of Odd Fellows 24
International New Thought Alliance 47
Irving, Sir Henry 6
Ivycliffe 32, 50, 59-63, 74, 93, 103

James, Bishop 37, 138, 158, 164, 166-168, 170, 171, 174
John, Augustus 160, 161, 168
Johnson, Violet 86, 87

Köllerstrom, Gustav 39
Köllerstrom, Oscar 39, 41
Krishnamurti 7, 8, 12, 20, 22, 23, 36, 46, 58, 61, 95-97, 123

Leadbeater, Charles Webster 1, 4, 8, 12, 15, 18-20, 23, 24, 28, 34-41, 46, 47, 51, 54, 58, 60, 61, 82, 95-97, 124, 127, 128, 154, 160
Leaf, Horace 98, 100
Liberal Catholic Church 24, 28, 36, 37, 39, 44, 49, 55, 57, 59, 82, 96, 97
Lilly, Lillian 159
Lingwood-Smith, Lily 60, 123

Machen, Arthur 1, 111, 167
Magic 7, 19, 23, 27, 28, 33, 36, 41, 59, 103, 119, 146, 149, 154, 158
Manor, the 40
Marie Russak 35
Marsh, Ngaio 167, 168
Martyn, Thomas H. 23, 24, 40, 41, 97
Marx, Karl 35, 76, 78
Masturbation 18, 46, 58
Melbourne 10, 13, 14, 18, 25, 39, 60, 75, 108-110, 117, 119, 123, 124, 127, 129, 138-140, 144, 153, 155
Menzies, Robert 130, 131
Mildura 125, 134
Miles, Arthur 83, 86-88
Mills, Revd Shapley 5, 11, 19, 37
Minogue, Henry 126, 130

Naturism 1, 16
Nehru, Jawaharl 159
New Thought 16 19, 24, 26-28, 32-34, 41, 43, 45, 51, 56, 59, 63, 73, 76, 79, 89, 93, 95, 102, 119, 122, 123, 134, 163
New Zealand 37, 63, 64, 67, 73, 75, 80-85, 87, 89, 91-95, 97, 102, 106, 119, 128, 129, 132, 173

Occult 2, 24, 41, 57, 62-65, 68, 74, 75, 80, 81, 83, 84, 89, 90, 98, 137, 138, 143, 144, 169, 171
Olcott, Henry 35
Old Catholic Church 24, 35-37, 39
Opium 45
Order of the Star in the East 12, 13, 23, 39, 40, 48, 52
Ordo Templi Orientalis 30, 33, 35, 41-45, 50, 55, 58, 62, 67, 68, 101, 103, 106, 137, 169

Pan 59, 111, 117, 154, 160, 167, 177
Pateman, James Harradine 28, 29, 33, 49, 55
Peace Pledge Union 166
Pillig, Gustav 111, 119, 160
Psychometry 65, 67, 124, 143, 146

Quimby, Phineas Parkhurst 16

Race 13, 14, 32, 77, 81, 108, 136, 159, 173
Ram Krishna Paramahansa 137
Redgrave, Michael 166
Redgrave, Roy 10, 19, 27, 136, 166
Reincarnation 14, 46, 91, 146, 154
Reuss, Theodor 35, 68
Rosicrucians 43, 45, 68, 83, 106

Schott, May 60, 104, 129
Seton, Julia 27, 28, 31, 34, 51, 93, 96, 123, 162
Sexual magic 27, 28, 41, 46, 103
Sharpe, Revd Arthur 150
Shirlaw, James Stewart 'John' 32, 50, 63, 74
Sickert, Walter 160, 168
Sister Veni Cooper-Mathieson 16, 17, 19, 24, 26-28, 31-34, 41, 44, 46, 49, 50, 52, 56, 65, 66, 93, 101, 119, 122
Sly, Bella (see also Mrs Field) 86, 128
Soper, Donald (Lord) 152, 162
Stables, Margaret 85-87, 92, 93

Stead, W.T. 2, 12, 99, 138-140, 143, 156, 173
Stephensen, Percy Reginald 134
Swedenborg, Emmanuel 156
Sydney 16, 19, 23, 24, 26-28, 31, 32, 34, 35, 39-44, 47, 57, 58, 59, 63, 67, 74, 75, 80, 82, 85, 86, 88, 94, 95, 97, 98, 99, 103, 105, 106, 110, 114, 119, 121, 124, 127, 129, 131, 132, 134, 138, 142, 152, 162, 167

Theosophical Society 2, 12, 13, 18-20, 23, 24, 35, 37, 39, 40, 42, 44, 46, 47, 49-52, 54, 55, 59, 68, 75, 82, 94, 95-97, 123, 124, 127
Thought-form 36
Tong, Philip Lew 10, 11
Truth 3, 26-28, 33, 34, 41, 63, 66, 68, 69, 72, 85, 91, 92, 101, 102, 112, 122-124, 129, 131-134, 150, 165, 173
Tweedale, Violet 2, 172, 173

Underhill, Evelyn 16

Victor, Grace 43, 46, 49
Vivekananda 137

Wedgwood, James Ingall 2, 8, 24, 28, 29, 34, 35, 37-39, 45, 46, 53, 55, 58, 60, 82, 97, 128, 138, 152, 166
Wilcox, Ella Wheeler 16, 47
Wilde, Constance 2
Wilde, Oscar 1, 2, 19, 20, 50, 55, 63, 110, 154, 177
Wolfe, Jane 172
Worthington family, the 66, 93, 94, 128

Yarker, John 35, 58
Yeats, W.B. 1, 26, 42, 143, 146
Young, Olive 85, 89, 90